HAWKEYE

HAWKEYE

THE ENTHRALLING AUTOBIOGRAPHY OF THE TOP-SCORING ISRAEL AIR FORCE ACE OF ACES

BRIGADIER GENERAL GIORA EVEN-EPSTEIN

Co-written with Ilan Kfir and Danny Dor

Translated from Hebrew by Anne Hartstein Pace

GRUB STREET · LONDON

Published by
Grub Street
4 Rainham Close
London SW11 6SS

A CIP record for this title is available from the British library

ISBN-13: 978-1-911621-96-6

Design by Lucy Thorne

Printed and bound by Finidr in the Czech Republic

Front cover painting:
The Yom Kippur War, October 20, 1973. Into the third week of the intense, bloody war with Israel fighting for its life, Israel Air Force ace then-Major Giora Even-Epstein takes on four Egyptian MiG-21s in one incredible dogfight. Flying a Nesher (Eagle), an Israeli variant of the Mirage V, of No. 101 Squadron, he dispatches the four camouflaged MiGs with the courage and skill that has typified his career as the top Israeli ace, ultimately bringing his total to 17 kills from the 1967 Six Day War, and placing him in the select pantheon of top jet aces worldwide.

American artist Roy Grinnell (1933-2019) created this striking painting of Epstein's incredible mission. Well-known for his work as the official artist for the American Fighter Aces Association, Grinnell received many awards and was well into his project to create a painting depicting each American ace's most significant action when he passed away on September 16, 2019. This particular work was privately commissioned by Mr Rick Turner as a tribute to his close friend, now Brigadier General Giora Even-Epstein, and is used here with the gracious permission of Mr Turner and Mrs Irene Grinnell.

To my dear family, and especially my wife, Sara,
who stood bravely with me in all my craziness.

CONTENTS

ACKNOWLEDGEMENTS

Co-writers:

Ilan Kfir is a journalist and photographer. He has been a senior writer for the newspaper *Yediot Achronot* (The Final News), and has written biographies of Bibi Netanyahu, the Israeli prime minister, Ehud Barak (once, the prime minister in 1999), and other senior people in Israel. All his books have been best-sellers in Israel.

Danny Dor is a professional editor, and was the senior editor for the publishing company Ceter (Crown) and the newspaper *Maariv* (Afternoon, or Early Evening). He also helped write the biographies with Ilan Kfir, as well as many other books that were best-sellers in Israel.

Translator:

Anne Hartstein Pace was born in St. Louis, Missouri and studied at Brandeis University in Massachusetts. She has been a professional translator for more than two decades, specialising in non-fiction subjects. She lives with her family in Jerusalem.

The author and publisher would like to thank the following people for their help and support with this book:
  Rick and Micah Turner, close friends of General Epstein, who were part of the project from the very beginning.
  Frank Olynyk, a well-known historian on aces who quickly answered historical questions.
  David A. Mersky, who helped with a lot of explanations for several Hebrew language, historical questions and place names.
  Irene Grinnell, for her permission to use her late husband Roy's painting for the cover.
  Peter B. Mersky, who helped edit the English translation and contributed his own knowledge of the Israel Air Force and its aces.
  Tony Holmes for introducing the publisher to this project.

TRIBUTES TO GIORA

"He had a greater hunger for success and for shooting down enemy planes than any pilot I've ever known. I attribute his incredible achievements in aerial combat to a quality that Giora possesses that I've never seen in any other pilots or anyone else: Giora is truly and absolutely fearless."

Brigadier General (ret.) Israel Baharav (an ace with 12 kills)

"To me, Giora is one of the finest combat pilots in the history of the air force. His ambitions focused on the area in which he was the best – aerial combat. He wanted to be the best in this field. He always preferred combat aviation, the framework that would enable him to train combat pilots, rather than instructional positions, which are part of the route to promotion in the air force. When Giora is in the air, in training or on an actual mission, he is utterly focused on the target. He hates to lose. A pilot who makes aerial combat a fine martial art."

Brigadier General (ret.) Ran Peker (seven kills)

"Every day that I let him go out, he downed three or four MiGs. A total of 11 enemy planes in the Yom Kippur War. Eventually I told him: 'You stay at headquarters, now it's my turn to go shoot down some planes…'"

Major General (ret.) Avihu Ben-Nun
(former Israel Air Force commander, four kills)

"As a member of Israel's national skydiving team, Giora raised the professional bar, increased the number of seconds of free fall before deploying the parachute and was one of the best, bravest and most unflappable skydivers I've ever seen."

Amos Shapira (skydiving instructor)

"Solo flight after 11 hours of flying. Took off well, landed well. Will be a good pilot…"

Colonel Eliezer 'Cheetah' Cohen
(primary flight instructor at air force flight school)

"Commander, leader… Watch him and learn… In the evenings on standby at Rephidim Air Base during the War of Attrition I saw him go to the helicopter landing zone and help evacuate the wounded and the fallen who arrived from the field."

Colonel (ret.) Arik Azuz
(commander of the Flying Dragon Squadron, two kills)

"The Phantoms that showed up in the War of Attrition 'threatened' the supremacy of the MiGs in aerial combat in the force. Very quickly, thanks to Giora Epstein and an elite group of pilots, this changed, and the rivalry between the Phantom and Mirage squadrons became much fiercer."

Major General (ret.) Eitan Ben Eliyahu
(former Israel Air Force commander, four kills)

"Thanks to Giora, air combat with the Phantoms often ended with victory by the Mirages. Ultimately, the Mirage pilots didn't learn how to contend with the Phantom crews, but vice versa."

Avraham Salmon (Mirage pilot, 14½ kills)

"In keeping with his character, Giora barely told me anything about all the planes that he downed. It was only from slivers of information I picked up from others that I realised the magnitude of his accomplishments and discovered that he was considered a very special combat pilot. His coolness under pressure became legend in the air force. Even when the children grew up, Giora hardly ever told them about his flight experiences and about the enemy planes he shot down. 'It's no big deal,' he would say when they asked him."

Sara Even-Epstein (Giora's wife)

"We got to be part of festive occasions in his life, but the most emotional one of all was the ceremony at the end of his final flight. Giora is not a man of emotions, but on his face I saw that this was a sad moment for someone who'd been called the air force's best combat pilot."

Nava Mosin (Giora's sister)

"In all my life, I never met a person as modest as Giora, someone without the tiniest drop of arrogance despite his elite status in the air force."

Yehudit (secretary, No. 117 the First Jet Squadron)

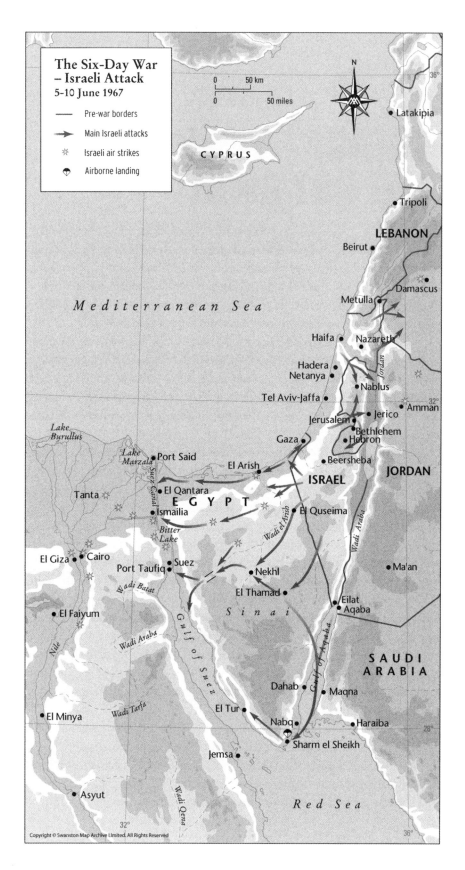

The Six-Day War
– Israeli Attack
5-10 June 1967

—— Pre-war borders

→ Main Israeli attacks

✳ Israeli air strikes

☂ Airborne landing

0   50 km
0   50 miles

N

Latakipia

CYPRUS

Tripoli

LEBANON

Beirut ●

Damascus ✳

Metulla ●

Mediterranean Sea

Haifa ●   Nazareth ●

Hadera ●
Netanya ●

Nablus ●

Tel Aviv-Jaffa ●

Jordan

Amman ✳

Jerusalem ●   Jerico ●

Bethlehem ●
Hebron ●

Gaza ●

Beersheba ●

JORDAN

Lake
Burullus

Lake
Marzala ● Port Said

El Arish ●

ISRAEL

Tanta ✳

● El Qantara

EGYPT

El Quseima ●

● Ismailia

Wadi el Arish

✳

Wadi Araba

*Bitter
Lake*

Ma'an ●

El Giza ● ● Cairo

Port Taufiq ●
Suez ●

● Nekhl

Wadi Batat

El Thamad ●

Sinai

Eilat ●
Aqaba ●

● El Faiyum

Wadi Araba

Gulf of Suez

SAUDI
ARABIA

● El Minya

Wadi Tarfa

Dahab ●

Maqna ●

El Tur ●

Nabq ●

Haraiba ●

Jemsa ●

☂ Sharm el Sheikh

● Asyut

Wadi Qena

Red Sea

Nile

Gulf of Aqaba

PREFACE – THE ONE THAT GOT AWAY

I have 17 kills – victories over enemy aircraft – to my name. Even though it's been more than 45 years since the last kill in the Yom Kippur War, I remember each one. Every detail, every pressing of the trigger or firing of the missile. I vividly recall the pursuit, the aerial manoeuvres, the moment when I saw the plane ahead of me crash and burn on the ground.

I also remember clearly the aircraft I failed to shoot down. There weren't many, but all are etched in my memory under the heading: The ones that got away… I have chosen to open my book with one of these. It could have been my first kill, but it didn't happen, and it would be several more days before my name was first written on the kill board of First Fighter Squadron at Hatzor.

It was the end of May 1967. The days of waiting and high alert in the lead-up to the Six Day War. Like the rest of the air force, the men of the First Fighter Squadron at the Hatzor airbase, a fighter squadron with delta-winged Mirage planes, were engrossed in preparations for Operation *Moked* (Focus) – to attack the Egyptian airbases and destroy the planes there. Briefings, preparations, drills, training. I was older than most of the pilots in the squadron, but in terms of experience as a combat pilot, I was one of the 'youngest' in the group.

In addition to the preparations for war, which we were all certain would come sooner or later, preferably sooner, the squadron kept planes on standby at all hours of the day to intercept Egyptian planes that crossed the border into Israel. The Egyptians had been sending a pair of MiG-21s each time, flying at high altitude, 50,000 feet, and at a speed of Mach 1.8, for photography missions over our nuclear reactor in Dimona. They took pictures and raced back into Egyptian territory. The code name the air force gave to this infiltration operation was *Efroah* (Chick).

Whenever such an infiltration was spotted, we immediately launched interceptors against them, but since the whole thing happened so quickly, the Egyptians always managed to cross safely back over the border, while we did not have permission to continue the pursuit into Egypt. The situation was already tense enough without adding aerial combat over Sinai.

The procedure was set: Two planes on the runway, pilots strapped into the cockpit and ready for take-off the moment the order was given. A second pair waiting for the engines on order, with the pilots in the squadron ready for immediate dispatch. When the first pair took off, the second pair boarded their planes, and a third pair, that has been waiting in the squadron operations room, moved to immediate standby for take-off.

I was in the second pair, together with the lead pilot, Lieutenant Colonel David Ivry, who years later would go on to become the IAF commander. We sat in our planes after the first pair took off in pursuit of a pair of MiGs sent by the Egyptians as a diversion. These MiGs flew south along the border near Mitzpe Ramon, while two other MiGs took off for a photography mission over the Dimona reactor. We were on standby, ready for immediate take-off, when suddenly we heard the order in our earpieces: "Launch! Pair of chicks at 50,000 feet. Mach 1.8." In an instant, I'm in the air right behind Ivry, who is armed with a French-made R 530 (Diamond) missile and a Shafrir-1 missile that homes in on engine heat and was developed by RAFAEL.

I had just one missile – a Diamond. After a few seconds, we jettisoned the drop tanks and started climbing. The Mirage accelerated to Mach 0.9, full afterburner, and climbed to 36,000 feet. I spotted the MiGs' white contrails, produced when some of the water in the jet fuel is emitted as the fuel burns and turns to vapor. The pair of Egyptian 'chicks' were flying toward Dimona.

As the drag on his plane was greater, due to the two missiles it was carrying, David Ivry stayed a little behind and I became the lead interceptor. In a flash, I analysed my situation and quickly calculated that I'd be able to catch them on their way out, when they headed back toward the border. I accelerated to Mach 1.2… 1.3… and climbed full burner to 48,000 feet.

Squeezing every drop of power out of the plane, I accelerated to 1.8 and climbed to 50,000 feet.

I had my eye on them, and the Egyptian pair was totally oblivious of my presence.

The two MiGs were trying to speed back over the border after completing their photography mission, and I came up behind them and locked my missile radar on the rear MiG. On the instrument panel in the cockpit, a blue light came on, indicating the missile radar had picked up the target. The missile made a beeping sound, a signal that it was ready for launch. Everything was ready, but rather than just press the button, I said over the radio to the controller back in the control tower, "missile locked on target" and requested permission to fire from my leader, and more senior pilot, David Ivry. Before Ivry could answer me, I heard the controller's voice: "Negative. Do not fire."

Hardly believing my ears, I again addressed Ivry, who by now was below me. "Request permission to fire."

The controller again intervened. "Negative. Do not fire!"

Now Ivry also ordered me not to fire.

The frustration I felt is hard to describe. I continued flying behind the Egyptian MiGs which still hadn't noticed me. Such a clear target, but the controller's order was even clearer. "Do not fire." I didn't know the reason why, but since I requested permission and was turned down, there's nothing I could do about it. A pilot with the rank of lieutenant does not disobey the controller and the order of a lead pilot.

The two Egyptian MiGs kept on flying west, unaware they had just been saved by that controller. Over Nitzana, they crossed into Sinai.

I came out of burner, slowed my speed, turned right, and began gliding toward the runway at Hatzor. Ivry landed ahead of me. I was seething but I didn't say a word. I had a score to settle with the controller who stopped me, and I was waiting for the debriefing at Kirya headquarters in the afternoon. When I entered the briefing room, an officer was waiting for me with a bottle of champagne. "I'm sorry," he said. It was the controller.

I was still furious. "How could you do that to me? I was locked on him. Why did you stop the launch?"

The controller explained the mistake. "I thought it was the first pair reporting, the pair that went after the Egyptian MiGs that patrolled along the border and had already crossed back into Sinai, and there was no permission to continue the pursuit westward." Also, since five pairs of our planes were in the air at the time because of the Egyptian MiGs, he had been concerned about 'friendly fire', that our own planes would be fired upon. David Ivry, who was present at the debriefing, did not explain why he had echoed the controller's order not to fire the missile.

That day I made a decision: Next time, if and when I find myself in a similar situation, I won't ask permission. I'll press the button to fire the missile and down the enemy plane.

And that is just what I did from then on, every time I was engaged in aerial combat.

There would be other kills that I 'missed', ones I could have had my name on, but just like how you always remember your first kiss, I always remember that first kill that got away.

Fortunately, after that one missed opportunity, there were many more that I *didn't* miss.

Giora Even-Epstein, 2020

1 NATURE BOY ON THE KIBBUTZ

I was born on May 20, 1938, at the hospital in Afula during a very turbulent period, the time of 'the riots' instigated by the Arab leadership in Mandatory Palestine[1]. Jewish communities were being attacked, the roads became death-traps, and the small Jewish Yishuv suffered a heavy bloody toll in the first major clash with Arab gangs. The women in the maternity ward in the Afula hospital, including my mother, hid behind the hospital's pillars whenever they heard gunfire from the direction of the nearby Arab villages. This was my first baptism of fire, as a newborn baby.

My parents came from Poland. My father, Hillel Epstein, was a member of the Hashomer Hatzair movement in the town of Wolkowysk, where he met Yitzhak Yezernitsky, later Yitzhak Shamir, who would go on to command the Lehi pre-state underground militia and later be elected prime minister of Israel. My mother, Chaya, was born in another town in Poland called Ulica, and like my father she was active in Hashomer Hatzair. They met for the first time in the early 1930s at a hachshara camp in Czestochowa that was part of the HeHalutz movement, in preparation for aliyah and kibbutz life. The youths of the hachshara had been issued permits – known as 'certificates' – for immigration to Palestine, based on allocations made by the British Mandate authorities, who restricted the number of Jewish immigrants. My father's application for a certificate was accelerated after he received a draft notice from the Polish army.

The first stop for the hachshara members was Kibbutz Ramat Yohanan near Haifa, where they learned the basics of farming in anticipation of their 'ascent to the land', or physical establishment, of Kibbutz Shamir and supported themselves by doing various types of labour: as dock workers at the port of Haifa, paving roads and other odd jobs. My father was one of the people who built Rambam Hospital in Haifa – one of the biggest hospitals in Israel. He also helped pave the road from Haifa to the Neve Sha'anan neighbourhood and worked as a docker. My mother worked in the children's house on the kibbutz. They married on Kibbutz Ramat Yohanan.

---

[1] British Mandate.

The *gar'in* (the group that immigrated together to Palestine) was composed of two groups, the Polish group and the Romanian group, but the attempt to merge them into one group did not go well. Eventually, the Kibbutz Artzi movement saw that it was hopeless and decided to separate them. The Poles were moved to Givat Ganim, a small Yishuv near Rishon LeZion, and added to the *gar'in* that was part of hachshara there in preparation for establishing a new kibbutz in the south that would be the southernmost Jewish Yishuv in Palestine, 13 kilometres south of Be'er Tuvia. The preparations for its establishment were undertaken in total secrecy for fear of the reaction of the British Mandate authorities and the Arab gangs. The hachshara members earned a living by working in construction in Rishon LeZion, and later as wagon drivers transporting iron and building materials. From time to time, they also worked in agriculture, mostly digging pits, planting orchards and watering trees.

The leaders of the Jewish Yishuv in Palestine and the Haganah[2] command planned the establishment of Kibbutz Negba as a secret military operation. According to the Haganah's plan, Negba, in central Israel, the sole Jewish kibbutz in the heart of a hostile Arab population – seven Arab villages and Julis, a large British military camp – was going to be the last Jewish Yishuv to be established as part of the 'Tower and Stockade' (*Homa U'Migdal*) method. The preparations were made at Kibbutz Givat Brenner, in central Israel far from the prying eyes of the British, who were deliberately making things difficult for the Jewish Yishuv in Palestine and had thwarted its settlement momentum. The guard tower and huts for the new kibbutz were prepared at Moshav Be'er Tuvia, the goal being to put up the tower and all the huts in a single night, since a law, in force since Ottoman times, prohibited the demolition of buildings that had a completed roof and a surrounding enclosure.

On the night of July 12, 1939, Negba was established: a tower, a few huts, and a wooden barrier that surrounded the brand-new kibbutz not far from the road that led to Camp Julis, which at the time was a major base for a British artillery battalion. In the morning, when the tower, huts, and stockade were seen by the British and the people in the nearby Arab villages, British police came to investigate the site, and the heads of the settlers' committee presented them with documents proving that the new kibbutz was built on Jewish land.

The first three houses on the kibbutz were built close to the tower. Made of silicate stones, these distinctive structures ultimately became a symbol of Negba's hold on the land. The mothers and children arrived some weeks after

---

[2] The main paramilitary organisation of the Jewish Yishuv in Mandatory Palestine between 1920 and 1948, when it became the core of the Israel Defense Forces (IDF).

the kibbutz first came into being. But even before that, the first two graves were dug on the kibbutz: On August 31, 50 days after its establishment, a truck departed the kibbutz, as it did every day, to bring back water from the Be'er Tuvia area. As the truck drove away, the scout in the tower followed its progress through binoculars, until suddenly there was a loud boom. The truck had driven over a mine planted in the dirt road north of the kibbutz. Two of the four passengers, Gershon Rogozhinsky and Avram Shak, were killed. The other two were badly injured. The first two victims of the long war to defend Negba.

LIFE ON A KIBBUTZ

I was about 14 months old when I came with my mother to the new kibbutz. My parents and other early members of the kibbutz said I was a curious child, one who had a strong desire to know and try everything. From my first day on the kibbutz, I lived together with the other children and our carers. We saw our parents in the evenings when they finished working. My father worked in the kibbutz orchards and my mother in the chicken coop. My mother also helped care for the kibbutz children, and would lend a hand in the kitchen, despite her total lack of cooking skills. She didn't even know how to make an omelette! There were no hired cooks on the kibbutz; all the cooking was handled by the female kibbutzniks. The menu hardly varied: boiled vegetables and semolina. Every day, semolina. There were often days when I couldn't bear to look at boiled vegetables and semolina anymore.

The kibbutz had a cattle shed, chicken coop and a sheep pen, but rabbits – which reproduce at a fast pace – were our main source of meat. Occasionally, we also ate chicken. There was often a rooster or chicken that got sick and had to be slaughtered right away. Beef was an even rarer commodity. Again, the only beef we ate came from sick cows that had to be slaughtered. An Arab slaughterer from the nearby village of Beit Afa would come to slaughter the animals.

In the carpentry workshop, they were building a merry-go-round for the kibbutz children, and it became a major source of entertainment for us. We would stick a piece of gravel inside the screw of the central axis and enjoy watching it get ground to bits. One day, my insatiable curiosity led me to stick my finger in the axis of the carousel, where it got crushed. I always excelled at mischief and pranks that often landed me in the kibbutz infirmary.

I was about five years old when a new sheep pen was built on the kibbutz. At the entrance there was a large wooden gate topped with a length of iron pipe, and behind that was a hayloft. We loved to climb the gate and cross from side-to-side by gripping the top bar with our hands and flipping ourselves over it. What we didn't know was that, on the inside of the iron pipe, there were electric wires running from one end to the other. One time, just when I'd climbed up the wooden gatepost which was about six metres high, my hands suddenly stuck to the wood and the iron bar. I was being electrocuted! The only thing that saved me was the fact that my legs were in the air, depriving this deathtrap of a grounding, so the electric current didn't kill me. The other kids shouted at me to move and I shouted back that I couldn't. Luckily, there was one older kid there, Eitan Arieli, who would go on to become the deputy commander of the 14th Tank Brigade in the 1973 Yom Kippur War. He picked up a long stick and hit my hands with it until they opened. While this saved me from severe electrical burns, I fell from the post and suffered a major concussion, which kept me bedridden for two weeks.

We enjoyed every minute on the kibbutz. There were always exciting new attractions that probably no children anywhere else in the world got to experience. The British soldiers from the big police fortress at Iraq Suwaydan invited us to a Christmas party at the police station. In the large yard there was a fir tree decorated with colourful paper balls. The soldiers served us cakes that tasted strange to us and gave out boxes of bright-hued sweets. We were in heaven. I wonder what they would have said if they knew that our parents on the kibbutz were responsible for the 'slik' – the hidden bunker, in which illegal weapons were stored – and that a company from the Palmach[3] militia permanently resided at the young kibbutz.

Entirely oblivious to the terrible war that was happening in Europe, we didn't have a care in the world. It was so far away, and our parents didn't share with us their worry for the families who were left behind. It wasn't until years later, when I was already grown, that I learned about the tragic fates of my parents' relatives who were deported to the concentration camps in Poland. Up until the start of the war, my father was in continuous contact with his family back in Poland, but then all contact suddenly ended. My father lost his parents, his brother and many first and second cousins. Two of my mother's siblings, a brother and sister who were in the Hanoar Ha'oved youth movement, managed to immigrate to Palestine before the German army occupied Poland. Her sister, Rachel, married Yitzhak Yaguri, a founder of Kibbutz Yagur, and her brother, Shlomo, one of the founders of Kibbutz Alonim, were sent to Europe after the war to aid in the immigration process for survivors. There Shlomo discovered that, out of their large family, only one half-brother,

---

[3] Founded in May 1941 as an elite fighting force of the Haganah.

their father's son from a previous marriage, had survived the Holocaust. Shlomo returned to Palestine with the devastating news that most of my mother's family had been murdered.

The curious child that I was, I eagerly awaited the start of first grade. My books and notebooks were ready long before the school year began. Books have always been an important part of my life. I learned to read before first grade and as a little boy I was fascinated by photographs and illustrations in books, especially ones of exciting faraway places.

My first grade teacher, Simha Levin, or 'Sashka' as we called him, was the best teacher we could have hoped for. He was the one who really immersed us in nature. We went out on nature hikes all the time, and thanks to him I got to know every plant, every animal, every insect and every flying creature. Sashka liked to take us to a big swamp where the plants grew all winter, not far from the village of Iraq Suwaydan, to introduce us to nature's wonders there, such as snakes, or nests of warblers tucked away in the brush. The learning was organised by topic, for example the topic of fire. We learned all there was to know about fire. At the end of each topic, we would put on a play about it. When we learned about trees, we learned the parable of the trees, from the Book of Judges, by heart. Sashka was a good friend of the poet Avraham Shlonsky who often came to the kibbutz and was a regular member of the audience at our plays.

Passover, the holiday that commemorates the exodus from Egypt, was a special experience on the kibbutz. Everyone came together in the dining hall which was in the big cabin in the centre of Negba and recited the Haggadah put out by the Kibbutz Artzi movement. The kibbutz choir sang and sang and sang. My father, who later on, after the War of Independence, was chosen to be in charge of the cultural committee (a very important part of kibbutz life at the time) had a special role. In Negba, the custom was for the recitation of the Haggadah to be divided among all the kibbutz members, and he was the one tasked with this responsibility. A few days before the holiday, my father prepared pieces of paper that he gave out to each person with the portion of the Haggadah they were supposed to read aloud. Some of them evaded this assignment, so my father, who was also responsible for overseeing all the kibbutz celebrations, read nearly a fifth of the Haggadah himself.

As a child I never missed the chance to attend a rehearsal of the kibbutz choir. The choir was conducted by kibbutz member Yisrael 'Yulek' Barzilai, who was supremely musical and turned the Negba choir into one of the best in the entire kibbutz movement. Thanks to Yulek, who went on to become a member of the Knesset and health minister, I was exposed to songs of Israel, songs of the Palmach, and classic Russian songs. I knew all the songs by heart. I had a special knack when it came to song lyrics. To this day, I think I still know all the words to Israeli songs. And I owe it all to those wonderful days with Sashka and Yulek.

I loved any kind of sport involving a ball – football, basketball, dodgeball – and athletics as well, but I was known as a nature boy above all. I was one of the shortest children my age, so I was nicknamed 'Pitzkeh' (Tiny), but it didn't bother me. In sports, I was one of the quickest – the child who needed three steps to match one step by the others, and still passed them. Practically every child on the kibbutz had a nickname. Yigal Hanegbi, my best friend in primary school until his parents left the kibbutz, was called 'The Specialist'. His father was a very important person on the kibbutz. It wasn't until many years later that I understood what his position was. He was the *mukhtar* (mayor) of Negba, a role similar to that of a regional commander in the kib- butz movement. On what came to be known as Black Sabbath, June 29, 1946, when the British turned dozens of kibbutzim upside down searching for Haganah weapons that were hidden in the bunkers – in reprisal for several major operations by the Haganah and Palmach, the biggest of which involved blowing up 11 bridges around the country – two battalions also showed up at Negba, but because of Yigal's father's ties with the soldiers, they didn't enter the kibbutz.

We lived in the children's house on the kibbutz, which we thought of as home. We didn't know any other way of life. The thing that really character- ised us was togetherness. We were a tight-knit group of 13 boys and girls. Even the shower was shared. There were no clear leaders in our group, but each one of us came to develop distinctive traits.

The routine was fairly set. The main carers would get us up in the morning and see that we washed up and brushed our teeth. Then came breakfast and lessons until noon. After lunch it was mandatory to get in bed for the afternoon rest. Then we would all comb our hair and dress nicely for the visit to our parents, in their small and modest two-room apartment. That's where I would also see my little sister Nava. For dinner, the children were back together again. Looking back, I think of my life with the kibbutz children as a most wonderful thing.

Ever since I was little, I have loved dogs. I had a dog on the kibbutz even before I started to walk. From that time on, I have cherished dogs, which always return the affection they are shown.

When I was seven or eight, my father was drafted into the Palmach as part of the quota that each kibbutz was obligated to supply. I'd heard the name

Palmach by then, but I didn't really know what it was. I just understood that he was in the army. He was stationed at Kiryat Anavim, and during the War of Independence, he was part of the Harel Brigade that was commanded by Yitzhak Rabin. My father was away from the kibbutz for two years. On weekends, by prior arrangement of course, my mother could speak with him on the kibbutz's one and only telephone, which was in the kitchen. On one of those occasions, I joined in the call too, and that was the first time in my life I had spoken on a telephone.

A few times, during school holidays, I travelled to visit him on the base. There I went around with the driver of Zvi Zamir, the battalion commander. Like everywhere else, the grown-ups were fond of me and liked the interest I showed in their training drills and in army life in general. As a child, I didn't understand why they were fighting each other with the shafts of hoes, and my father explained that this was how they trained in the Palmach. On my last visit with him, we rode down from Kiryat Anavim to the coastal plain in an armoured vehicle. This was not long before the road to Jerusalem was blocked.

Ahead of the UN declaration of the establishment of a Jewish state, relations with the neighbours in the Arab villages worsened, and we children were no longer allowed to wander close to them. The Arabs, who for years had been our good neighbours, started to harass the kibbutz. Their flocks of sheep entered Negba's agricultural fields and ruined them. On the kibbutz, people began to dig connecting trenches, and a heavy Besa machine gun was installed atop the water tower. The large pit by the kibbutz entrance where they had planned to build a swimming pool was converted into a hidden shooting range. The kibbutz members and the people from the Palmach hachshara held target practice there. After each round, they collected all the casings so as to avoid the notice of the British, and we children vied to see who could manage to pull out the bullets that were fired into the pit's defensive wall. Not long after that, the pit was used as an emergency water reservoir.

In May 1948, as the British Mandate was about to end and the British were preparing to leave the country, the soldiers from the Julis military camp came to say goodbye to us. It was an artillery base, so they spread their cannons out along the avenue of Ficus trees on the kibbutz, allowing us to freely climb on them. We were a carefree bunch of kids who loved to play and get into mischief.

The 1948 Passover Seder was the last major event on the kibbutz before the situation changed. As usual, Yulek oversaw the preparations and conducted the choir. The rehearsals took place in the children's storeroom and

I didn't miss a single one. I sat there fascinated, while Yulek yelled at people who sang off-key and made everyone start all over from the beginning. During breaks in rehearsal, I heard Yulek talking about the security situation. He had received reports from the Mapam[4] leadership that David Ben-Gurion was going to declare the establishment of the state and then the Egyptian army was expected to immediately invade. None of us children, however, thought for a moment that life as we'd always known it was about to change beyond recognition.

---

[4] Left-wing political party in 1948 – now the Meretz Party.

2 WAR AND EVACUATION

Our personal paradise changed overnight.

As a 10-year-old, I wasn't much aware of the dates on the calendar, but that day, May 14, 1948, was unusual and especially exciting. Yulek travelled that morning to Tel Aviv, and we children noticed the special excitement among the adults, who in the afternoon gathered around a big radio, from which we all heard the familiar voice of David Ben-Gurion declaring the establishment of a Jewish homeland in Palestine. We were proud that our Yulek was there, with the nation's leadership.

That evening he returned to the kibbutz, called an urgent meeting and informed everyone that the national leadership had information that a war would start that very night. The Egyptian army was going to invade the newborn country. It was a stormy meeting. Yulek announced that buses would come to pick up the children and mothers and evacuate them from the kibbutz. There was shouting for and against, and it was decided by vote that all the children and some of the mothers would be evacuated.

The carers immediately started to prepare provisions for our evacuation. They packed clothing and personal items as if we were heading off to summer camp. At one in the morning, a convoy of buses arrived, escorted by soldiers. My mother was not being evacuated that night, and she asked me to look after my little sister Nava, who was also evacuated. My mother, and other mothers, told their children, "See you tomorrow," held back their tears and waved goodbye to us. The men and the mothers of older children remained on the kibbutz. The mothers of babies and young children were evacuated. My father had been drafted into the Palmach and wasn't on the kibbutz at the time of the evacuation.

The convoy of buses left Negba using low headlights. On the way north, there were checkpoints and the soldiers waved to us. We drove to Kibbutz Givat Brenner, and they put us up in the children's house there. We got up early in the morning, eager to know what had happened on the kibbutz. It wasn't until a few days later that we were told about the Egyptian assault that involved tanks and armoured vehicles, as well as Spitfires from the Egyptian air force.

In the first assault, the dining hall, the pit that was intended to be a pool, and houses were hit. The big lawn of the kibbutz was filled with craters from shells and bombs. In this offensive, which was repelled when the Egyptians had practically reached the fences, seven of the kibbutz's defenders were killed, including the fathers of three of the evacuated children, and about 30 were wounded. About 200 Egyptian soldiers were killed in the first attack.

Kibbutz Negba was the last stronghold standing in the way of the Egyptian column that was advancing eastward, aiming to cut off the Negev from the centre of the country. The Egyptians made a concerted effort to conquer Negba before continuing on. The saga of Kibbutz Negba, 'Negba-grad', would ultimately become part of the heroic lore of the War of Independence, with the awareness that the prolonged battle to seize the kibbutz halted the Egyptians' eastward march, and later made it possible to deploy a strong enough force to stop the advancing Egyptian column.

Five days after the evacuation, May 20, was my birthday. I had waited for it with great anticipation, but no one had time to even think about celebrating. After two weeks at Givat Brenner, they moved us to Herzliya. There we were housed in a high school, that we came to think of as Little Negba. The classrooms were our living quarters and where we had our lessons. During the first lull in the fighting, most of the women who'd remained on the kibbutz were evacuated. My mother was among them. The only women still at Negba were young single women who served as nurses, medics and cooks.

We got into a routine of school, as if we were still at home on the kibbutz. There were 15 children in our group. When we'd been there a few months, they brought us some of the animals from the kibbutz, including one of the horses that had been evacuated from the bombed-out stable. I was thrilled when I saw that my dog Kushi was with the animals that were brought to us. My whole class adopted him and he followed us everywhere. We were sad to learn that most of the cows from the cattle barn had been killed in the bombardments.

Adults from the kibbutz who came from Negba to visit us in Herzliya were careful not to tell us exactly what was happening on the kibbutz. They hid the truth from us – that most of the kibbutz buildings had been hit and that some of the kibbutz members, including parents of evacuated children, were killed in the battle for Negba. A little booklet published on the 10th anniversary of the battle said:

"There wasn't a single thing on the ground that wasn't destroyed, burned or damaged. There wasn't an inch of earth that wasn't strewn with shrapnel and bullets. The ground was tilled with the plough of destruction. Twenty-five thousand shells were dropped on us. One hundred and fifty airborne bombs in 27 bombardments by Egyptian planes. Above ground, Negba ceased to exist. Underground, Negba hung on in trenches and bunkers, positions and tunnels. Negba's defenders lived deep in the earth. There they walked, ate, slept, fought and also died… The quiet village surrounded by shady trees, with white houses and green lawns, had suddenly become a raging battlefront. The first line of fire in a fateful life-or-death war. A stronghold that was clung to by the fingertips until death."

On July 12 – how symbolic that the second and even bigger attack on Negba occurred precisely on the one-year anniversary of the kibbutz's founding – after the first lull in the fighting, achieved through UN mediation, the Egyptians attacked again, with much greater force. The Egyptian army surrounded Negba, which was situated on a plain, and controlled all the surrounding hilltops except for those on the eastern and north-eastern side. The Egyptian force numbered in the hundreds, with dozens of tanks and armoured vehicles and Spitfires, which along with converted Dakota bombers circled over the kibbutz unhindered. Arrayed against them were a few dozen people from Negba plus a company from the Givati Brigade of about 70 fighters, and a force composed of another 30 fighters, who arrived as reinforcements. The second attack was also halted after a few hours. Most of the tanks drove over mines that had been scattered in the open areas outside the kibbutz fences, and by the end of the day of combat, the Egyptians had retreated, leaving behind about 250 dead. The defenders' losses totalled five dead and dozens wounded. In the course of the war, and when the pressure from the Egyptian army was at its most intense, the kibbutz members debated several times: Stay or evacuate? The decision was virtually unanimous: We fight to the end for Negba-grad. The kibbutzniks clearly drew inspiration from the heroism of the Red Army in the fierce battle for Stalingrad in World War II.

During one of the lulls, we were taken to the kibbutz for a visit. I didn't recognise our Negba. Aside from the three silicate buildings at the entrance to the kibbutz, no house in Negba has survived the heavy bombardments. It made us angry when we heard from our parents who had stayed to defend the kibbutz that the neighbouring Arabs had also joined in the assault on Negba. I could not understand how they could have done so. How they could have been so ungrateful. We recalled how just a few months before the war an Arab from one of the villages had shown up at the kibbutz with his young son who had somehow gotten a piece of eight-inch pipe stuck in his head.

In the welding workshop, they gripped the boy's head in a vice and managed to free it. The father couldn't thank us enough. And now? Was he also among the forces that charged the kibbutz fences? We weren't friends with the kids from the Arab villages, but we knew them. We also knew Abed, the Arab who had been employed as a guard in the fields by us for years, very well. We would always see him galloping by on his horse and he would wave hello to us. Abed, we were told, had also joined in the attacks on Negba. After the war he fled to the Gaza Strip, and as we later heard, the score with him was settled when the Israel Defense Forces (IDF) seized control of Gaza in the 1956 Sinai Campaign.

Summer holidays arrived. My favourite place to hang out was the small airport in Herzliya, where for the first time in my life I saw a Messerschmitt – one of the planes that Israel obtained from Czechoslovakia after the war started. Another time, I witnessed an accident when a Messerschmitt crashed on the runway in Herzliya. I found out later that the pilot of that plane was Modi Alon, who did not survive the crash. Modi Alon, the Israel Air Force's first fighter pilot and the first commander of the First Fighter Squadron, had returned that day, together with Ezer Weizman, from attacking the Egyptian forces in the Ashdod area. At that point in my life, the experience of being around the Herzliya airport did not spark in me the yearning to fly.

After nine months in Herzliya, they moved us to an enormous building in the middle of some fields and orchards in Ness Ziona. The building had formerly been the home of a wealthy Arab *mukhtar*, and it looked like a palace out of the *Tales of the Arabian Nights*. It had dozens of big rooms and a huge roof. We children lived in rooms in the estate and the adults in cabins that had been built close by. The palace was surrounded by many acres of orchards. There were all kinds of fruit trees. Our life there was very similar to our kibbutz routine; it was as if we were still at Negba. We also returned to cultural activities in an attempt to recreate the Friday nights on the kibbutz.

The biggest show was the production of Avraham Shlonsky's 'Mickey Mouse' staged by our Sashka. I played the lead of Mickey Mouse and the show succeeded beyond all our expectations. After Ness Ziona, we were invited to perform at the Mograbi Cinema in Tel Aviv, and one of the people in the large audience was Vera Weizmann, wife of President Chaim Weizmann. She came up on stage and gave me a kiss on the forehead.

The war ended at the start of 1949, but the return to Negba was still far off. The kibbutz had been completely destroyed, and of all the structures we once knew, only the water tower survived, though it, too, was perforated all over from being hit by numerous shells. It bore silent witness to the ferocious battles. Negba had to be rebuilt and we were happy for every extra day we got to stay at our palace in Ness Ziona. We hoped we could go on staying there for a long time. Wherever we went, we heard people talking about us with admiration: These are the children from Negba. The name of the kibbutz had become legend in the War of Independence. A symbol of fortitude in the face of the Egyptian army. American friends of the kibbutz bought a new Scania truck to replace the one that was burned in the war, and we also received shawls from the US Army and paraffin heaters on which we dried our wet clothes during the Ness Ziona winter, which was harsh, rainy, and muddy. In Ness Ziona, I lost my dog Kushi, who just disappeared one day. We looked everywhere for him, to no avail. Years later, at a kibbutz movement convention in Rehovot, a little white dog suddenly attached itself to me and wouldn't leave me. When we went back to the kibbutz, I took him with me.

BACK TO THE NEW NEGBA

In 1950, two years after the evacuation, we returned to Negba. We didn't recognise the place. All the surrounding Arab villages had been abandoned and after the war, all the houses there were bulldozed and the land readied for agriculture. The war wounds were still visible everywhere. The kibbutz had lost a number of members, but the biggest loss that people talked about was the Palmach regional commander –Yitzhak Dubnov, nicknamed Yoav – who was a special figure on the kibbutz and was killed in the first bombardment of Negba on May 15. Two children in my class had lost their fathers in the war, but they hardly ever spoke of them.

We started to get used to the new Negba. The children's house we once knew, the parents' houses – all of these were gone. New houses were built in their place. Each one had four rooms – one room per family. Now that we were 13 years old, we moved into the local kibbutz school, about 500 metres south of our kibbutz, a place that was like a small kibbutz unto itself, with classrooms and small huts for the teenagers who came from five kibbutzim in the area.

The kibbutz rehabilitated itself. A new group of *olim* from South America was introduced and as we were approaching high-school age, the kibbutz was reformed into a high school to serve several kibbutzim. Some 'outside children' also came to Negba, including some who were Holocaust survivors. One of them, Yossi Peled, grew up to head the IDF's Northern Command.

From time to time, donors from abroad would come, accompanied by people from the Jewish Agency who had brought them to see 'the kibbutz that defeated the Egyptians…' The visitors were so impressed and excited that they gladly opened their wallets, and signs went up on the school bearing the names of the foreign guests.

At that time, we started going to the youth group camps and that's where we were exposed to the ideology and values of the Hashomer Hatzair movement and its mother political movement – Mapam. We learned the songs of our movement, and we also learned to put down the other youth movements. The grown-ups' political battles trickled down to us, and we were raised on a hatred of Ben-Gurion and Mapai. I had a problem with the attempt to brainwash us with love for Mother Russia. The death of Stalin the dictator in 1953 was a major event for the kibbutz. An enormous photograph of the Russian leader was hung up in our school dining hall, surrounded by olive branches that were painted black. Some of the girls in my class were weeping, but I couldn't keep from laughing about the whole thing. I did not share their adoration for him.

In Hashomer Hatzair at the time, there were three age groups: 'Bnei Masada' who were the youngest, 'Tzofim' for the pre-teens, and 'Bogrim' for the older kids. The transition from one group to the next was always an occasion for a ceremony where the insignia and coloured neck scarves for that group were given out, accompanied by motivational talks from the counsellors. I was the only one who received them later on, not with the rest of my class. I was told that it was because I did not embrace the group's spirit. I was very hurt, but it was true that I had a negative attitude during group discussions that involved ideological brainwashing. I had my own opinions, and the older I got, the more confident I became in defending them.

I loved my years at the kibbutz school. Classes until noon, and then after lunch, we worked in the fields. I worked in the pig barn, the chicken coop, the vegetable garden and the dining hall. And I was the first one who was given the job of 'mekima' – waking the younger children at four in the afternoon and preparing them to see their parents. I got them dressed, and also acquired skills like combing and braiding the girls' hair. I was a bookworm before that term really came into use. I read voraciously, maybe 100 pages an hour. I devoured all the books in the kibbutz library and at the school, and through reading, I acquired vast general knowledge. I read a book a day. There wasn't a single book in the kibbutz library that I hadn't gotten my hands on.

My childhood heroes were Winnetou, Old Shatterhand, Old Firehand and the men of the Wild West – all characters from adventure books by Karl May. I galloped with them on wild mustangs through the American West, and I fought alongside them against the hostile Indian tribes that threatened the pioneers of the American frontier. I also loved tales of the forest like Robin Hood and Ivanhoe. Ever since that time, green has been my favourite colour.

At school, there were Gadna (pre-army training) lessons. We had Gadna Sayarim – a scouting youth group. Other places also had air force Gadna, and later on, a lot of pilots entered the air force after first being exposed to it through the Gadna. That didn't come to our school. Someone had apparently decided that the air force Gadna would go no further than somewhere around Givat Brenner. But I started to gain a love for flying through books.

In the last years of high school, I was especially into books about war heroes, and I was particularly fascinated by books about pilots. I knew by heart all the tales of the battles of Douglas Bader – 'the amputee pilot' – and the hero of the Battle of Britain, and all about Pierre Clostermann, the French flying ace who flew in the uniform of Britain's RAF in that same war, and who was later called France's top pilot by Charles de Gaulle. I was drawn to history books about aerial combat, and I learned how the light patrol planes of Germany, France, and England, whose job at the start of the First World War was to fly across enemy lines and direct the artillery, had evolved into fighter jets that began engaging in dogfights with one another.

Pilot solidarity was so high in those days that whenever two enemy planes first crossed paths, the custom was for both pilots to straighten up in the cockpit and salute each other. This gentlemanly gesture stopped being made after an instance when a German pilot was saluting the French pilot who passed him, and the latter pulled out a gun and shot him. Then the Germans were out for revenge. Pilots began carrying pistols and rifles, and, later, machine guns, and the patrols turned into dogfights. This is when the first aces – pilots who downed at least five enemy planes – were crowned.

I also knew by heart every dogfight of Alan Deere, a New Zealand-born pilot who served in the RAF during World War II and wrote a book about it called *Nine Lives*. I was surprised to find a book about a Russian amputee pilot, Alexander de Seversky, just like the British had. I often imagined myself as one of those fighter pilots. Little by little, from reading about all these pilot heroes, my own dreams took shape. By 12th grade I'd made up my mind: I would be a fighter pilot, like my heroes.

3 NOT FIT TO BE A PILOT

I was 17 when my first draft notice arrived. There was no question in my mind where I wanted to go. It had to be the pilot course. Though our childhood heroes had been the paratroopers, heroes of the reprisal operations that captured the imagination, most of the boys in my class went into the tank corps. Maybe because the tank school, Julis, was right across the road. Only two guys volunteered for the paratroops; all I wanted was to become a pilot. In addition to physical fitness and other good qualities, I have incredible eyesight, something that is a great asset for a fighter pilot. I can see twice or three times as far, maybe more, than anyone I know. I apparently inherited this from my mother. I remember that we kids were standing next to the school one time, which was about 500 metres away from the kibbutz houses, and I told the boy next to me that his father had just come out of the room. He looked and didn't see anything. There were many times when I saw things from a distance that my friends who were with me couldn't see. I was even able to read the numbers on the planes that flew over the kibbutz.

Thanks to all the stories I'd read about the greatest pilots in history, I'd also learned to identify from the ground any aircraft that flew overhead, and a lot did pass by because the plains around Kibbutz Negba were part of the training zone for the air force planes from Hatzor and Tel Nof. I knew all the types in the air force, and I was especially drawn to the fighter jets. Every plane that passed over Negba attracted my attention, and I followed it with my eyes as it descended in preparation for landing at the nearby Hatzor airbase. One day, I noticed a formation of four Mosquitos, which were relatively new in the air force. These were the kind used in World War II to mark ground targets with white phosphorus rockets. Suddenly, I saw that one plane had lost its two engines and was plummeting toward the ground. One of the two crewmen bailed out and then his parachute opened. The plane broke up in the air. One wing fell next to the children's building. Other parts were scattered in the fields. We raced toward the wreckage and found the aircraft's nose planted in the earth. The second crewman was lying dead by the plane's exit door.

Another time, when I'd already completed my army service, a pilot of a

Super Mystère who was about to land at Hatzor ejected after birds flew into the plane's engine. The plane continued its forward trajectory, without an engine, until it landed intact in the kibbutz's pear orchard. Fortunately, it happened minutes after the people working there – my father among them – had left for lunch.

When I went to the draft office after receiving my first call-up notice at the end of 11th grade, I told them I was volunteering for the pilot course. I was sent to Tel Nof for the preliminary tests for acceptance to the air force. After a long day of medical examinations and psychological tests, I returned to the kibbutz feeling that I'd easily passed all the medical exams. I'd also been tested on composition, something I'd never been that strong in, but I convinced myself it wasn't something they'd disqualify a flight candidate for. All the other tests had gone very smoothly. Even though, in the name of the principle of equality, there were no matriculation exams on the Hashomer Hatzair kibbutzim, we occasionally compared our knowledge with that of the children in city high schools, and we had nothing to be ashamed of.

My class enlisted in two stages. The girls were drafted in June and the boys went to work on the kibbutz and were drafted later. Before our enlistment, we prepared a show of poems and classic tunes to which we added lyrics that described our life growing up on the kibbutz. We performed at the three kibbutzim that were served by our school: Negba, Kfar Menachem and Ruhama.

I waited every day for the letter from the army, and finally it came. A brown envelope with a military postmark, and inside a single sheet that made me very happy. I'm reserved by nature and don't generally let my emotions show, but this time I couldn't contain my happiness. I'd been accepted on to the pilot course.

On August 18, 1956, I donned an army uniform for the first time and was summoned to the air force booth. In those days there was no *gibush* stage (trial period for elite units) at the start of the course, and we all went to begin regular infantry basic training at Bahad 4 in Tzrifin. Basic training was supposed to last two months, but a week before the end we stopped training because the Sinai Campaign had begun with the paratroop battalion's capture of the Mitla Pass. With training halted, we were dispersed to the different air force bases. I was sent to Hatzor and assigned to the technical division as an assistant to the munitions personnel. My job was to check the electrical contacts inside the engines of the rockets carried by the Mystères. My work was timed with the activity of the pilots, who took off armed with rockets and returned an hour later without them.

When the war ended, all the cadets designated for Pilot Course No. 25 were sent to Tel Nof to start the course. I was informed that I was not joining them. The decision was final, and no one bothered to explain why. I felt like I was going crazy. No one would tell me why I alone, out of all the cadets who had passed the preliminary tests and basic training, was not going to start the course. At the Hatzor base I tried talking to anyone who might be able to give me an answer. Everyone said they'd check into it, but no one ever got back to me.

At one point, I went to one of the young pilots, Lieutenant Ran Peker, who was in charge of the new cadets in the pilot course, and asked him why I wasn't joining the others. He promised to look into it, and after a while he came back and told me that they'd found some medical issue and that I had to go through a medical committee for approval. I went through all the medical tests again and was told to go back to Hatzor and wait patiently. They would contact me there to tell me what was happening.

Pilot Course No. 25 began at Tel Nof with ground training, classroom lessons and introductory Piper flights. Meanwhile I was stuck at Hatzor, frustrated, not knowing what was happening with me. All I knew was that it was some kind of medical problem, something to do with the heart, and that my case would be reviewed by the air force medical committee.

While I waited in Hatzor I was sent to the base carpentry shop where, together with other soldiers, I made lockers for the soldiers at the base out of ammunition crates. At the Hatzor carpentry shop there were two expert carpenters, true craftsmen, who let me assist in the preparation of a wooden model of a Mystère, which was to be given as a gift from the base to Ezer Weizman, who was finishing his time as Hatzor's commander.

There was still no answer from the medical committee.

From the carpentry shop I was moved to the First Fighter Squadron, as a mechanic's assistant. I served as an apprentice to the experienced mechanics, and I worked with them to reassemble a damaged Mystère using new replacement parts from the plant in France. Before long, I went from being an apprentice to an advanced mechanic and fuelling Mystères. The high point of my various technical jobs came when I ran a Mystère engine while sitting in a locked cockpit. It was a wonderful illusion. I felt the power of the plane, the noise of the engine. But I was still just a mechanic who prepared the aircraft for take-off. I wanted so badly to be the one who sits in the cockpit and speeds down the runway for take-off. I had faith that day would come.

4 IF NOT A PILOT THEN A PARATROOPER

After the Sinai Campaign, the air force was in urgent need of pilots and new pilot courses opened at a faster rate. Course No. 25 kept advancing. Course No. 26 was about to start and I was still waiting for an answer from the medical committee. Then Course No. 26 began, and I was still outside. Back to another medical committee, and once again, told to wait. I saw Ran Peker again, now he was a young squadron pilot and also in charge of the new cadets of Course No. 26, and I told him what was going on.

"I want to be a combat soldier," I told him. "If they won't accept me into the pilot course, I want to volunteer for the paratroops." Ran promised to help, but it seemed the air force wasn't keen to release me to the paratroops. My scores were apparently very good and the air force still wanted to keep me. They offered me any job I wanted: controller, air force Gadna instructor, anything that would keep me in the air force, just not as a pilot.

I insisted on leaving and requested a meeting with Motti Hod, the base commander. Ran Peker helped me get to him. Hod, a kibbutznik himself from Deganya, welcomed me very warmly. He was enthusiastic about my determination to be a combat soldier, and said he would help me move to the paratroops. He didn't understand why the air force refused to release me and promised to check into the matter. A week later I received permission to transfer to the paratroops. But there was still another hurdle I had to overcome.

The brigade administrative officer for the paratroops, Major Baruch Levy, brother of future IDF chief of staff Moshe 'Moshe-and-a-Half' Levy, called me in to see him and explained that if the air force was adamant about not accepting me to the pilot course for health reasons, I might not be suited for the paratroops, either. To be sure that I had no medical problem that would prevent me from being a paratrooper, he sent me to the air force medical committee. I passed all the tests and was given written approval saying that I was fit for combat in any IDF unit. With this paper in hand, I requested a meeting with Dr Baruch, the flight surgeon who, of course, didn't remember me. I asked him why, if I was in such excellent health, I couldn't go back to the pilot course.

Dr Baruch, whose signature was on the medical permit I received, opened my medical file, number 6519 (in those years, medical files were a very closely guarded secret in the air force so I had no idea what was written in it), looked through it, spotted my medical problem, and read his own recommendation not to permit me to join the pilot course because of a problem that was found with my heart. He read what he himself had written just a few months earlier, and immediately insisted that I give him back the permit that he had issued. I couldn't figure out how the same doctor who disqualified me from becoming a pilot could approve me to be a paratrooper, when the physical demands in the paratroops were greater than in the pilot course. I had the chutzpah to ask him to explain to me the logic behind his decision. He refused and just repeated his demand that I return the letter. "I won't give you the letter," I said and rushed out of his office with the letter that was meant to go to the administrative officer of the paratroops.

In those days, there was no cardiologist in the air force, and the opinion of Dr Baruch, the flight surgeon, was enough to dash my dreams of being a pilot. A doctor who was not a cardiologist, and who did not see any need to add the expert opinion of a cardiology specialist to his findings regarding my case.

I made up my mind: I'll go to the paratroops, but I'll keep on fighting from there against Dr Baruch's medical decree. I left for the paratroop battalion training base at Beit Lid, near Netanya, more determined than ever that one day soon I would return to the pilot course in Tel Nof.

5 IN EROL'S COMPANY; IN RAFUL'S BATTALION

I joined the paratroops. Since I'd already completed basic training in the air force, I didn't have to go through another course of basic training, and I was attached to Daled Company with guys who had begun their army service in November. The company commander was Aharon 'Erol' Eshel, who was married to a woman from Negba and lived on the kibbutz. Erol, a star figure in the paratroops who later became a good friend too, did not tell me that my medical file contained a recommendation that I report back to the medical committee for check-ups every four months. If I'd known about it, I certainly would have done as it said, but I had no way of accessing my medical file, and I had no idea that such a possibility even existed. I came to the paratroops with the idea that this was where I would serve. But the dream of becoming a pilot hadn't faded.

In my first year in the army, I grew taller by three inches. The physical effort we put in during this time was very hard. There were a lot of kibbutzniks in Daled Company. It was an especially fine company with real quality people. I came into the company a few months after the Sinai Campaign and the paratroops' battle at the Mitla Pass. Most of the company's staff members, including Erol, of course, had parachuted at Mitla and taken part in the fierce fighting there. To me, they were all true heroes. There were several members of the national volleyball team in the company as well, and most of them were from kibbutzim, too. One of these was Arie Selinger, who went on to become an acclaimed manager who coached three national women's volleyball teams – Israel, Japan and the United States – as well as the Dutch men's team.

Traditionally, the volleyball players chose to serve in the Nachal Brigade, at the recommendation of national coach Micha Shamban, but this time, having made the decision during a flight from Paris to Israel, the team members opted to volunteer for the paratroops. Not surprisingly, the paratroops volleyball team won the IDF championship that year. We also took first place in tug-of-war and krav maga[5]. Our krav maga coach was known as 'Laughing

---

[5] A self-defence martial arts programme that originated in Israel.

Aimi'. His odd nickname dated from the time of the illegal immigration to Palestine near the end of the British Mandate. He was said to have swum 20 kilometres in the sea in order to guide a ship carrying immigrants. As a result of that effort, his facial muscles froze so that he always appeared to be grinning.

After a year, our two companies were merged into one and the best soldiers were sent to the squad commander course and the rest to the corporal course. It was the outstanding company in the brigade in the various sections of training. Rafael 'Raful' Eitan was the battalion commander and Marcel Tobias, a veteran of the French Foreign Legion, was the deputy battalion commander. They believed in serious training, lots of navigating, and tough marches, but without jerking us around for no good reason.

I excelled at hurling hand grenades, thanks to all the practice I got as a child trying to toss stones into a distant barrel. At the firing range, I came in second in the company. My sharp eyesight helped me with sharpshooting. Later on, after my achievements as a combat pilot, Raful liked to boast of how the air force's biggest ace was actually a paratrooper. At the time, we were not involved in any real military operations apart from one instance. During one training session in Wadi Ara, we were suddenly sent to the north, and we were briefed on a mission to seize the Syrian outpost at Tel Azaziat. That evening, as we were about to set out and cross the border, a messenger arrived on a motorcycle: the government had not approved the operation.

During the squad commander course, operations were combined with training. The company was stationed by the Mekorot water company plant not far from the Gaza border, and went out on ambushes. The local Arabs knew when the paratroopers were out on a mission and when the Golani soldiers were out, and they planned their theft of the farming equipment from the nearby kibbutzim accordingly. We lay in ambush and waited for them. When they realised that we'd seen them, they left their camels and quickly fled back into Gaza.

The most popular site for an ambush was not far from the UN position on the border of the Gaza Strip. The UN personnel were always watching films, and from the ambush location you could watch along with them. One day, a report came from one of the moshavim about a calf that was stolen from the cattle shed. It was a rainy day, so we weren't thrilled about going out to search for the stolen calf. Then the Bedouin officer, Amos Yarkoni, who would go on to become commander of Sayeret Shaked which was an army unit that would scout ahead, made one long mooing sound, and the missing calf came running back.

The squad commander course was nearing its end. Four gruelling months with hardly any break. The final march, from Tze'elim to Beit Lid, was supposed to be the last stage of the course before we were certified as squad commanders in the paratroops. It was planned to go for three nights – one night of navigation as a squad, a second night of marching as a division, and then a company-wide march on the third night that would end at Beit Lid. The marches also included raids, camouflage and other types of drills.

On the second night, we were assigned missions, and the other division set out to conquer the Beit Guvrin police station and mark Xs in chalk on the vehicles there. Two of the soldiers decided to make a prank of it and disguise the fact they were paratroopers. They removed the rubber bands from their trousers' legs so the trousers covered their red boots. The officer at the guard post by the entrance started to ask questions and the pair knocked him out. The division burst in, made a scene inside the police station and some of the soldiers commandeered vehicles and drove north with them. A few days later, one of the command cars was found on a cliff and could not be retrieved.

The incident did not go without a response. Haim Laskov, the officer commanding Southern Command at the time, summoned Raful and told him that if he didn't dismiss his 'Indians' from being commanders, the entire company, including him, would go to prison. Our division's planned raid was cancelled and we continued on the march toward Beit Naballah. When we got there, we found the soldiers from the other division sitting inside the base at Beit Naballah with their two squad commanders, who were officers with the rank of lieutenant – Dan Shomron and Danny Wolf – surrounded by a fence of concertina wire and military police sentries. A debate arose over what we should do, and we decided that we were joining them.

That same night, trucks came and took us to Beit Lid, where the paratroop battalion base was located.

We hadn't been at the base for four months. We'd spent that whole time in the field, in training. Our personal gear, the mattresses and beds were all in storage, and the commanders informed us that in two hours we had to be ready for the commander's inspection with an area cleared of all grass, paths marked with plaster, and tents erected. We decided spontaneously to refuse the order. There was absolutely no way we could manage that in just two hours. We lay down with the gear, and our commanders called the battalion police from the base to arrest a few soldiers whom they suspected of inciting the whole company to rebellion. When they arrived to make the arrests, we swarmed them and blocked them from reaching the soldiers. A big commotion began. Someone from the battalion command summoned the military police from a nearby base. The military police officers surrounded the encampment and announced that the company's soldiers were under arrest. In those years, there was no love lost between the military police and the paratroops, and there were plenty of times when a paratrooper was arrested on the road for a missing hat or unpolished boots. Seeing the military police officers approaching the encampment, the young paratroopers clutched their weapons and threatened to kill them if they didn't get away from there.

Raful, the battalion commander, and Erol, the company commander, were called to the site. Raful blasted us for our behaviour and said we had shamed the battalion and the paratroop brigade. The soldiers of the company protested about the humiliating treatment they'd received. Someone managed to get copies of Form 55, a transfer request, and we unanimously decided to sign them. We sent a delegation to Raful and placed the signed forms on his desk: a request by all the soldiers of Daled Company, graduates of the unfinished squad commander course, to immediately leave the battalion. We were all ready to go to prison. Of course, we didn't get to go home that weekend as planned, as the whole company was confined to the base.

The loser in this whole thing was the battalion, the brigade, and the IDF. The company was supposed to have sent 50 candidates to the officers' course. In the wake of the events that weekend, many of them decided to forgo the course. I didn't plan to go to the officers' course, either. On the other hand, I didn't want to remain in the battalion as a squad commander. Fortunately, the paratrooper school was looking for people to take the course for paratrooper instructors, and after a short break, I was on my way to Tel Nof. The way I saw it, a paratrooper instructor who also specialises in parachuting was the closest thing I could get to flying.

6 FELLAH AND SHEPHERD

The paratrooper instructor course lasted four-and-a-half months and I enjoyed every minute of it. I loved jumping, and I loved teaching paratroopers about jumping. I met some wonderful people at the parachuting school, and some of them became my close friends. Amos Shapira was one group ahead of me. Biatsky was one course behind me. In the parachuting instructor course, I started doing skydiving, too. In 1955, Israel had been represented at the World Skydiving Championship in Moscow with Raful and Topol on the team, but the whole field was still in its infancy.

We'd started our training by static-line jumping[6] exiting the plane as you would for a free-fall dive. The next stage was exiting at a higher altitude for three seconds of free-fall diving, then five seconds, and so on. When we reached the stage where we were free-fall diving for 30 seconds, the plane had climbed to 6,500 feet. I floated in the air like a bird before opening the parachute and it was incredible. My love of free-falling would stay with me for decades. Even when I became an experienced pilot, I kept on doing it – both within the army and with a private club that I helped found. As a free-fall diver, I learned to control my feelings in the air and to feel like I was my own master. I thought of free-falling as the noblest sport imaginable. It was like flying an engineless plane, with my limbs and my body as the controls. I finished the parachuting instructor course as the outstanding student.

After a year at the parachuting school, I completed my army service and returned to Negba. I came back to the kibbutz without pilot's wings, but with hundreds of jumps to my credit, including many dozens of free-fall dives. I came back with the goal of continuing to live on the kibbutz. This was my home. From here I went to the army, and to here I returned. Negba had always been a warm home for me, a place that was nice to live and work in, but deep down I hadn't come to terms with the failure of my efforts to get into the pilot course, and I often watched enviously as the fighter jets took off or landed at the nearby Hatzor airbase. I could have been there. In the air.

---

[6] Static-line jumping is when the parachute cord/strip is connected to the aircraft so when you jump it is automatically pulled to open the 'chute, as opposed to a free fall when pulling the 'chute is up to the individual.

Dr Baruch was and remained the one standing between me and my dream. The problem was that, in those days, he was considered the supreme authority in Israel on aviation medicine. He'd been certified in the field at a medical centre in London, and no one dared question his authority. The air force's aviation doctor was essentially a one-man medical committee whose decisions were extremely difficult, if not impossible, to challenge.

In the paratroops, they knew my medical story and encouraged me to keep up the fight, but the day I took off my uniform, I understood that only a miracle could get me back into the pilot course. After my discharge from mandatory service, there were two obstacles keeping me out of the pilot course – Dr Baruch's expert opinion, and my age. The air force did not accept pilot candidates over the age of 24. I was just 21 then, but I was very doubtful that the main hurdle before me would be removed before three years were up.

On the kibbutz I joined a group that worked in the sheep pen. Two of the kibbutz old-timers who had been in charge for years of the kibbutz sheep pen had retired, and a new young group, of which I was a part, stepped in to take their place. The work was very physical, it was one of the hardest jobs on the kibbutz, but we were young and we wanted something challenging. We got up before dawn for the milking, we cleared away the piles of rubbish each morning, we took the animals out to graze, we looked after the young lambs, and we brought them back to the pen for the evening milking. All the members of the group developed strong arm muscles from the strenuous milking, and regularly carried an awful stench from the residue that stuck to their clothing after each milking. Other kibbutzim had already installed milking machines that lightened the workload considerably, and we decided that Negba should progress with the times and bring a milking machine into the sheep pen. We brought this request up at the kibbutz assembly, and we were turned down. Too expensive, they told us. We responded with a protest strike after which they decided to throw us all out of the sheep pen.

From the sheep pen, I moved to working in the fields. I lived in a shared room in a cabin whose floor was piled high with discarded sunflower seed shells. Every once in a while, we cleaned the room, just when the shells were about to reach as high as the beds. We were a close-knit group that worked well together, laughed together and had a lot of fun together. For our dinner one evening, we decided to help ourselves to some of the tempting items that were stored in the kibbutz kitchen's refrigerated room. The room was kept locked but by pressing with a knife on the pulley of the inner door, we were able to get it open.

In shorts and topless, I went inside to look for meat, but then suddenly we heard someone approaching the kitchen. The guys who had come with me hurriedly shut the door and fled. I was left inside. I couldn't open the door from the inside and I immediately started to feel the cold. To keep warm I started moving crates from one side of the room to the other and I used one of them to bang on the door. Maybe someone would hear me. After I'd been trapped for several minutes, with the cold really starting to grip me, my friends heard me knocking and let me out.

For a while, I was also a shepherd, riding on a horse and leading the sheep to pasture. One day, one of the sheep stepped on a viper and was bitten. Luckily, the sheep hadn't been shorn yet and the venom didn't penetrate. I wasn't afraid of snakes. At one time, I was keeping seven vipers. In the alfalfa that grew near the kibbutz entrance gate there were long black snakes, non-venomous ones that ate mice. Sometimes I would catch them and they would sink their teeth into me. It felt like a pinprick and nothing more.

I liked working in the fields. By five in the morning, I was in the field, enjoying the sunrise and the pastoral quiet all around. I was enchanted by nature's wonders – seeing deer sprint by, finding porcupines hidden among the vegetation, the moles that burrowed in the ground, and other wild animals.

During the time I worked in the fields, an episode occurred that entered the kibbutz lore and has often been recalled at kibbutz celebrations and at various occasions in my life. I was working on a heavy tractor, a Caterpillar D6 with treads. The tractor had two engines – the main engine and a smaller engine that was used to start the big engine by winding a rope. One evening, the fuel in the small engine ran out and it couldn't be used to start the big engine. I ran to the kibbutz to fetch a fuel can. I got on a Ferguson tractor there and made my way back to the field. I got the D6 started, but now I had a problem: How was I going to bring back both tractors? I put the D6 on the road that led to the kibbutz and put it in gear. I drove the Ferguson ahead of it and then stopped every few dozen metres, waited for the D6 to catch up, adjusted for a defect it had in the right tread – the vehicle had once gone over a mine – and kept on. In this way I manoeuvred the two tractors and got both back to the kibbutz. In the dining hall they saw two tractors arriving and hastened to prepare dinner for two people.

I kept on doing my reserve army duty as a parachuting instructor, and on one free-fall dive, I ended up breaking my fibula. With my leg in a cast, I couldn't go on working in the kibbutz fields. I spent a month-and-a-half doing bookkeeping. There was another time that I broke a leg. By then, I was already a pilot. I went up for a jump directly after playing football, without changing my shoes. When I stood up at the end of the jump, I felt a click in my foot and ended up in a cast once again. This happened just a few days before my wedding to Sara, so I had my leg in a cast during our wedding ceremony on the kibbutz. While I waited for it to heal, I passed the time doing handicrafts. People brought me sheaves of wheat, and from the straw, using a razor and glue, I constructed miniature houses and pagodas.

7 IN ETHIOPIA WITH EMPEROR HAILE SELASSIE

One day, the IDF parachuting school contacted me and asked me to do two months of reserve duty with officer's pay for an important assignment. The honour guard of Ethiopian Emperor Haile Selassie was coming to Israel for a parachuting course, and they wanted me to be there. Not only because of my experience as an instructor, but also because of my English.

Why would a kibbutznik know English? My English teacher in high school had been part of a *gar'in* that made aliyah (immigration) from the United States to Kibbutz Kfar Menachem. He taught us English through American folk songs by The Weavers, Pete Seeger, and others. Also, the year that I was serving at the parachuting school, I didn't go out that much. I preferred to watch films, and they improved my English as well.

Nearly the entire honour guard from Ethiopia came to Israel. One person who was missing, though, was one of its most famous members – marathon runner Abebe Bikila, who was training for the Olympics games in Rome, where he went on to win the gold medal after running the entire course bare-foot. He was the first black athlete to win an Olympic gold medal for distance running. Later on, when we went to Ethiopia, I got to meet him, too. The Ethiopians were slender and tall and incredibly fit. It was a pleasure to watch them easily running around Tel Nof. Working with them was a tremendous experience, despite the language barrier.

The Ethiopian cadets completed the course and were awarded their para-trooper's wings in a special ceremony. We were invited to come back with them to Ethiopia to put on a parachuting exhibition. In the briefing ahead of the trip, we were told that we wouldn't travel there in uniform. We would wear civilian clothes, and for the dives we would wear regular jumpsuits. The Ethiopian emperor was determined to keep our visit and our mission a secret.

Where was I going to find a suit? The solution was to be found in the kibbutz clothing storeroom. There were lots of suits there. I tried some on and found one that fit. In the storeroom I also found a leather suitcase that belonged to Yulek, and I used it for the trip.

In Addis Ababa we performed a number of free-fall dives, to the delight of the leaders there, including the emperor himself, who attended one of the jump performances with his entire entourage. His golden throne was placed in the centre of the field where we landed. At the end of our time there, the emperor held a reception for us in the palace. Up to then, my idea of a palace was the big Arab house in Ness Ziona. However, the Ethiopian emperor's palace was incredibly opulent and glittering with gold. In one corner there were tigers in gold cages. The emperor, in dress uniform, shook hands and exchanged a few polite words with each one of us. Aware of the strength of my hands from working in the sheep pen, I shook his hand gently. Each of us were given a gift of sterling silver cufflinks emblazoned with the Lion of Judah, the symbol of the empire.

When I was in Ethiopia, I had a very interesting encounter. Douglas Bader, the famed World War II amputee pilot, also happened to be in the country. One of my childhood heroes. I spotted him in the dining room of our hotel. I went over to him, introduced myself and shook his hand. He shook hands with me, but didn't show much emotion. He was a famous pilot, a living legend, and I was just a young skydiver.

On the way back to Israel we landed at Lake Tana, source of the Blue Nile. There, I bought five wooden figurines and a bottle of Coca Cola. It was the first time in my life that I ever tried the famous American drink, and I decided to bring a bottle back to the kibbutz. It was a major attraction. In the dining hall, they set up an exhibit of the African figurines and the bottle of Coca Cola.

I was 23 when the kibbutz received a request from Hakibbutz Ha'artzi, the national kibbutz movement, to send two members for two years of permanent army service. They called this 'percentages for service in the standing army'. In the IDF of the early 1960s, there was a serious shortage of officers and good people in the permanent army, so the kibbutz movement set a 'volunteer' quota for the kibbutzim, which were asked to send a certain number of reservist soldiers for an extra two years of duty. I decided that I wanted to return to the army. I loved kibbutz life, but by nature I'm someone who needs challenges and excitement. This was something the kibbutz did not offer at the time. There was also another reason, of course: the jump training was done at the Tel Nof airbase. That's where the flight school was located, too, and I believed that I'd have an easier time from there resuming my fight to get back into the pilot training course, despite Dr Baruch's position.

Giora, you're going back to being a jump instructor, I told myself, but don't forget that somewhere along the way, the pilot course is also waiting for you.

8 EPSTEIN BECOMES EVEN

In December 1961 I returned to regular duty at the IDF parachuting school. It was a challenging period, and one of the peaks was the World Skydiving Championship in the United States. This time, the IDF took the event very seriously and brought in a skydiving instructor from France named Bonfils. He was about 40. He was supposed to teach us new methods and instruct us on the ground and in the air. We trained non-stop. Aerial manoeuvres of spins and somersaults, with a big T on the ground made up of large red panels. One red panel – spin left to right. Two panels – right, left, right, somersault. It didn't take long for us to discover that this French 'expert' had no idea whatsoever about skydiving.

As the pace of training accelerated, we kept improving. I enjoyed every minute, and my performances in the exercises and precision landing on target were among the best in the group. We practised jumps from 5,000 feet, free floating in the air for 20 seconds, and starting aerial manoeuvres. We made a lot of progress in precision landings on the cross. The parachutes we used were fairly primitive compared to the general standard. Two open chambers and steering rings. We practised style and gliding a lot.

At the end of the training, five of us were chosen for the final squad that would compete in the world championship: Topol, Biatsky, Talman, Schwartzy and myself. Topol was the commander of the parachuting division. There were also three more with us: delegation commander Marcel Tobias, the parachute folder, and the pilot.

Before departing for the championship, I had to deal with a real dilemma: changing my surname. At the time, David Ben-Gurion insisted that anyone officially representing Israel abroad must leave Israel with a Hebrew surname. A demand that one couldn't argue with. So I received a new surname: Even. It was the closest thing to Epstein. More than 50 years would go by before I went back to using my original surname again.

After another training session, we set off on the long trip to New York. We flew to Paris in a twin-engine Nord transport from the air force, with a stop-over in Rome. When we landed in Rome, we were taken to a hotel on the banks of the Tiber River with canopy beds. I'd barely settled in when I heard one of the guys complaining that the toilet wasn't working, so I went to see. It was a bidet. From Rome we flew to Paris, and Marcel Tobias, who knew Paris from the time he served in the French Foreign Legion, took us to a burlesque show at the Crazy Horse, and to a jazz concert by black American musicians that really wowed me. At the jazz show we sat on the floor and were joined by singers Esther and Abi Ofarim, a couple I adored, who were living in the City of Lights at the time. From Paris we took a commercial flight to New York, then from there we travelled to Boston, and then to Orange, Massachusetts, where the world championship was being held.

Orange was a small town of 6,000 people with one main street and a number of small streets running off of it. A small town that became a meeting place for skydivers from all over the world. The teams from Russia and the Eastern European countries were comprised of military personnel, including some women, all of them professional skydivers. The Russian team was accompanied by a Communist Party commissar whose main job was to keep a close eye on the skydivers to watch they didn't get too envious of the wonders of the Free World. Other delegations from the Communist Bloc countries also had such commissars with them. But that didn't stop one skydiver from the Romanian team from falling in love with an American participant and deserting to the West when the competition was over.

Next to the town was a small airport where we took off for our dives. Every day there were competitions in different styles, with international judges monitoring the dives and awarding points based on performance. The top places were taken by the Russians, the Czechs, and the Americans. The Israeli team placed right in the middle out of 24 countries, a fine achievement compared to the championship in Moscow where the team had placed close to last. Talman notched an impressive achievement by coming in seventh in gliding to the target. He was one of the IDF's top jump instructors. Years later, he was killed in a car accident.

Among the members of the Israeli team, I excelled at performing aerial manoeuvres before the 'chute opened. At the time, I had logged about 300 dives, compared to an average of 1,000 for the competitors from the other teams. The world championship event was a big step forward for the sport of skydiving. For the first time, we were exposed to exhibition dives by large groups. We were light years away from that ourselves. There was an Olympics-like atmosphere at the competition that led to lasting friendships. We became especially friendly with the American team, and during the competition, we toured New York with them. One night, there was a special performance for all the competitors by the American folk singer Pete Seeger. I knew all of his songs by heart and at the end of the evening, I taught him to sing *Hava Nagila*.

In addition to participating in the world championship, we also visited Oshkosh, Wisconsin, where a big annual air show was being held. We saw all kinds of aircraft there, both civilian and military, including some that had made history in wars in which the United States took part. On the way back to Israel, we had a stopover in Amsterdam. A visit to the Van Gogh Museum and, at the other end of the cultural spectrum, to the city's famous red-light district, were my parting experiences from the trip to the World Skydiving Championship. The most exciting thing I brought back to the kibbutz were the blue jeans I'd bought in New York – part of the youth fashion revolution, which was something we on the kibbutz had only read about in the newspaper.

9 BACK TO THE PILOT TRAINING COURSE

I returned to the parachuting school in Tel Nof. From time to time at the base I ran into guys who'd gone through the basic pilot training course with me. By now, they were pilots with five years' experience under their belts. I felt there was no reason why I shouldn't be entitled to earn my wings too. I resumed the fight with full force, and enlisted the help of anyone I could think of to prove that I was fit for the pilot course, and that the only thing stopping me was the opinion of the flight surgeon. Some of the senior personnel at Tel Nof were familiar with the story of the parachuting instructor Giora Even-Epstein who'd fought for his right to serve as an air force combat pilot. Some of them tried to cool my fervour. "You're tilting at windmills," they told me. "You're wasting your time," they said. My age was starting to work against me, too. Soon I would turn 24 – the cut-off age for starting the pilot course.

But I didn't give up. I roamed the air force headquarters, and tried to put connections to use. To keep pressing and trying to convince them. The person who helped me the most was the paratrooper brigade's physician with whom I became friends. He managed to access my medical file and was the first to tell me about the medical findings it contained. I have what's known as 'athlete's heart' – a condition sometimes found in people who do a lot of sports, in which the left chamber of the heart becomes enlarged. My EKG did show this uncommon finding, but the paratroops doctor did not think that was any reason to disqualify me from the pilot course, and he promised to talk with high-ranking IDF medical officers to see what could be done about my case. All he asked was that I be patient and give him time. He also revealed to me that my medical file contained records of periodic summonses that had been issued for me to appear before the air force medical committee. No one had ever told me about them, so I had never reported back to the committee. Thus, I'd missed a number of opportunities to try to right the wrong that was done to me.

Meanwhile, I continued working at the parachuting school. I was approaching 500 jumps, many of them free-fall dives, while breaking the records for starting altitude and hang time in the air. I was part of a team that developed new parachuting methods, such as ways to fly and parachute equipment to fighting forces on the ground, including auxiliary weapons and vehicles. We developed methods for parachuting jeeps and command cars. The parachuting school gained world renown, and senior officers from foreign armies would come to Tel Nof to learn from us.

One day we put on an exhibition of parachuting a command car for a visiting French general. In a complex manoeuvre like this, the plane is flying with the rear door open and the command car is standing on a wooden surface tautly strapped down and with its rear part attached to the pull parachute. Above the target, the crew released the straps and opened the parachute that pulled the vehicle out of the plane. In the air, three one-ton parachutes immediately opened to lower the cargo slowly and prevent it from crashing to the ground. Two paratroopers followed immediately after that. Their job was to land as close as possible to the command car and free it from the harnesses. In the earlier trial jumps, the command car's landing had gone smoothly. This time things went horribly wrong. The other instructor got tangled up inside the plane, and only I jumped out after the command car.

As I exited the aircraft, I could see I was very far from the target X where the French general was waiting. The wind was very strong, and when I saw from the air that the command car was being swept along the ground by the parachutes after it landed, I understood right away that it hadn't landed correctly and that the ground crew hadn't been able to release the 'chutes. Close to the ground, I released myself from the 'chute harness and finished the dive as if parachuting into the sea. I landed about two metres away from the French general, and I noticed the ground officer standing there with the wind-speed meter, looking ghostly pale.

"What's the matter?" I asked him.

"The wind speed is 32 knots," he replied.

The manoeuvre should never have been attempted in such conditions. Parachuting is normally only permitted in wind speeds up to 12 knots. That was the strongest wind I've ever parachuted in.

On the ground I saw the upside-down command car being dragged along by three large 'chutes, with the supply personnel furiously chasing after it, trying to no avail to free the vehicle from the 'chute harness. The command car was dragged hundreds of metres until it finally came to a stop in a wadi and they were able to free it.

Another time I had a very close shave. When I opened my main 'chute, the canopy was tangled up and twisted around the cords. I had my legs down and opened the reserve 'chute. I bunched it up and tossed it to the side just as we'd drilled. The reserve 'chute got tangled with the main 'chute and above me was just a small 'chute canopy. I descended to earth at a dizzying speed. I was wearing a crash helmet that Marcel had bought for us in America. Upon landing, my head struck the altimeter that was attached to the reserve 'chute. I took a hard hit to the face and eyes. I was sure that I'd lost my sight. The medic and ground officer raced over to me. They both were sure I was a goner. A few minutes later, I was able to shake it off and was okay. An engineer who analysed the speed of my descent found that it was comparable to a fall from a seven-storey building.

My ongoing struggle to get back in the pilot course was starting to bear fruit. The paratroopers brigade doctor talked to the chief medical officer, Colonel Dr Baruch Padeh, and with expert cardiologists, who agreed that I'd been arbitrarily disqualified from the pilot course without a thorough cardiological work-up, or any findings that supported that decision.

Eventually, Dr Baruch received an order from the chief medical officer to call me in for another round of exams. The chief medical officer had apparently decided to make me a test case. I wasn't the only one who'd been kept out of the pilot course due to athlete's heart. The air force had been compelled to forgo a good number of potential pilots who'd been found to have a similar problem, and somebody figured that my case could be used to formulate a policy about their other candidates. So every morning for a week, I reported to Tel Hashomer Hospital for tests that examined my heart's capacity to function under conditions of reduced oxygen. During the tests they kept lowering the air pressure and measuring my heart function, recording the effects on my EKG. The doctors who conducted the tests were surprised by how little oxygen my heart consumed.

The results of the tests done at the Tel Hashomer cardiology department were unequivocal: I was fit for the pilot course. I'll never forget that Thursday afternoon in September 1963. I was called to the telephone at the parachuting school, and Aharon Yoeli, the flight school commander, said to me: "Sunday morning at 8:00 a.m., report to me at the flight school." At last! My battle was over. I was starting the pilot course.

Later on, I learned that the call came after a senior air force committee, headed by the chief of the air division, had discussed my case, reviewed the test results from Tel Hashomer, and decided I could be admitted to the course. Dr Baruch had also been invited to the committee and was informed of its decision. A total knockout victory. I was 25-and-a-half when I started the course. A year-and-a-half older than the official maximum age at the time. Here, too, I set a precedent.

Having finally triumphed over Dr Baruch, there was still one hurdle left for me to overcome: the kibbutz assembly. My period of regular army service was due to end in December 1963 and I was supposed to return to the kibbutz then. I went to the kibbutz secretary and put in a special request that I be allowed to extend my time in the regular army and join the pilot course.

I expected to have the full support of the kibbutz members who all knew how badly I wanted to become a pilot and how hard I'd fought to get to this moment, but that's not what happened. A bunch of people thought it was time for me to return to the kibbutz, which was in need of good labourers. Kibbutz Negba couldn't let Giora Epstein go. I asked for a chance to speak.

"I could come back to the kibbutz and decades from now go up on the hill (into the cemetery)," I told everyone. "I've been dreaming of the pilot course since I was 18. Everyone here knows that's always been my goal." My heartfelt words convinced the doubters and, by a majority vote, the kibbutz members approved my request to join the course.

What would I have done if the kibbutz had not given its permission? That would have been a big dilemma. I dearly loved the kibbutz, but my desire to be a pilot was just as strong. And so, seven years after I'd begun Pilot Course No. 25, I returned to Pilot Course No. 46. Seven years in which 21 pilot courses in the air force had been completed. I could have been a veteran pilot by this time.

That Sunday I reported to the flight school. Seven years older than most of the cadets who started Course No. 46 with me. Most of them had just begun their military service. I was already a sergeant major in the regular army. There were five phases to the pilot course. The first, known as the preparation phase, was made up of three parts: the preliminary stage, which included basic training, ground studies, Piper flights, and solo Piper flights. The preparatory stage, which included infantry training, training on what to do if captured, and a parachuting course; and classroom lessons – eight subjects that we studied in preparation for flights in the Fouga Magister, a French-built twin-engine jet trainer. Then came three more phases that included flights in the training aircraft: the primary phase, in which you learned to fly. The basics phase followed with more advanced flights, including a solo flight, instruments, navigation, night flying, and aerobatics. Then the advanced phase – aerial manoeuvres in preparation for combat training.

Whoever successfully passed all of these phases received his pilot's wings.

I joined the final third of the preliminary stage of the course, and had just a few days to learn all about the Piper aircraft. I managed to do that, and then the stage of Piper flights began. First, you flew with an instructor, and then you made a solo flight. When a cadet received permission for the solo flight, it meant he could advance to the next stages of the course. I loved flying from the very start. My squadron commander in the preliminary stage was Eliezer 'Cheetah' Cohen, who went on to become one of the air force's top helicopter pilots and later an El Al pilot.

My solo flight went cleanly, and I was certain that I'd passed. After landing, as I was taxiing on the ground, I briefly let go of the control stick. The Piper, as I learned, has a tendency to drift to the right. The plane's nose struck a pole near the runway and the aircraft was slightly damaged. Since this happened after the solo flight, it didn't affect my score, but that didn't stop my friend Yalo (Aharon Shavit) from joking years later at an air force event in my honour, "How could they have let Giora keep flying after he crashed the Piper into a pole?"

Course No. 46 was about to start the preparatory stage, and I thought that with all my military experience, I should be able to skip the infantry training and parachuting course. It was an unusual request to make, and I was told that they would look into it and get back to me. A few days later, I was given this reply: "Your course is going on a break now for a week. Course No. 45 is currently doing the parachuting course. You have one week – if you pass the exams on the study material, you'll go to the primary phase – straight to the Fougas."

I crammed for a week studying all the material to be ready for the Fouga flights. I went over and over the material and memorised it until I felt like I really knew the plane well. I earned excellent marks on all eight exams and was passed to the primary phase, together with Course No. 45. The flight cadets who reached the primary stage got a special privilege: They no longer ate in the general dining hall of the base, but in a separate dining hall where the menu was the same as that given to air crews. I couldn't stand the food in the base dining hall and wouldn't eat there. Having already served two years in the regular army and earned the rank of sergeant major, I just couldn't bring myself to sit there. In the preliminary stage, I had reached an agreement with the staff: I marched to the dining hall together with all the other cadets, but I didn't enter. I remained outside, where I ate apples sent to me from the kibbutz, and in the evenings, I went to the kitchen of the parachuting school, where they made splendid meals for me.

In the first days in primary phase, we received instruction on the Fouga from the course commander and squadron commander. The Fouga squadron

was parked on the large asphalt surface in the north-western section of Tel
Nof. During the first lunch break, a Willys pickup truck came to give us a lift
to the dining hall. There were six of us cadets plus an instructor. We piled
into the back while the instructor, who was a pilot, sat in the cab next to the
driver. When we'd driven a short way, the truck stopped and the instructor
got out of the cab, walked around the back to where we were sitting and
pointed to me: "You, get into the cab…" I got in, and then I saw that the
driver was none other than Yalo, Aharon Shavit, a fighter pilot who had
downed two Egyptian Vampire aircraft during the Sinai Campaign. Yalo had
been grounded for some reason and assigned as a cargo pilot in 103 Squadron,
where he'd met me as one of the parachuting instructors. Later, he was
appointed commander of the Fouga squadron in the primary phase.

I said hello to him like we were old friends.

"Quiet, look straight ahead. What are you doing here?"

"I'm in the course," I said.

"Report to my office at 16:30."

I went to his office as instructed. Yalo was sitting behind the desk, and
there were two glasses of whisky in front of him. I told him that alcohol didn't
agree with me.

"You're not drinking alcohol. You're drinking whisky."

Then he asked again what I was doing there. I told him about what had
happened over the last seven years, about my fight and my long wait to get
back into the pilot course. From that day on, we remained close.

Flying a Fouga is nothing like flying a Piper. After a few flights with an
instructor seated behind me, I felt like I had full control of the plane for take-
offs, landings, and circling. I loved flying. I loved being in the air, controlling
the aircraft. We reached manoeuvring altitude and performed simple aerobatic
manoeuvres. At a relatively early stage, I started to fly solo. On one of those
flights, I passed over Atlit and was supposed to turn south and head down
along the coastline, and then turn sharply inward when I was opposite Pal-
machim to land at Tel Nof. As I neared Tel Aviv, I received a warning about
an approaching thunderstorm and cumulonimbus clouds – storm clouds with
rising and falling currents. I spoke with the controller and he directed me on
a big bypass to the east, in pouring rain and zero visibility. I executed the
flight perfectly and landed smoothly in terrible weather conditions. Another
flight test that I passed with flying colours.

The stage where we moved on to flying in close formation was considered
much harder and required the ability to pilot and retain control and maintain
your position within the formation. When flying in formation, the distance

between the aircraft is very small and each pilot must carefully maintain his position. The Swedish air force had devised a system for assessing a pilot's ability based on flight performance in close formation, which Israel also used. I did well in this stage and passed it, too.

We moved on from the primary phase stage to the basics phase. Yalo, our squadron commander, worked closely with us and flew with us. We practised navigating and did low-altitude flights at 300 feet from one point to another. I really enjoyed the basic part of the course. We'd do five or six manoeuvres in a row. Loop, dive, pick up speed, do another loop and start all over again. I loved the Immelmann turn, a manoeuvre named after a First World War German pilot I'd read about. You start with a loop, and then at the peak altitude, you do a somersault. We also learned how to do a barrel roll, where you raise the nose a bit and do a half-roll to end right-side up, but going in the opposite direction The Fouga was capable of executing a loop at the relatively low speed of 250 knots.

In basics, we started doing night flights. We quickly advanced to 'blind flying' with instruments, flights in which the cockpit canopy is covered with cloth and you fly using the altimeter, speedometer, course deviation indicator, and artificial horizon, which shows the plane's position in relation to the horizon, and is the main instrument used when flying on instruments. This stage was not easy for me. I'm not considered a 'smooth' pilot, and I felt that instrument flying was not my strongest side. I had no problem with navigation, though.

The basics phase ended and we moved on to the advanced phase. Of the dozens of cadets who'd begun the course, only a few reached this stage. Here the demands were much tougher. You do simulated combat flying, perform simulated attacks, practise shooting and quick take-offs. By this point, we were just two cadets sharing a room. When I started the course, there were five of us.

We were taught about vertigo, the condition where the pilot loses his sense of orientation. It happens most often at night in the dark, but also when weather obscures visual references, when the pilot is convinced he's flying straight even when the instruments show that he's flying upside down. The instruments are always right, but the pilot doesn't always trust them against what his senses are telling him. I took to heart the important lessons about vertigo and how to get out of it. As soon as the pilot realises he's experiencing vertigo, he must lower the pilot's seat and believe only the instruments and the artificial horizon, even if they are at odds with what he feels to be right. It's important to aim the aircraft toward populated areas where the lights from the buildings provide a clear indication of where the ground is. Once you straighten out, the vertigo passes.

I didn't personally suffer from vertigo, but later on, I was actively involved in several incidents related to this dangerous phenomenon. The first was during my first night flight in a Dassault Ouragan on the OTU course, the operational training squadron. This was a solo flight, since the Ouragan was not a two-seater with seats for cadet and instructor. I flew in total darkness at an altitude of 15,000 feet until the first point of light in the Arava, Moshav Hatzeva, where I turned right toward Be'er Sheva on the way to landing at Hatzor. As I made the turn, I felt the plane give a big shudder, as if something had happened. Then I realised that another plane had passed very close to my Ouragan.

I raced after him and called on the radio, "Who's over Hatzeva?"

"It's me, Erlich," I heard a voice that sounded sluggish and not very clear. "For the last five minutes, I don't know what's with me."

I realised that he was experiencing vertigo, and I had to get him out of it.

I flew in front of him and told him he should fly behind me in formation, and I led him all the way to Hatzor for landing. I let him land ahead of me. He did a 'kangaroo' landing in which the plane lands on the nose wheels instead of the main wheels. The plane jumped into the air and when it returned to the runway, the two main tyres burst. I couldn't land so I circled in the air for another half hour until they cleared the runway. In the debriefing, he couldn't explain what had gone wrong with him.

The second incident occurred a few months later, when I was a young pilot flying a Super Mystère[7] in No. 105 the Scorpion squadron. On one of my first night flights, three of us were flying south toward Hatzeva, where we would turn right toward Be'er Sheva, strike a target in the Halutza firing range, and then return. I was in an internal position in the formation, and the leader was a reservist pilot. Over Hatzeva he made a 90-degree turn instead of a 35-degree turn followed by a spin and straightening out.

"You have vertigo," I called to him on the radio, and I also warned the third pilot in the formation to move to the side so he wouldn't collide with him. Once he was over the city of Be'er Sheva, with all the lights below, his vertigo completely cleared up.

The air force firing range at Halutza is notorious for cases of vertigo. Night strikes on ground targets in the light of flares often cause pilots to lose their sense of orientation in space. Many pilots' lives have been saved because they adhered to the rules for escaping from vertigo. Over my years in the air

---

[7] Another French fighter, comparable to the North American F-100 Super Sabre.

force, I knew quite a few pilots who were affected by vertigo. Not all of them managed to get out of it.

There was another serious incident that I experienced – during the advanced stage, the cadets from my course took turns serving as duty officers for the new cadets from later courses. On the night of April 29, 1964, it was my turn, and I made sure to have dinner ready for the cadets from a navigators' course, who were supposed to return from a night navigation over the Big Crater (*HaMakhtesh HaGadol*). I kept waiting for them to arrive, and after a while, when they hadn't yet shown up, I went to sleep in the room for the officer on duty. At four in the morning, I was woken up. Aharon Yoeli, the school commander, wanted me to get all the cadets out of their room. I woke them and brought them outside. They stood on the ramp at the entrance to their living quarters, and Yoeli stood before them, on the ground. Lower than them. We noticed right away that four cadets were missing.

"Where are your comrades?" Yoeli asked them.

No one answered.

"I'll tell you," he went on. "They're all buried deep in the crater now."

The Nord aircraft used for night navigation had crashed in the Big Crater. Nine people were killed. The crew, the instructors, and four cadets. No one survived.

The instructors in the course, except for Yalo, were all younger than me. They had taught me to fly, and I had gotten to know them as pilots and as people. There was one instructor who liked to do the manoeuvres I was supposed to do as a cadet. He would move the stick and do the manoeuvres together with me. When I saw this was the situation, I just took my hands off and let him do it. Afterward, he would question me as if I had done the drill. At the party marking the end of that stage of training, I told him what I thought about it, and he laughed. He was killed in the Six Day War.

10 FROM TOP OF THE CLASS TO...THE HELICOPTER SQUADRON

For me, the most exciting phase of training was the preparation for aerial combat. Pursuing the enemy in formation, and one on one. I felt that my performances were good, that I was living the battle. This was the kind of combat pilot I'd always aspired to be.

The course was nearing its end, and speculation began as to who would be named the outstanding cadet. I didn't have any special ambitions of such, though I had a good opinion of my flying abilities and my performances in the air. The day before the ceremony in which we were to receive our wings, all the cadets were invited to a private talk with the flight school commander. When we started the course, the commander was Aharon Yoeli. Toward the end of the advanced phase, we got a new commander, Yaakov Agasi. He reviewed with me all of my marks and evaluations.

"Very nice, you're the outstanding cadet in the course, and as you know, you're going to the Rolling Sword squadron, the helicopter squadron."

I was totally dumbfounded. I'm a combat pilot. The outstanding cadet. Since when was the top cadet assigned to helicopters?

In its early days, the helicopter squadron was not considered the elite of the air force. The helicopter pilots were either veteran pilots of light aircraft or those who had left the fighter pilot course and were reassigned to helicopters.

It's doubtful if at that time there was a case similar to mine, of the top cadet in the combat pilot course being assigned to the helicopter squadron. I had started out as one of the oldest cadets ever to be accepted into the pilot training course, and I completed it in record time – just 13 months. After the initial shock, it suddenly dawned on me – I had Dr Baruch to 'thank' once again. In his final medical summary, he must have written: 'Approve Giora Epstein for the pilot training course. Medically fit for helicopters only…' With helicopters, there would be no issues of high G-force and low G-force, conditions he thought could hurt me as a combat pilot.

End-of-the-course talks between the commander of the pilot course and a cadet in the course are a matter of routine, even with the top cadet of that course. But that wasn't the case in my talk with Colonel Yaakov Agasi after he surprised me with the news that I was being assigned to the helicopter squadron. I spoke with emotion, with frustration and anger. I told him about all the years I fought to get into the course; the seven lost years since I was first accepted into Course No. 25; how I'd made almost 500 jumps in the parachuting school; competing in the World Skydiving Championship and the hundreds of hours I'd flown in a Fouga in the pilot course. I proved that I'd never had any problem with G-forces.

Agasi listened, asked questions and showed empathy.

"Commander, what can I do?" I asked.

"The authority for assigning pilots belongs to Shaya Gazit, head of the instruction department. Tomorrow you all get your wings. Tomorrow night is the graduation party. Pilots from all over the air force will be there. Shaya Gazit will be there, too. Find him, explain the problem to him, and ask him to cancel Dr Baruch's recommendation. I can't do anything."

Our graduation party was held on November 19, 1964, in the auditorium of the Tel Nof cinema, not outside on the plaza, because it was pouring with rain that day. My family and friends from the kibbutz came to the ceremony and saw Ezer Weizman, the air force commander, hand me my wings and a wooden frame with a miniature plane made of bits of metal and inscribed: 'Giora Even-Epstein, outstanding cadet.'

After the ceremony I kept my eyes on Shaya Gazit, and at the right moment I went up to him. I repeated my story to him. I'd finished the course as the outstanding cadet, as a combat pilot, why should Dr Baruch say that I can't be a combat pilot?

Gazit reassured me. "Don't worry. Tomorrow you're starting a week-long break. Come by my office in the Kirya [the Israeli Pentagon] and we'll talk."

That night, the course graduates drank and drank. I was the only pilot of the eight who graduated that stayed sober. I don't touch alcohol. I walked around with a cup full of cola, and whenever someone tried to pour something into it, I showed him that it wasn't empty yet.

The next morning, a Friday, I showed up at Shaya Gazit's office in the Kirya in Tel Aviv. "I've gone over your file," he told me, "and I'm taking care of it. Go relax in Netanya and stop by here on your way back."

I went off to Netanya feeling optimistic. I believed the problem was solved.

A week later I came back to Shaya Gazit, who informed me that my file had been sent to an expert cardiologist, a three-star general in the American army. "But in the meantime, you go to helicopters," he said.

Once again, I felt like I'd just been hit over the head with a sledgehammer. I tried to persuade him to change the decision.

"I'm the first top cadet from the pilot course to go to helicopters. The first in the history of the air force… If I start out in helicopters, will they let me switch to combat later?"

Gazit was unfazed. "You have my word. This is all temporary. If your file comes back with a recommendation that you can be a combat pilot, you'll immediately go to the operational training unit [OTU]. I'll make sure of it."

I wasn't ready to give in.

"Why should I start with helicopters at all? Maybe I could stay in your office and work with you in instruction. If a positive answer comes, I'll move from here to combat. If the answer is no, I'll go to helicopters."

"There's no need. You have my word. Go to helicopters," Shaya Gazit replied, ending the meeting.

I walked out of his office satisfied, and stupid. Satisfied by his promise, and stupid because I hadn't requested a written summary of the interview.

I reported to the helicopter squadron. I was assigned a private instructor, a former Mystère pilot who'd switched to helicopters. I practised on a Sikorsky S-58, a helicopter with the huge engine of an American B-17 bomber. It wasn't long before I did my first solo flight and after a month-and-a-half, I was certified as an operational co-pilot.

Two months after I started flying in the helicopter squadron, the winter ball took place at Hatzor. This was sort of a competing event to the regular air force events at Tel Nof. The whole air force came to enjoy a night of music, performances, drinking, and throwing pies at each other.

I met pilots from my course, who told me that they hadn't yet started to fly in the operational training unit. As we were talking, Motti Hod, head of the air force general staff, passed by. He was happy to see me. "So, I see you're in the OTU."

"No, I'm in helicopters."

"How can that be? Your medical file came back from America two weeks ago with a recommendation that you fly combat planes. After your file came back, the assessment committee decided that you're transferring to the OTU and ordered the Tel Nof base to transfer you."

I thought I was going crazy. No one had talked to me or said anything about this.

The next day, I got hold of Haim Naveh, commander of the helicopter squadron.

"Haim, why am I still in your squadron?"

"As far as I know, you're supposed to be a pilot with me."

I told him that I'd spoken with Motti Hod and that he'd said Tel Nof received an order to transfer me.

The squadron commander denied there was any such order.

I got angry.

"Listen, stop lying to me. Motti told me exactly what happened."

At this point, he finally stopped lying and admitted that medical approval had arrived from the United States, and that Menachem Bar, the Tel Nof commander, had received an order to transfer me to the OTU. Menachem had held a meeting of commanders, where it was ultimately decided that, with my talents, the air force was best off keeping me where I was, so as to upgrade the helicopter squadron, rather than make me into another combat pilot. They'd gone ahead with this move at my expense.

"I don't care what you all think. I came to the air force to become a fighter pilot."

The squadron commander tried a new tack.

"We're going to put together a four-pilot team that will travel to France to learn about the Frelon helicopter and bring it to Israel. You'll be part of the team. The youngest pilot on this important team."

That didn't move me, either, of course. "They can take their precious Frelon and…" I thought, holding firm.

"From this moment on, I am not willing to fly anymore until a final decision about me is made. I'll take it all the way to the prime minister if I have to," I informed the squadron commander.

I requested permission to meet with Menachem Bar, the Tel Nof commander. I went to his office, went over my whole story again, and got the impression that he was hearing it for the first time. I sensed that the situation was uncomfortable for him. Throughout the meeting, he avoided looking me in the eye. When I finished my explanation, he replied tersely, "That's all very nice, but we've decided that for the good of the air force, it's better for you to stay in helicopters."

I reacted furiously. I started shouting at the base commander. A young second lieutenant, who'd just finished the pilot course, shouting at a colonel.

Menachem tried to calm me down.

"Whom do I need to speak with to get the approval, to Motti Hod?"

"You can't speak with Motti."

"Then whom can I speak with?"

"With Ezer Weizman, the air force commander."

An appointment was scheduled for me with Ezer Weizman. Yardena, his bureau chief, showed me into his office. In those days, Ezer Weizman was a legend in the air force. A popular commander, a gregarious type who personally knew most of the pilots in the force. People always said that he kept a file with a page on each pilot in the air force, and that each time he was going to visit one of the bases, he would review his notes to refresh his memory about the pilots' names, and surprise them by also knowing the names of their wives, and other information.

I repeated my story to him. It seemed to me that Ezer had heard about my problem. I told him that, unlike what happened with Shaya Gazit, whom I'd believed without getting anything in writing, I was not going to budge without a letter that said I was going to the OTU.

"I'll just sit here and wait until you decide. Give me any assignment you want. If you want to charge me with refusing an order, that's fine. I won't accept any more lies."

Ezer smiled and pressed the intercom. "Yardena, we have a customer for tea every day at ten…" Then he turned to me. "Get going to the squadron. I'll let you know."

An exercise was planned for the next day – the biggest drill ever done by the helicopter squadron. It would last a day and a night and include transporting forces from the paratrooper brigade. Everyone assembled for the briefing. I attended, though I wasn't paying close attention like the rest of the pilots. I sat down in the back row. I had no intention of participating in the drill.

About five minutes into the briefing, the squadron commander was called to the phone, and right after that, I was called over as well. The squadron commander, looking pale, handed me the receiver. "Here, he wants to talk to you."

"Listen, you piece of shit," I heard a familiar voice. "I didn't sleep all night because of you. Grab your rags and get yourself over to OTU on the double. I don't want to hear from you again!"

It was Ezer Weizman. That was another reason he was so popular in the air force.

I went to the helicopter squadron commander and told him that, now, I was ready to take part in the drill.

"Over my dead body," he replied angrily.

But, in the end, since he was short of pilots, I did take part in seven flights. When the drill was over, I bid farewell to the other pilots in the squadron over soda and wafers in the club.

I waited for Course No. 46 to finish and for the graduates to go to the OTU. That training was only going to start in a month-and-a-half. I made use of the time. I refreshed my skills flying a Piper and served as the Tel Nof cargo pilot. They were very pleased with this arrangement because the veteran pilots really disliked being assigned to cargo flights.

While waiting for the course, I also got to spend a lot of quality time with Yalo. He was older than me, but we developed a special friendship. I loved the man for his serious side and for his special sense of humour. I was ready to do any job: to be a driver transporting the air crews, to be a guest pilot in the reservist Fouga squadron, where reservist pilots, including some El Al pilots, served on Fridays. I was a second lieutenant who'd just finished the pilot training course, and Yalo let me fly with them, on simple flights mostly. I took part as a guinea pig with the leader of the air force's aerobatic quartet. I had 220 hours of flying time in the Fouga, and I think I did well.

11 A FIGHTER PILOT AT LAST!

At the end of December 1964, we started in the OTU. In its early days, after the departure of the Machal (foreign volunteer) pilots, who were the heart of the force during the War of Independence in 1948-1949, the Israel Air Force did not have any organised training programme. Menachem Bar, a senior member of the force at the time, is credited with instituting some order and methodology in the pilot training course and operational pilot training, and he also established the OTU for training pilots who had just completed the pilot course. At first, this was done in the remaining Messerschmitt aircraft used in 1948; later Spitfires and Mustangs were used, and when I finished the pilot course – Ouragans. Bar later became the commander of the Tel Nof air base.

While waiting for the operational course to begin, I got to spend time at home on the kibbutz. It was a rare opportunity to be with my parents and my two sisters, Nava and Zahava. My parents had always supported my ambition to get into the pilot course, no matter what, even when it looked hopeless. Even though we hadn't spent a lot of time together, I had a good relationship with my sisters – Nava who was born in 1943 and Zahava, the youngest, who was born during the War of Independence. Like me, they had each spent most of their lives on the kibbutz with the group of kids their age, and we would mainly see one another during visits to our parents' house.

At this point, I had learned to fly a plane. Over the next four months, I learned how to be a combat pilot. So far, I had flown the Fouga. Now I was in the cockpit of the Ouragan, a French-made fighter jet. This was a huge leap for someone fresh from the pilot course.

We practised flying in formation and protecting the formation. We learned all the main flight formations for combat flying: tight, offensive, and defensive. In a tight formation, everyone flies in nearly the same line, very close to one another – only a few metres apart. In this formation, you practise spins and turns. The next stage – offensive combat formation. The basic formation for an offensive is with a quartet of planes that are divided into two pairs: numbers one and three in the formation are the leaders, with numbers two and four guarding the leaders from behind at a distance of several dozen metres. In a defensive combat formation – everyone is spread out in one horizontal row, with a distance of 100-150 metres between planes. Flying in formation is a preliminary step to training for aerial combat. 'Dry' (not involving live ammunition) drills in which cameras replace the guns and can show which aircraft downed its rival and won the dogfight. Each pilot tries to reach the six o'clock position, his rival's rear sector, to sit on his tail and bring him down. Photographing the other plane from this position counts as a kill.

Dogfights are planned down to the last detail. It starts with a briefing in which the combat conditions are determined, and the altitude restrictions are set. The battle begins when the two aircraft – one flown by an experienced pilot, and the other an OTU cadet – are close to one another. The leader issues the command "cross turn" and the two planes move away from each other at a 90-degree angle. As soon as the leader decides the distance is large enough, he says over the radio, "Inward turn". The two aircraft turn back to face each other, maintaining a safety range of 1,000 feet of altitude between them. As they proceed through drills, they take photographs and switch off roles. Usually, a training dogfight lasts 17-20 minutes from take-off to landing.

One method of aerial combat is called 'Beurling'. It's named after George Buerling, the Canadian fighter pilot[8] who flew in the RAF in Europe and Malta, where he set a kill record. His technique was unique. He would estimate the enemy plane's course and open machine-gun fire – not directly at it, but in front of it. In this way he gained an advantage in dogfights over Malta during World War II. With 27 German and Italian planes downed, the pilot earned the nickname 'The Falcon of Malta'.

For me the Ouragan was a big step up. It was the main fighter jet used by the French air force after World War II: an aircraft with thin, straight wings, two 30-mm cannons in the nose and a gyro gunsight that required target assessment by eyesight.

After the phase of aerial photos and intercept manoeuvres, we moved on to the firing range, practising bombing and shooting. Circles were painted on the ground. The smallest had a 12-metre radius, and the largest had a 100-metre radius. The pilot would fly to the target area at a certain altitude, lower the nose, place the sight on the target and, at a certain speed, release the ordnance. The altitudes at which we practised bombing targets were low. We would release the ordnance at 2,500 feet, and immediately head out. And no

---

[8] Flight Lieutenant George F. Beurling, with 31 kills scored mostly over Malta in 1942. He died in the crash of his light transport in Rome while headed for Israel in 1948. Sabotage was suspected. See *Malta Spitfire* (Grub Street, 2011) for more information about Beurling.

matter what, we couldn't descend toward the target below an altitude of 500 feet to avoid the danger of being hit by shrapnel or small-arms fire.

The thing I loved the most was practising dogfights. I felt that I was improving from one dogfight to the next, and successfully implementing what I was learning from the instructors, especially from the best ones. I brought down several of them, and I was also brought down more than once. There's a special challenge to downing your instructor.

Dogfights took place at a minimum of 12,000 feet, and the entire process was taken into account when assessing the battle. Not just the 'kill' but how you construct the dogfight from beginning to end, without exceeding the limitations placed on you like velocity, G-force, and more.

I received high marks in all the parameters of the course: dogfights, flying in formation, target practice, and aerial photography. At the end of the course, the commander told me I'd been selected as the number one cadet. This had a big practical advantage. The top cadet can choose whether to stay with the Ouragans, or to move to a squadron of Mystères or Super Mystères. The latter was the fastest and most advanced of the three, second only to the Mirage in its operational capabilities in the air force at that time. I chose to join No. 105 Squadron, the Scorpion squadron at Hatzor, which flew the Super Mystère, and would for a long time.

The training in the Super Mystère squadron was generally similar to the training in the Ouragan squadron. The difference was just the plane, itself. Again, I had to familiarise myself with the aircraft, learn how to fly it in formation, fly photography missions, and fire at targets. To me this was all routine, and I waited impatiently to get to the dogfight stage.

I had my first dogfight in the squadron against a respected, veteran reservist pilot. It didn't take me long to bring him down. We readied for a second go-round, and soon I brought him down again. As soon as he landed, he went straight to Nissim Ashkenazi, one of the deputy squadron commanders, upset.

"You said you'd give me a beginner pilot…" Incidentally, both deputy squadron commanders, Ephraim Ashkenazi and Nissim Ashkenazi, had started the pilot course with me in 1956.

My natural flying ability enabled me, even before I had much experience, to down less-skilled pilots who were older and much more experienced. Against the better pilots, I still had to gain experience, as the following story will show.

After I'd defeated the veteran reservist pilot in the dogfights, the squadron commander, a pilot with a big reputation in the air force, decided to go one-on-one with me in dogfight training too. Within a minute, after a few manoeuvres, I was at his six o'clock position. The reason they call it a 'dogfight' is that just as fighting dogs try to grab their rival from behind by the back of the neck, the same happens in an aerial dogfight. Each pilot tries to get on his adversary's tail, referred to as the six o'clock position. You want to get 200 to 450 metres behind the other aircraft and then fire your guns.

The squadron commander began making evasive manoeuvres to keep me from downing him.

We descended to a low interim speed, 240 knots, and he drew me into a situation in which he had the advantage over me with better control of the aircraft, due to his greater experience. At an altitude of more than 12,000 feet I lost control of the aircraft and went into a spin.

In fighter jets, entering a spin is one of the most dangerous situations for a pilot to be in. The aircraft is spinning on its horizontal axis without the pilot's control, a situation that can lead to a total loss of control and a crash. My plane wasn't responding to steering, but I remained calm and attempted to stabilise. The squadron commander saw that I was in a spin and started to shout over the radio: "At altitude 6 [6,000 feet], you jump. You're in a right spin… You're in a left spin…"

I was totally focused, waiting for the plane to do two or three more turns and for the nose position to change so I could take it out of the spin. The shouting was disturbing me.

"Stop shouting, you're distracting me," I said on the radio. After about 30 seconds, I managed to stop the spin and get out of it. I landed at the base, and during the follow-up debriefing the squadron commander really laced into me for having gotten caught in a spin and lost control of the aircraft. I was grounded for two weeks. Normal procedure after such an occurrence.

Two weeks later, I returned to flying. Regular flights at first, photography and more. I used the time to practise how to deal with spin situations. All of my experience with skydiving and mid-air control manoeuvres helped me get out of the spins I put myself in. Each of these drills lasted seconds, but I never got nervous for even a fraction of a second. At no point did I ever think of ejecting. The lesson I drew from that event was that there are ways to get out of a spin. The pilot mustn't lose his cool and has to be able to tell what type of spin he is in.

In the Super Mystère squadron I met Arik Azuz, whose background was similar to mine. He had also come to the pilot course after service in the paratroops. He was a big fellow and a real stickler. He taught us about the structure of the aircraft in great detail, down to the mechanical level. The

Super Mystère's engine is similar to that of the Mirage. Later on, when we joined the Mirage squadron, No. 119, the Bat Squadron, and got to the stage of learning about the engine, we saw our instructing officer knew less about the engine than we did. During one lesson, we stopped him in the middle, telling him, "Either you go study, or we'll have to teach you".

During my time in the Super Mystère squadron, there were a number of ejections due to technical problems. Five aircraft were abandoned in the air and the entire squadron was grounded. One of the abandoned planes did not crash, and thus the problem was discovered. All of the Super Mystères were sent to Israel Aircraft Industries (IAI) to have the defect repaired. Incredibly, it was a wooden tube in the fuel system. The planes were very gradually returned to service and the number of flights was reduced to the minimum.

One day, I was summoned to the squadron commander's office, where a team from the army magazine *Bamahaneh*, a reporter and photographer, was waiting. The reporter was Yadin Dudai, who went on to become a professor at the Weizmann Institute of Science and one of the world's leading neuro-scientists. The photographer was Miki Astel. They told me they'd come to do an article on a fighter pilot who had 500 parachute jumps and had competed in the World Skydiving Championship.

It was obvious this was not a private initiative on the part of a journalist or the editor of *Bamahaneh*, and that the go-ahead had come from air force headquarters, perhaps from the air force commander himself, but I immedi-ately told them I couldn't do it. I couldn't have them publish an article about a pilot with 500 jumps, when I only had 498. I needed two more dives to hit that round number. "I'll only do this after I have 500 jumps recorded," I said.

The air force was very eager for this article to appear, so they decided to let me do two more jumps. Since the rules say that pilots are not to risk their lives skydiving, special permission from the air force commander was needed. The squadron commander and base commander didn't have the authority to approve it.

I was given permission to do two regular jumps. The first one was really a regular jump. Before the second jump, I insisted, "This will be my 500th jump – I want to mark this round number with a free-fall dive."

Once again, permission had to be obtained from the air force commander, and it came through. The *Bamahaneh* team accompanied me to the plane and the photographer Miki Astel took dozens of shots – on the ground, in the plane, and as I left the plane for the dive. The military censor wouldn't allow my face to be shown. All the pictures had to be in profile, and only my first name could be published. This was my 271st free-fall dive and the skydiving instructors who sent me up were all my former pupils. The reporter, who was waiting for me on the ground, remarked to me after I landed that I didn't look very excited.

"Sure I was excited," I replied, and my words were quoted in the article. "But not the way you think. I was excited because, at last, after such a long time, I could jump again."

The article about the fighter pilot with 500 jumps, in which I was identified only as Giora, got a big response, one of which was most unexpected and painful.

A few years after the article came out, during the War of Attrition in the south in September 1969, Captain Giora Romm's Mirage was hit[9]. He ejected and was taken prisoner in Egypt. During the ejection, his arm and leg were very badly injured. During the harsh interrogations he was subjected to, he told the Egyptians he'd broken his leg during the ejection because he wasn't skilled at parachuting. The interrogators, who believed he was hiding information from them, suddenly pulled out the issue of *Bamahaneh* with the story about the pilot Giora who had 500 jumps to his credit.

"You're lying," they said angrily. "You said you don't have any experience parachuting?" Giora Romm of course denied his supposed 'past' in the paratroops, but the interrogators weren't convinced. "If you're lying about the parachuting, you're lying to us about other things," they insisted, and continued subjecting him to torture.

Giora Romm returned from captivity after three months and told me about the interrogations and torture he went through because of that article in *Bamahaneh*. He returned to flying, took part in the Yom Kippur War and reached the rank of major general in the IDF.

In August 1966, after more than a year in the Super Mystère squadron, we were given the choice between becoming instructors for the flying school or switching to the Mirage. I was up front about my ambition to make the switch. The Mirage was the plane of my dreams. The best fighter jet in the air force. My request was accepted. I went to start training with the Bat Squadron, commanded by Ran Peker.

---

[9] Retired Major General Romm was the IAF's first ace with five kills in 1967. His well-received memoir about his service and especially his experience as a POW was published in English in 2014 under the title *Solitary*. He commanded No. 115 Squadron flying A-4s in the 1973 war.

12 LOVE AT FIRST SIGHT

The Mirage was the 'ace' of the air force's fighter jets. It had downed more enemy aircraft than any other plane in the history of the Israel Air Force. For me, it was love at first sight – the way the delta wings attached to the fuselage; the high, noble nose. I knew this was the plane for me. The fighter jet with the top capabilities. Years later, when its fame had faded a bit and the Phantoms the air force received toward the end of the War of Attrition took its place as the air force's leading aircraft, I retained the same affection for the Mirage; whose performance never let me down, even in my most difficult dogfights. The air force eventually took it out of service in 1982.

From my very first training flights on the Mirage, I had good control of the aircraft. It was similar in many ways to the Super Mystère, but the Mirage had a performance edge of about 30 per cent over the Super Mystère. It was a gorgeous plane. When you get into it, you feel like you're a part of it. It was as if they took a pilot, sat him down on a Martin-Baker Mk. 4 ejection seat, and built the plane around him.

When I flew the aircraft, it felt like all I needed was to think what I wanted to do, and the Mirage would do it. Of course, it did have its problems, and you had to be a very experienced pilot to know how to extract the maximum from the aircraft. There was another problem: The high position of the nose obstructed the view of the runway during landing. If the pilot didn't control the plane well enough, he ran the risk of smashing the plane's tail on landing.

We were still on the training course for switching to the Mirage when the IDF declared a *konenut gimel*, the highest state of alert, due to a deterioration of the security situation on the Jordanian border, and the attempt of the Palestine Liberation Organisation (PLO) leader Yasser Arafat to set up 'Fatah land' in the Arava, on Israel's eastern border. The air force prepared for Operation Sumu (named after an Arab village on the West Bank). Our course was temporarily halted and we went back to our previous squadrons. I returned to the Super Mystère squadron at Hatzor. On August 16, 1966, we were sitting in the aircraft holding area by the runway when we saw a Mirage come in to land, along with another plane with a different silhouette. A MiG-21F.

The MiG landed next to us and we ran to get a close-up look at it. A jeep full of security personnel came over from the vicinity of the control tower. One of the men in the jeep was so excited that his Uzi slipped out of his hands. An Arab pilot exited the MiG and was immediately taken away. The aircraft was towed into one of the hangars and hidden. It wasn't until hours later that we heard the story behind the landing of the Iraqi air force MiG whose pilot had decided to desert to Israel. We weren't aware that this was the high point of one of the major Mossad operations at the time, under Mossad chief Meir Amit. There was so much secrecy surrounding the operation that very few people knew about the Iraqi pilot's arrival. Ran Peker, the squadron commander, who was sent to meet the plane that was coming from Jordan, had almost intercepted it when it approached Israel's eastern border. At the last moment, Ran was told that it was a friendly aircraft on its way to land at Hatzor.

The IDF launched Operation Sumu, and in this operation Yoav Shaham, a brigade commander in the paratroops, was killed. In the operation, Ran Peker downed a Jordanian Hunter after a long dogfight on November 11, 1966. Three days after the operation, the high alert was cancelled and we returned to the Mirage squadron for more training.

Later on, I was involved in two incidents in which the life of PLO leader Yasser Arafat, who was in my sights, was saved. The first was in 1968, when I was an instructor in the OTU. We set out to strike two suspicious Mercedes cars that were driving in northern Jordan on the road from Irbid to Amman. I spotted them from the air. One was a black Mercedes and the other was blue. The order was to fire at the blue vehicle. I locked onto the target and the Mercedes was hit and went up in flames. When I landed, I was told, "Idiot, Yasser Arafat was in the *other* Mercedes!"

But my 'affair' with Arafat did not end there. Four years later, in 1972, when I was a deputy commander of the Super Mystère squadron, we were assigned a mission to attack a two-storey stone building in the town of Qaba-tiya, Lebanon. Arik Azuz, the squadron commander, was away overseas and I was filling in for him. The order I received said that a gathering of senior Fatah commanders was supposed to take place at the location. These were the years when the PLO was establishing itself in southern Lebanon, after being expelled from Jordan in 1970.

I had a discussion with headquarters about which type of munitions to use in the strike. For this type of target, you would usually go with 250-kg bombs, but since the aerial photos showed there was a school adjacent to the target, the use of bombs was ruled out. I said that the building could only be blown up with rockets equipped with wall-breaching warheads. I believed that this way we could carry out the mission with a direct hit on the building without risk to the nearby school.

"Negative" was the response I got. I was not given permission to use the rockets. The only option I was given was to strafe the house with my 30-mm cannon. From the start I was sceptical that this type of munitions would be enough to bring the building down on top of the people in it, but I had to obey the order.

I led a quartet of Super Mystères. We flew over the Golan Heights and descended toward Qabatiya from the north-east. We did one flyover. Then we began firing from 600 metres to 200 metres, taking care not to hit the school and civilians. We fired at vehicles parked near the school and hit the second floor of the building hard. The first floor sustained hardly any damage.

We landed back at the base without knowing whether the people who were in the building had been hit. In the mess hall, Benny Peled, the head of the air force command staff who was considered the heir apparent to Motti Hod, the air force commander, came over to me and said, "Tell me, how is it that you're given the go-ahead to kill Yasser Arafat and you don't do it?" My explanation that I'd asked permission to use wall-breaching rockets and been turned down was to no avail.

The training on the Mirage was scheduled to last four months. The squadron had three two-seater Mirages, in which each cadet performed three training flights with an instructor sitting in the rear seat. After that, we moved on to flights in a single-seat Mirage.

In the squadron there were three attractive operations secretaries. One of them tried to catch my eye, but my head was so caught up in the training flights that I didn't realise that the female soldier who was being extra nice to me was actually flirting. This was Sara, a beautiful girl from Bat Yam. After a while, it finally dawned on me and we started dating. At the time, she had another suitor, Aviam Sela, a pilot in the Defenders of the South Squadron (and years later one of the pilots who took part in the strike on the Iraqi nuclear reactor). Apparently, she ended up choosing me. She told me later on that friends in the squadron had tried to match us up, but she had the impression that I wasn't interested, that flying was all I thought about. She also told me that she first became interested in me even before we met in the squadron. She'd read the article in the issue of *Bamahaneh* about the pilot with 500 jumps, and asked a friend of hers who served with her in the army, a girl from Kibbutz Negba, to bring her to the kibbutz for the weekend so she could meet me.

As it turned out, that weekend I had to stay at the base and wasn't at the kibbutz. We really clicked when we took a trip up north together in a rented car. From then on, we were a couple. There was one time, later on, when we were flying in a Piper to the Afula area, together with another friend, Reuven Rosen. Sara was sitting in back and I did all kinds of aerobatic manoeuvres. She was terrified and yelled at me to stop, and when I didn't stop she kicked me hard in the back. It didn't hurt, because I have a very high pain threshold, but that's when I learned that Sara could also bite back when necessary.

Before Sara, I had a girlfriend on the kibbutz who wanted for us to get married badly. But I was totally focused on the goal I'd set for myself: to finish the pilot course and become a fighter pilot. I told her I didn't feel ready for that kind of relationship. She understood, and ended up marrying a classmate of ours.

By the time I met Sara, I was already a pilot, so the fervour to finish the course was behind me and apparently, the time had come to start thinking about having a family. I brought her to the kibbutz for the first time to meet my family. She was warmly welcomed, but to the kibbutzniks, at first, this city girl might as well have just landed from the moon. The way she dressed was too fancy and fashionable for their taste. But right from the start, she formed a strong bond with my parents and my two sisters. Her parents in Bat Yam also welcomed me very warmly right from the start. Her mother was very pleased by my readiness to help out with all the household chores, and whenever I came to visit she prepared special foods, like calf liver.

Sara's parents had managed to flee Poland after it was occupied by the Germans, and made their way east all the way to Siberia. They both made aliyah illegally with forged immigration certificates and, like many other displaced persons from Europe who came to this country they passed through the Atlit immigrant detention camp. Later on, they were adopted by the Shaham family of Ekron, whose son Yoav grew up to become a paratroop brigade commander and fell in Operation Sumu in 1966. Eventually, Sara's parents moved to Tel Aviv. Her father worked at first for Elite, a candy company – there was always plenty of chocolate in their house, even during the austerity period – and later for Israel Military Industries.

After her mandatory national enlistment, Sara was sent to serve at Kibbutz Ma'ayan Baruch. She quickly fell in love with kibbutz life and wanted to remain there for the duration of her service. But after her mother came all the way up north to see her and talked her out of it, her kibbutz adventure came to an end. She was transferred to the air force and assigned to be an operations secretary in the Mirage squadron at Tel Nof, which was commanded by Rafi Har-Lev. The pilots who were there at the time later said that she was the one who taught them to slow dance, as well as ballroom dancing with the lights dimmed. There she also found her first serious boyfriend, Meir Shahar, a pilot who was later killed after his plane was hit during an attack over the military airport in Damascus on June 5, 1967, the first day of the Six Day War.

In December 1966, at the end of our initial Mirage training, we were assigned to different fighter squadrons. I went to No. 101 – the First Fighter Squadron – at Hatzor. Sara finished her army service, and our romance grew. Ran Peker, who always took credit for bringing Sara and me together, once told me that he'd made two big mistakes in his career: Fixing the two of us up and letting me slip away to the First Fighter Squadron.

Once I joined my new fighter squadron, a squadron that played an important part in my life as a pilot in the air force, I was four months away from being certified as an operational pilot. Four months of training at the highest level during which I honed my capabilities as a fighter pilot. The practice dogfights against other cadets and commanders were thrilling. This was a very high-level squadron with really excellent pilots, some of the best in the air force. I learned something from each one of them, and kept improving.

In March 1967, I was certified as an operational pilot in the Mirage squadron, and a month later, I was also 'certified' as Sara's husband. We had a small religious ceremony presided over by the rabbi in Gedera. A few days before the ceremony, Sara took me to a very fancy jewellery store in Tel Aviv to buy rings. We walked into the store, I was in uniform, and the owner – his name was Kashi – beamed with pride when he saw me.

"You're a pilot?" he asked.

"Yes."

"Then you get a discount."

Sara smiled gratefully, but her smile disappeared when she heard my response: "No discount needed. You need to make a profit, too."

At 29, I was getting married at an older age than most of my friends, who'd married when they were much younger. My adventuresome impulse had pushed aside all else; I had to become a fighter pilot before I felt ready for other things like a home and family. Sara moved in with me at the Hatzor base. I was still a member of Kibbutz Negba, so my whole salary went into the kibbutz coffers. We planned to hold a large wedding party on the kibbutz, a month after the ceremony in Gedera. Who imagined that between these two events, the ceremony in Gedera and the planned party on the kibbutz, the Middle East would be transformed in the span of six days?

13 WAR AND MY FIRST KILL

In May 1967, the Middle East was seething. Egyptian army divisions had begun streaming into the Sinai Desert, and Egyptian President Gamal Abdel Nasser expelled the UN observers who had been posted along the border since the Sinai Campaign. He also blockaded the Straits of Tiran, and in a meeting with Egyptian pilots at the Bir Gifgafa airfield, Nasser boasted, "Hey, Rabin, *ahlan wa'sahlan*, we're waiting for you…"

The tension started to build two months after I joined 101 Squadron at Hatzor. The atmosphere on the air force bases was totally different from the atmosphere in the world beyond the bases. The public was gripped by terrible anxiety, partly due to the stammering of Prime Minister Levi Eshkol and the ministers' hesitation in deciding on a pre-emptive strike. Never before in the country's history had top generals accused the political leadership of being paralysed by fear and cowardice. Major General Ezer Weizman, chief of the Operations Branch, angrily hurled his general's insignia on the desk of Prime Minister Eshkol and shouted at him in frustration. We, meanwhile, were secretly preparing for Operation *Moked* (Focus) – a surprise attack on the Egyptian airfields, an operation that had been planned months earlier. Every fighter pilot in the air force knew the operational plan for his squadron, and which targets he was to attack.

In the squadron, I was responsible for the orders. I was very familiar with the specific group of targets we'd been given. There was a separate order for each part of the operation: strikes on airports and military convoys, and dog-fights. We had aerial photos of the Egyptian airfields and they were updated daily with photographic sorties. The Egyptian air force had gone into heightened readiness, and more planes were deployed to the forward airfields in Sinai.

I wasn't afraid at all of the coming war. I was confident in our ability to defeat the Egyptian air force, and the air forces of other Arab countries, if they also got involved. I didn't have experience yet in facing Egyptian pilots, but I wasn't impressed by their displays of power as seen in cinema newsreels. We knew that the Egyptian MiGs, especially the Soviet-made MiG-21, the Egyptian air force's main interceptor aircraft, were very technologically advanced, but my basic attitude had always been that it's the quality of the pilots and not the planes that decides the battle.

I had no doubts about our qualitative edge. Our pilots were both better pilots, and better fighters. The Israeli pilots, especially the kibbutzniks and moshavniks who were the majority in the air force at the time, came from the kind of patriotic upbringing and love of the land that gave them a basic advantage over the enemy pilots. Israeli pilots from an urban background were a rarity at the time in the air force, but they, too, had that combination of being a good pilot and a good fighter. We had better flight capabilities, we were quick-thinking, and had excellent coordination and spatial orientation.

The new Egyptian MiG-21s were considered technologically superior to the French Mirage, but from the time I came to the certification course at Tel Nof, and of course after I was assigned to the First Fighter Squadron in Hatzor as a fighter pilot, I became attached to the Mirage, and saw it as a winning aircraft. Its capabilities and mine were ideally matched. To me, it was the best plane in the world for dogfights. Small, agile, quick, with incredible manoeuvring ability. Give it a good pilot and it would achieve the optimal performance in its designated mission – dogfights.

While we were on high alert, all the combat squadrons maintained full crews, including reservist pilots. At the daily briefing each morning, orders were refreshed, the latest aerial photos of the Egyptian airfields were presented, and we studied maps of flight paths and how to reach the target. Every day we were tested on different flight-related subjects – for example, the word 'fire' would be written on the board, and we had to write down all the actions we pilots had to take in the event that a fire broke out on the aircraft from being hit by enemy fire; or we had to say how we would deal with a drop in oil pressure in the engine.

In the briefings, we went over and over every possible detail about the targets in Egypt. We had to know by heart the Egyptian airbases at Inshas and Cairo West, as well as Almaza airfield in Damascus, which we would also attack the moment Syria got into the war alongside Egypt. Ezer Weizman, who had been the air force commander until not long before the war, along with Motti Hod, who succeeded him, and other officers from the general staff, had prepared the air force for war long before Nasser went crazy.

As soon as the vaults were opened at air force headquarters in the Kirya and the details of Operation *Moked* were revealed, I knew which formation and which quartet of planes I was assigned to, who the leader was, and who were the pilots flying alongside me. The three-week waiting period was an excellent time to really get to know all the reservist pilots who'd been assigned to the squadron. I was older than most of them, but as a pilot I was still considered a 'kid'. We spent our free time between briefings and training competing in volleyball and basketball, the regular pilots versus the reservist pilots.

The plan for Operation *Moked* said that 12 Mirages, four from each squadron, would remain on the ground on intercept alert. We were the only ones who, at the moment the war began – 07:45 on June 5 – were still on standby on the runways, while all the rest of the air force was flying over targets in enemy territory.

On June 4, all the base commanders were summoned for a briefing at air force headquarters in the Kirya. Motti Hod briefed the commanders, flanked by senior officers, including Colonel Rafi Sivron – considered the main planner behind Operation *Moked* – for an early morning strike on Egypt's military airfields, with the sun in the east behind the attackers and right in the face of the enemy pilots, who, according to intelligence reports, would be in the mess halls on their air force bases at that hour.

The night before the attack, I slept at Hatzor. I was awakened at five in the morning. We went to the squadron headquarters for a briefing. In the briefing, the squadron commander went over what we'd been told in earlier briefings: Everyone takes off except for the four planes that are on 'immediate standby'. The first morning of the war was entirely taken up by attack missions. The Mirage pilots searched for prey to intercept in the air but found hardly any. Very few Egyptian planes managed to take off that morning. Of those that did, most did not make it back to land.

At some point, we were ordered to take off to patrol the skies over the Negev. We didn't have a defined target. As we were patrolling, we received an order from the controller to fly eastward. There was a report of enemy aircraft coming from the direction of Jordan and flying toward the nuclear reactor in Dimona. From a distance, I spotted two planes. These were not enemy aircraft. I identified two Ouragans, and reported to the controller that the 'targets' were two of our Ouragans.

"Negative," he replied.

We approached the reactor in Dimona.

"Break now," the controller ordered, adding the code word that meant a Hawk missile was about to be launched – a surface-to-air missile (SAM) from one of the missile batteries installed to protect the Dimona reactor.

"It's ours!" I called once more to the controller. The second Ouragan that came from the east and was also mistakenly identified as an enemy plane also warned, "It's ours".

I broke north. I was two kilometres from the plane, and saw the Hawk missile that was fired at it. Then came the hit and the plane exploded in the air. I didn't see a parachute opening in the air. In the debriefing afterward at Hatzor, we learned that the Ouragan pilot who was killed was Yoram Harpaz. The second pilot in his formation was Israel Baharav, who landed safely. They were returning from a strike on a military airbase near Amman. In the course of the attack, Harpaz had apparently hit a high-tension line and was severely jolted by the electricity, which was why he hadn't responded and flew over a no-fly zone – the nuclear reactor in Dimona. The strict security directives that prohibited any flight near the reactor had superseded logic and common sense in this case.

In the afternoon, we took off for an attack sortie on Cairo's international airport. Since the military airfields in Egypt had already been hit and temporarily shut down, Egyptian planes that were in the air that morning, as well as those that were sent up after our aircraft, were landing at Cairo's international airport, which had not been bombed on the morning of the operation.

David Ivry led the formation. We flew at an altitude of 6,000 feet over Cairo, and as we descended toward the target – the runways of the international airport – I noticed Egyptian fighter jets hidden beneath the wings of passenger airliners. The order was unequivocal: We do not attack any passenger jets at the airport. Only runways. The controller reported to us that there were Egyptian planes in the air and I asked David Ivry for permission to take them on in a dogfight.

"Negative" was the response. Our mission was limited to bombing alone. On the way back home, we passed over the Suez Canal, a blue-green strip of water glinting in the sun. The yellow desert beyond. Each plane that returned with any munitions released it over a parked Egyptian train. We did the same. After us, another quartet, a formation from the Bat Squadron led by Ran Peker, came in to land. He reported that he spotted Egyptian fighters that were in the air when he and his pilots came in for a shooting sortie at the Egyptian airport. Unlike us, Ran Peker had strafed the Egyptian fighter jets that were hidden among the civilian aircraft and destroyed some of them.

In the post-mission debriefing, I asked Ivry why he hadn't let me get into a dogfight with the Egyptian planes. I found the answer he gave me less than convincing. I'm an idiot, I thought, I should have fired at the Egyptian planes. But still I accepted what Ivry told me: Our mission was to attack the airfield and not the enemy planes. The leader in the field is always the top commander of the mission. He is the one who will have to provide a reckoning of his decisions.

June 6, the second day of the war. We sat in the underground hangar on standby as the second pair in the squadron. I was in plane 56, paired with Amos Lapidot, the squadron commander, who was number 1 and the leader. At 04:15 we got the order to take off as a second pair toward the west, though we still hadn't been told exactly what our mission was. As we climbed, I heard on the radio that the first pair was being directed toward targets in the El-Arish area. I saw that Amos Lapidot, the leader, did not react, and continued flying toward the sea. I told him about the mission in El-Arish that I'd heard over the radio. After some repeated urging from me, he contacted the controller, and we received orders to fly toward El-Arish. As we arrived over the city, we were told to fly a pass near the airfield, next to which there were supposed to be enemy aircraft. Above the field we came under heavy anti-aircraft fire, but we didn't see a single enemy plane. We turned toward the north, and I spotted a trio of Sukhoi Su-7 ground-attack jets, lined up and coming in from the south.

We weren't there alone. There were two more Mirages in the air that descended upon the Su-7s. Soon there was a Sukhoi leading the line with a Mirage right behind it. Another Sukhoi sat behind the Mirage, and then another Mirage behind that Sukhoi. The third Sukhoi was on another side, and it also was being chased by a Mirage. Fortunately, the two Sukhois were downed and the third Sukhoi continued trying to flee to the west, still being chased by the Mirage.

Since there were no other targets, I told Amos Lapidot that I was joining the pursuit of the fleeing Sukhoi. Yochai Richter, who was chasing the Sukhoi, hadn't been able to close on the plane. He fired a missile, a Shafrir-1, that hit the ground, and he also fired all his bullets without hitting the plane because of the distance. At this point he called that his ammunition was gone, and he was returning to base. After Richter left, I kept chasing the Sukhoi. Bit by bit, I closed in on it. We were flying at extremely low altitude, about 50 feet, at a speed of 700 knots, above the dunes south of Yamat Bardawil heading west.

When I came to within 400 metres, I raised the trigger cover and tried a short volley. Nothing fired. I checked the switches and found that the cannon switch wasn't in the firing position. For a moment I had acted as if I were in a training dogfight, whose results would be decided by the evidence on film, and not in a real battle.

I adjusted the switch as I closed to within 200 metres and fired a short volley, right into the centre of the engine. Immediately, there was a huge explosion and the plane's entire tail disappeared. The front section of the Sukhoi, including the cockpit, kept moving forward, nose up, before flipping over and crashing into the ground in a moment. No one could have ejected from a situation like that.

I had downed a Su-7. It was my first kill in a dogfight. I pulled up immediately to avoid damage from the explosion and turned toward home. I climbed back to altitude and found Amos Lapidot over El-Arish. He didn't know where I was. I reported to him and joined him on the way back to land at Hatzor.

I told Sara about the kill. She was excited. I wasn't, really. To me, it didn't feel anything like what I'd seen in other pilots who had downed enemy planes. I knew from previous events in the squadron and from the stories the pilots told, what great excitement there was after a kill. Two months before the war, the First Fighter Squadron had been involved in the big aerial battle over Syria in which six MiGs were downed, three of them by pilots from our squadron – Avner Slapak, Iftach Spector and Benyamin Romah. At Hatzor, everyone kept talking about the buzz flight over the base, about how the pilots went wild and whooped with joy afterward in the squadron club. Similar scenes took place at Ramat David and Tel Nof after kills.

I remember that I stood there at the base, full of admiration, yearning to be in that position myself. Now here I was, only I behaved differently. No buzz over the base. No ecstasy, no whoops of joy. I talked about it with Sara. She'd been called up in the reserves to serve as an operations secretary for the Mirage squadron at Tel Nof, but just before Operation *Moked*, all the air force bases were closed. No one could go in or out. She remained in Hatzor and was immediately recruited as an operations secretary on the base.

"I don't get why everybody gets so worked up from downing a plane," I told her. "Everyone's so excited and congratulating one another, making toasts. Another one from the squadron who downed a plane. Of course I'm happy that that I got the kill, but it doesn't give me that ecstatic feeling."

To this day, I think Sara never did quite understand it.

Throughout the war, Sara served in the operations room for No. 101 Squadron. After the war, she told me that for her it was a big relief, because she continually heard my voice over the radio and knew that I was okay. "If I hadn't been able to hear you, I would have gone out of my mind with worry," she told me after the war.

On the third day of the war, June 7, we were dispatched to attack an Egyptian armoured column that had set up an ambush for a column of AMX tanks on the corridor between Bir Gifgafa and Ismailia. Our tanks were taking a lot of hits from an Egyptian SU-100, an armoured vehicle equipped with a double-barrelled anti-aircraft gun that was being used to attack tanks. As soon as I spotted this armoured vehicle I dropped a 500-kg bomb, which landed right on top of it, penetrated it, and blew it up.

On the way back, the controller directed us toward the sea.

"There's a vessel, I want you to find it."

The leader's radar wasn't working well, and I was the one who spotted the ship. It was a medium-size grey ship with a large number of antennas on it. We reported to the controller that we didn't see any identifying signs. No name, no flag. There were no people on deck either. He instructed us to quickly leave the area.

We obeyed, of course. Later, we learned that a pair of our Mirages was sent to strafe the ship, and three torpedo ships were also sent out from the Ashdod port to attack it with deck guns. Thirty-four crew members were killed and 174 were wounded. Only after the attack did Israel discover, in emergency cables from Washington, that this was the American spy ship USS *Liberty* (AGTR-5) which had been mistakenly identified as an enemy ship.

In the six days of fighting, I completed 13 sorties, mainly attacks, against Egyptian armoured convoys. In one of them, I was attacking a large Egyptian convoy between Bir Tamada and Bir Gifgafa. There was a set method: you hit the head and the tail and then the convoy is stuck, because to the sides there are only sand dunes that offer no avenue of escape. In the debriefing we reported that we hit an Egyptian armoured division that was a source of pride for Nasser. The successful strike on this division hastened the defeat of the Egyptian army. In the course of the war, no one from my squadron downed more than one plane. Pilots that had notched kills prior to this war, didn't get any more this time.

During the war, an intelligence report was received saying that the Egyptians had moved an SA-2 anti-aircraft missile battery into place to protect the city of Suez. The battery was set up in a wadi near the canal. We didn't have precise information on its location, but we knew more or less where it was deployed.

In the briefing ahead of the assault, we were told that it was very effective at an altitude of 6,000 feet. We set out as a trio of planes. We passed over the city of Suez and the controller directed us to go west. There were Egyptian destroyers there that fired anti-aircraft weapons at us. But we flew low, at the altitude of the destroyers, and the gunners were unable to lower their guns enough to get us. We spotted the missile battery, descended for two rounds of strafing at low altitude, nearly at the altitude of the buildings in the city. We hit the brains of the missile battery. In that attack, I was a part of another historic event for the air force: the first time an SA-2 missile battery was destroyed by air force aircraft.

On that day our squadron lost two pilots. Benyamin Romah, who was killed by anti-aircraft fire in one of the attacks west of the Suez Canal, and Yair Neuman, the first religious pilot (simply a devout Jew, not a rabbi) in the air force, who was killed when his plane was hit during a dogfight. We also lost David Baruch from Kibbutz Yad Mordechai, who was sent up at night to intercept an Ilyushin Il-28 bomber. He identified the target, readied for the attack and then over the radio a shout was suddenly heard – "Oh!" Then nothing more. No further contact. It was clear that he'd been hit and crashed. We went out to search for him in the area where his plane was presumed to have gone down. I flew in a Piper along with Dan Sever, the deputy squadron commander. We flew as far as the Mitla Pass, but we couldn't find any wreckage. It wasn't found until after the war, and then Baruch could finally be buried.

Twenty-five air force pilots were killed in the Six Day War. The heart-stopping sight of a military vehicle outside the house, followed by the base commander and a military doctor getting out of the car, became the greatest nightmare for every air force family. I knew that Sara had this same fear, though we hardly spoke about it. She was very busy as an operations secretary in the squadron, but once when I did ask her about it later, she said that she always had a deep belief that I'd emerge unscathed from all the dogfights in the war.

On my final sortie during the Six Day War, I set out with David Ivry to attack an Iraqi brigade that was meant to serve as reinforcement for the Syrian army along the Petroleum Road in the Golan Heights. Ahead of us was a pair of Mirages from the Tel Nof Mirage squadron, No. 119. We saw one of them fire at a munitions truck, which then blew up. The Mirage, which was flying very low, was also hit in the explosion. The pilot, who was the Tel Nof commander, managed to gain altitude and then eject. Meanwhile, his lead plane had to turn back because its fuel was almost depleted.

I kept an eye on where the parachute was headed. Luckily, that pilot landed on the back slope of a hill near the road. I saw that he was limping – he must have been injured when ejecting or when he hit the ground. Not far from him I saw Syrian soldiers starting to run toward him. I reported to the controller and to David Ivry, the flight leader, that I could see him, and we stayed nearby to protect him. Whenever the Syrian soldiers moved closer to him, we dropped a bomb near them and fired our cannons at them. After a few minutes of this, the controller informed me that one of our helicopters was now above Lake Kinneret, the Sea of Galilee. I flew toward it and guided it to the place where the pilot had landed. We kept on firing at the Syrians until the helicopter was able to land and rescue the pilot.

On the way back home I noticed that my fuel level was dropping fast. I decided to land immediately at Ramat David. The mechanics found 16 bullet holes in my fuel tank, one of them just 40 centimetres behind my head. They patched up the holes in the plane and refuelled it, and then I took off for Hatzor.

A few weeks after the war, the air force celebrated the great victory with a lavish party at the Diplomat Hotel in Jerusalem. At the party, air force commander Motti Hod gave out certificates to the pilots who had downed enemy planes. When it was Giora Romm's turn – he had downed five planes in the war, the emcee mistakenly called for 'Captain' Giora Romm to come to the stage, even though he was still a lieutenant. The crowd started shouting, "Captain! Captain!" And in a spontaneous gesture, Motti Hod awarded Giora Romm the rank of captain. When my name was called, 'Captain' Giora Even (apparently it was mistakenly written this way on the certificate), the crowd again shouted out "Captain! Captain!" But unfortunately for me, I wasn't present at the party. That day, I had to remain on standby at Hatzor. So I remained a lieutenant and missed my chance for a spontaneous promotion.

The air force set up a forward base at the airfield in Bir Gifgafa – which was given the biblical Hebrew name Rephidim. Four Mirages were permanently stationed there to take turns patrolling the Sinai skies. In the beginning, right after the war, the living conditions at the former Egyptian base were awful and the planes were also left exposed on the runway. Eventually, a shelter was built for the planes and one of the existing buildings was fixed up to house the pilots and ground crew. Natan, a civilian employee of the IDF, one of the veteran construction workers at Hatzor, who was as tall as a professional basketball player, was in charge of the project. He built a bathroom and shower for us and attached the mirror at the height of his head. Avner Slapak used to joke that we had to jump up to look in the mirror for shaving.

We were the first foursome to go down to Rephidim: Dan Sever, Ran Avshalom, Ron Huldai and myself. Four kibbutzniks. Along with Ron Huldai – a friend of mine since the pilot course, though he was two courses behind me – I decided that we had to deal with an urgent problem: We slept on iron beds with springs, and we woke up every morning with terrible backaches.

The first Saturday, right after we'd arrived in Rephidim, we took an Egyptian pickup truck and went off in search of normal beds and mattresses. We found some in a storeroom at Bir Tamada. Big sturdy beds with thick wool mattresses. The Egyptian pilots hadn't been bothered by back problems, apparently. The grateful teams that came after us congratulated us for our action.

The Rephidim base developed quickly and became a key centre of activity for the IDF deployment in Sinai. The commander of the airbase was Colonel Eliezer 'Cheetah' Cohen, and close by, there was an armoured brigade commanded by Shmuel 'Gorodish' Gonen that was responsible for ongoing security in the sector. The standby alert planes were meant to be dispatched in emergencies. The patrols around the canal were done by quartets of Mirages that came from the centre of the country and from Ramat David.

Being on standby at Rephidim wasn't easy. It was divided between three Mirage squadrons (Nos. 101, 117, and 119). Each time there would be two planes on standby for 90 minutes, with the pilots sitting in the cockpits. The Mirage cockpit was cramped and uncomfortable. Crammed behind the seat was a parachute and an inflatable lifeboat with oars, and after sitting there for an hour-and-a-half, your bottom and back were stiff and sore. After a while, we reduced the sitting time in the cockpit to an hour, and later on we took it down to just 30 minutes.

At Rephidim, being in Sinai, we were also faced with a new challenge: sandstorms. There were days when the storms were so strong that we had to cover up the standby planes so sand wouldn't get in and make them unable to fly. Of course, in such conditions, there was no point even being on standby. It was impossible to take off. Arkia Airlines started operating a daily flight to Rephidim, and one day, when Huldai and I were flying back from Rephidim on one of these flights, I directed Ron's attention to a lovely blonde and blue-eyed stewardess, and he struck up a conversation with her. That conversation led to a romance and marriage.

Speaking of marriage, remember the religious ceremony Sara and I had with the rabbi in Gedera, and the promise to have a big wedding on the kibbutz soon afterward? The big event had to be postponed due to the war. We finally found time to do it in August 1967.

In October, we went with two other families to Eilat for vacation. A belated honeymoon. We joined an army jeep tour of the Moon Valley. We drove through the wadis and ate lunch with local Bedouins. We were on the way back to Eilat, when the sky filled with coal-black clouds. Minutes later, we were caught in a huge downpour. The wadis in that area turned into lakes, so we had to walk ahead of the vehicles to test the depth of the water to see if the cars could pass. When we reached the road that descends from the fortress to Eilat, we saw that it was impossible to go any further with the vehicles. The road had totally disappeared in the flood. We went all the way back down to Eilat on foot. The next morning, the normally clear blue Red Sea had turned brown from all the earth that was swept into it.

Our belated honeymoon was suddenly interrupted. We were summoned back to the base to assist in the search for survivors from the navy destroyer *Eilat* that had been struck by sea-to-sea missiles in an Egyptian ambush as it sailed off the coast of Port Said. The destroyer sank, and 47 crew members perished when it went down. We were dispatched to the disaster zone and fired illuminating flares over the sea to help in the search for sailors. The next day I flew a Piper down to Eilat and picked up Sara.

After the war, I remained in the Mirage squadron at Hatzor for another four months, and then I was supposed to leave for the flight school, which had moved from Tel Nof to Hatzerim. David Ivry, with whom I'd flown many operational flights, and who was the first commander of the flight school in Hatzerim, was eager for me to join him there as an instructor. Sara and I weren't that keen to leave Hatzor, which was convenient for her job as a medical secretary at Kaplan Hospital and also close to the kibbutz, our second home. As soon as an opportunity came up to be an instructor in the OTU in the Ouragan squadron, I chose that over Hatzerim.

In December 1967 I was an instructor in the Ouragan squadron. I also flew operations in the Ouragan and maintained my flight fitness in the Mirage squadron. After the Six Day War, the Ouragan squadron was given responsibility for securing the border with Jordan in the Beit She'an area, where it had to guard against terrorist infiltrations and attacks, including shooting attacks from the Jordanian army. Every morning, when a foot patrol set out to open a corridor along the border fence, we kept two Ouragans ready for take-off in case anything happened. One day, I was dispatched to assist a patrol that had come under attack. The controller told me that the terrorists who'd attacked the patrol had fled into a banana grove. I dropped two bombs on the banana grove. I don't believe anyone there could have survived.

On one sortie in the Beit She'an sector, we fired at targets across the border and then I climbed to 10,000 feet and headed south toward Hatzor. To save fuel, I reduced the power and switched to cruise flight. When I wanted to add more power to the engine, I saw that the engine wasn't responding, so I decided to glide down to land at Ramat David. The Ouragan has thick straight wings like a glider and has excellent gliding capabilities. I managed to land safely on the runway at Ramat David, and the technical crew at the base that examined the plane found a problem with one of the two fuel pumps that send fuel to the engine. The Ouragan has two fuel pumps – the main pump and a second auxiliary pump that's activated during take-off and landing. The mechanics discovered that a brass pipe that connects the two fuel pumps had been struck by a Kalashnikov bullet fired at me during the strike in Jordan, and as soon as I switched to cruise flight, an air bubble formed so that the pipe was letting air into the engine instead of fuel.

In July 1968, Moshe Levy, who was the commander of the parachuting school at the time, asked me to join the Israeli skydiving team that was training for the world championship in Austria. I'd known 'Moshe-and-a-Half' for a while, and he knew about my achievements in free-fall diving, especially when it came to style and gliding to the target, aspects in which I was considered the best. In the past, after I'd received permission from the air force commander to make two more jumps to get to 500 for the *Bamahaneh* article, I'd pressed for and obtained permission to keep doing skydiving in my free time. "If you're letting me jump for the article in the paper, there's no reason I shouldn't be able to keep on doing it," I argued, and so I went whenever I had the chance.

Even with the War of Attrition on the southern front, and even though at this time I was an instructor in the OTU in the Ouragan squadron and was often on standby alert duty in Rephidim, the air force gave me the OK to compete on the skydiving team. The problem for me wasn't the air force, but the imminent birth of our first child. Sara started having contractions on the morning of July 24, 1968. I took her to Tel Hashomer Hospital. Her doctor was Dr Benjamin Kelner, the physician used by the pilots' wives, due to his unique background: he'd been a cadet in Pilot Course No. 13 before switching to medical school. After Sara was admitted, I thought I had enough time to do a skydive before the birth took place. I drove to Tel Nof and by the time I got back to Tel Hashomer, I was already the father of our daughter Adi. Everything had happened so fast that I never made it to the delivery room. Sara didn't object to me leaving for the world championship, but I only realised later on just how angry she was with me. Both for not being there with her for Adi's birth, and for choosing to go off to the world championship instead of staying home and helping her during those first weeks after the birth.

Having received the OK from Sara and the air force I flew to my second World Skydiving Championship. This time it was held in Graz, Austria. Most of the competitors were veteran skydivers I knew from the previous tournament. The Russians and Czechs, drawing on a long free-fall diving tradition, were the best. The Russian record-holder had made 3,000 jumps. I had a little more than 500. In the competition, we witnessed a thrilling battle between a Czech and an Australian skydiver. In their first four jumps, both landed exactly on target. In the fifth and deciding jump, the Czech won by just a half-metre.

I became good friends with skydivers from other teams, even with the Russians and Czechs whose freedom of movement outside the competition was very limited, as they were under the watchful eyes of commissars for fear they might desert. Despite the close supervision, there were several cases of desertion. Also, all the Eastern Bloc countries had cut off ties with Israel after the Six Day War, so for the competitors from those places, it wasn't such an easy thing to connect with us. During the competition, on August 20, the Russian army invaded Czechoslovakia. The jarring images from Prague, where thousands were in the streets facing the Warsaw Pact tanks, affected the mood at the competition. The tension between the Russian and Czech teams was hard not to notice. The Czechs were extremely anxious and consumed with following the news from home. The competition became secondary to them. However, one of them dared to openly criticise the Russian invasion.

Our performance in Graz fell far short of that of the leading teams, but I achieved the top results on our team.

14 DOGFIGHTS IN THE DESERT

On July 20, 1969, a new stage of the War of Attrition in Sinai began: the air force entered the battle. Up until then, the government, primarily Defence Minister Moshe Dayan, had tried to keep the air force out of the war, but the escalation in Egyptian activity in the form of relentless shelling of the IDF strongholds on the Suez Canal line and the commando raids on patrols and buildings, ultimately forced a change of policy. Given the IDF's clear disadvantage in artillery compared to that of the Egyptians, the IAF was seen as the only factor that could restrain the Egyptians in the south.

Before the change of policy, the IAF had focused on patrolling the canal on the Tassa-Baluza corridor. These missions were most often carried out by aircraft that came from bases in the centre of Israel or from Ramat David in the north. The Mirages remained on standby at Rephidim in the Sinai in the event of infiltration by Egyptian planes.

We continued making high-altitude aerial photography flights around the canal and deep into Egypt. Throughout this time, before the serious air strikes in Egypt began, there were a few incidents in which the Egyptians sent planes up in the air against our jets. Nearly all of these dogfights ended with the downing of the enemy aircraft.

The permanent standby situation in Rephidim resulted in a heavy workload for the pilots in the Mirage squadrons who bore the brunt of the operations; at some point reserve pilots were also added to the intercept rotation at Rephidim. Only on weekends were all the squadrons fully staffed when reserve and additional emergency crews arrived. There was another reason that the air force didn't enter the fight in the south at full force. At the time, the Americans had begun to supply the Israel Air Force with A-4 Skyhawks, and then F-4 Phantoms, as the American Nixon administration tried to mediate between Israel and Egypt to reach a ceasefire at the Suez Canal. As long as the mediation attempts continued, the Americans had imposed a firm veto on the active use of the new aircraft.

Before the massive air strikes west of the Suez Canal began, most of the air force's activity on the southern front was done by the AH-1 Cobra and

CH-53 Sea Stallion squadrons. The helicopter pilots landed near the bombarded strongholds, often under heavy fire, to evacuate the dead and wounded. A large field hospital was erected at Rephidim to treat the wounded, and on nights when I was on standby at Rephidim, I often helped the medical teams take the wounded off the helicopters and transport them by ambulance to the military hospital. One night, we had to unload the bodies of 14 soldiers from one helicopter. Even for me, someone who had seen a lot of terrible things and lost many friends, it was a very difficult sight.

The situation at the canal worsened. In June 1969, the Egyptians accelerated the pace and intensity of their artillery strikes. Every day there were new black-framed obituary notices in the papers with photographs of the young soldiers who were killed in the strongholds or on the patrols between them. Under growing public pressure in light of the hundreds of dead and thousands of wounded in the south, the Israeli government had to come up with a response. Meanwhile, the Egyptians also increased their commando raids, and for the first time in the War of Attrition, brought in Su-7s for attack sorties. They would fly in low, release their bombs, and race back into Egypt.

In March 1969, I had returned to the First Fighter Squadron as a deputy squadron commander, and four months later, in the third week of July 1969, the air force readied to enter the fight at the canal front. After heavy pressure from the air force command on the general staff, and ongoing pressure on the politicians, the green light was given to use aircraft to attack ground targets west of the canal, with the immediate mission being to neutralise the Egyptian artillery batteries that were causing heavy losses.

The big air force operation began on July 20, 1969, and was directed first of all against the few SA-2 surface-to-air missile batteries that were scattered about the area. This was immediately followed by massive air strikes against all the Egyptian artillery, tank, and infantry targets west of the canal. As per the operational plan, the number of standby interceptor teams at Rephidim was increased. From the usual four planes, we moved to six. The three pairs were: Yoeli-Shohat, Epstein-Benaya and Spector-Gordon. In the afternoon, in the break between our attacks, the Egyptians sent up several attack formations on the eastern side of the canal. Yoeli and Shohat were the first to be dispatched toward Ismailia and we followed right behind to the encounter east of the canal. We took off at 12:15.

We accelerated and jettisoned our drop tanks. Near the canal we spotted a quartet of MiG-17s that was returning westward. Yoeli and Shohat closed in on the rear pair. Yoeli fired and downed the first MiG and Shohat started duelling with the second aircraft. The first two MiGs broke contact and vanished to the west. The remaining MiG crossed the canal heading west, surrounded by four of our planes. The battle – four Mirages versus a single MiG – took place over the Egyptian city of Ismailia. Yigal Shohat fought with him for a few minutes at low altitude, maintaining a good distance behind him the whole time, but at very high G force, and didn't hit him. The gyroscope of the Mirage has a certain flaw that became apparent in this dogfight; It sinks and disappears inside the glass of the gunsight. As a result, Shohat fired and fired until he was out of ammunition, and the MiG kept on flying. At that point, Shohat pulled out of the dogfight and headed back to base, while Yoeli, who was below him, came in at a side angle and announced that he was going in.

He couldn't hit the MiG, either.

Now it was my turn.

I went after the MiG, closed to within 300 metres and started firing. At a speed of 400 knots, the G force was very high and the gunsight was sunken. Pursuing him at the height of the palm trees, I tried a few volleys, and saw that even though I was behind him, I didn't score any hits, but I did cause him to change direction. At that moment, I fired a long burst that struck the plane's tail as he turned. The MiG immediately stopped manoeuvring, but there was no fire and the aircraft didn't explode. I pulled out of the dogfight and told Benaya to enter. Benaya entered, but at that moment the MiG turned over and plunged to the ground at a 90-degree angle. I followed it until it crashed. The pilot was still sitting in the cockpit until the moment the plane hit the ground. Either he'd been hit or had lost all controls. This was my second kill, and my first in the War of Attrition.

The aerial activity above the canal continued, but in the month that followed that kill, I didn't notch any more. Having lost a good number of planes in dogfights initiated by us, the Egyptians were generally careful not to be lured into the traps we set for them. On September 11, I planned to leave with Sara on holiday, to make up for the previous trip that was interrupted when I was called back to the squadron. Once again I had been called up. I took off in the afternoon in Shahak (Mirage) No. 59, in the Epstein-Gonen formation, heading to western Sinai between Tassa and Baluza.

We climbed to 20,000 feet and were over the Mitla Pass when the controller called over the radio, "Hurry to Abu Rudeis for the encounter."

Over Abu Rudeis I noticed explosions on the ground.

"Where are the attackers?" I asked the controller.

"Over the sea, on the way back to Egypt."

I was 25 miles from them when I spotted them. Four aircraft on the way back to Egypt.

"Eye contact," I reported.

"Eye contact?!" The controller couldn't believe I could see them from such a distance.

We jettisoned the big drop tanks and began the pursuit. As we dove, we accelerated to 700 knots and raced into Egypt. I passed Mach speed. When we got close to them, I saw that it was a quartet of Su-7s that had entered a deep canyon and was flying very low and fast. One pair in the lead and the other behind. All at high speed and low altitude in a canyon with lots of turns. We were behind them. We crossed the Suez-Cairo highway, flying low beneath the high-tension power lines and gradually closed in behind the second pair. I closed on the rear plane of the pair and fired my cannon at it from a range of 250 metres. The plane exploded and almost immediately struck the ground inverted. I didn't see the pilot eject. He must have been hit by the cannon or not had enough time to get out.

It was my third kill, and my second in the War of Attrition.

His leader, who was about a hundred metres ahead, didn't see what happened and kept on flying.

"He's yours, take him down," I said to Gonen.

Gonen began firing. Suddenly, I saw explosions below us that looked to me like anti-aircraft fire coming at us from the ground. I warned Gonen but he said it wasn't anti-aircraft fire, it was his bullets. I saw that he was too far from the Sukhoi. I called to him to stop firing and get closer to the other plane, but Gonen replied that his ammunition was finished and he was pulling out. I went in after the Sukhoi right away. I raised the trigger guard and prepared to fire at him, and at that moment, he realised what was happening and ejected from the plane as it flew fast and low. I pulled up and watched as he plummeted to the ground, his parachute not fully open. It's hard for me to believe that he could have survived. This event was not credited to me as a kill.

There were still two more Su-7s flying ahead of us, and they may not have been aware of the battle that went on behind them, but now we were approaching the Egyptian military airfield at Belbeis. The forward pair was close to landing. We turned east and flew fast and low, then before the Great Bitter Lake, we gained some altitude in preparation for landing at Rephidim. There were other dogfights that day in which 11 Egyptian planes were downed, and one of the Mirage pilots, Captain Giora Romm – the IAF's first ace – was shot down over Egypt and taken prisoner.

The routine continued. Being on standby and being dispatched into the air. At one point, a Mirage quartet was transferred to the Ophira airport in Sharm el Sheikh, after the Egyptians moved a MiG-21 squadron to the military airfield in Ghardaka, from which they could attack the southern part of Sinai. If they tried it, we would be there.

While we were on standby at Ophira, we received our first air-to-air missiles, the AIM-9H Sidewinder with an AIM-9B body, an advanced infrared warhead, with a two-second burn. The eight missiles we received replaced the AIM-9Bs we had which weren't good enough. One common problem with them was a burn that was too short, and a terrible lack of precision. If we fired the missile from a distance of 800 metres, it wouldn't come within range to blow up the plane and would fall to the ground. The Sidewinder was developed during the Cold War between the United States and the Soviet Union and was considered reliable.

In the 1960s, two Sidewinder missiles had been stolen and smuggled to Russia. The Russians copied the missile and, on the basis of the information they acquired, developed a nearly identical missile called the Atoll, which was also very highly regarded. In the Six Day War, the IDF got its hands on some Atoll missiles, which were then used by RAFAEL (Israeli defence company) to improve their missiles. Toward the end of the War of Attrition, RAFAEL finished developing an outstanding new air-to-air missile, the Shafrir-2, which also began to be incorporated into fighter squadrons. During the Yom Kippur War, we also had upgraded Sidewinder missiles that were an improvement over the earlier model.

For us, the time we were on standby at Sharm meant working in much worse conditions. There was only one air conditioner on the whole base, and the temperature always seemed to be near 50°C.

One day, the first pair of Mirages was sent up. They flew around but didn't spot any enemy planes. After they landed, my number two, Shmuel Gordon, and I were sent up. After just a short time in the air, I saw a pair of MiG-21s. We jettisoned our drop tanks and drew closer to them. When I was 800 metres away, I fired a Sidewinder missile. The missile passed below the MiG. I kept on in pursuit and closed to within cannon distance when suddenly, I sensed a shadow pass in front of me. It was my number two, who had cut ahead of me without telling me while I was turning right in pursuit of the two MiGs. They were in the front, he was behind them and I was behind him. Gordon wasn't able to bring them down. At this point I told him to pull out and let me continue the dogfight. Gordon didn't hear me.

Colonel Yehezkel Somekh, the commander for the sector, had come down to Sharm with us. He was listening to the radio the whole time and heard Gordon's shouts and my calls to him to pull out and let me continue the battle.

After a few minutes of this, the commander had had enough, and ordered us to halt the pursuit and return to base. Gordon didn't hear this order at first either, and I had to repeat it several times until I could tell he heard it.

Back at the base, I found out why the missile I fired had missed. The connector that brought the main missile body and the warhead together broke when I jettisoned the drop tank. Therefore, there was no way the missile could hit the target. The second missile was also knocked out of position as a result of the hit.

The state of alert at the Ophira airfield didn't last long. We returned to Hatzor. At that time, air force commander Motti Hod had an unusual idea. He created elite interceptor teams. In each of the three Mirage intercept squadrons, he identified a group of pilots who were his top team, the ones that would achieve the best results in every dogfight. I was on standby at Rephidim, the second deputy squadron commander for the Mirage squadron, filling in for first deputy squadron commander who was away in America, so effectively I was the commander for a month as well. After 12 days in Rephidim, I went home for the weekend, when I got a phone call.

"The air force commander would like to speak to you."

Motti Hod: "Giora, if you want us to put you on offensive manoeuvres, make sure you have the right guys in Rephidim…" I understood what he meant. Not every pilot on standby in Rephidim was suited to be part of Motti Hod's team.

That weekend, the standby team at Rephidim was composed of reservist pilots and guys from the emergency back-up crews. Not exactly the top tier. I ended my home leave and flew a Piper back to Rephidim. The air force commander's instruction had immediate operational implications: The seven reservist pilots and back-up crews were taken off the squadron list.

At Motti Hod's initiative, integrated interceptor teams were established with a mix of Mirages and Phantoms. In late 1969, the air force had received the Phantoms. Nicknamed 'Sledgehammer', they were meant for attacking and for dogfights, and on March 16, 1970, the first joint Sledgehammer-Mirage operation was launched. There were four of us – Shmuel Hetz, commander of 'The One' Phantom squadron, No. 201, and Eitan Ben Eliyahu flying Phantoms, and Menachem Sharon and I flying Mirages with No. 101, the First Fighter Squadron. This was the elite team that Motti Hod had envisioned. Pilots who were all highly regarded by the air force senior command.

Following a joint briefing, we took off and flew at very low altitude toward the canal. As soon as we pulled up higher, we were directed by the controller to an engagement with a patrol of MiGs. I made the first eye contact and reported it immediately to Shmuel Hetz, who told me a few seconds later that he saw them, too.

The Sledgehammers gained altitude as Sharon and I went after the MiGs. The group of four MiGs split into two pairs. Each one of us went after one pair. Sharon pursued his pair but did not get in close range. I raced right into missile range and fired a Burkan missile when I was 800 metres behind one of the MiGs. The missile exploded close to the MiG. I was sure the plane was hit and would fall. I left that one and focused on the second MiG. I fired my cannons at it from 400 metres but failed to hit it. The Mirage has two 30-mm cannons whose trajectories cross at 400 metres, but whatever I tried was to no avail. I was right behind him, in the correct range, firing my cannons, but the shells kept diverging and not hitting the target. We received an order to disengage and I broke eastward. I climbed higher and started flying toward the canal, and on the way I asked the controller to direct me to meet up with the rest of the formation.

"They're in combat," he told me.

I returned to the battle and saw a new quartet of MiGs. I was flying amid the palm trees of Ismailia. Too low to fire a missile. The cannons were still failing to hit the MiG. Hetz approached and flew beside me.

"I'm getting out. Take my plane," I told him.

Hetz went in after the MiG, but soon lost eye contact with the Egyptian plane. At some point, Eitan Ben Eliyahu had also tried to shoot the MiG from a difficult angle and missed. The Phantoms had now left the scene. The MiG that Sharon was chasing, apparently the one that was damaged by my missile at the start of the fight, hit the ground. Then we heard the controller tell us to cease the fight and return to base. I came back frustrated and angry. It really was a superb team, but besides me, none of the others had seriously threatened the Egyptian planes. Eitan Ben Eliyahu fired and missed. Hetz and Sharon didn't even fire. The MiG that hit the ground was credited to Sharon as a kill.

I went back to the squadron and told the mechanics to bring the calibration instruments to check my Mirage's gunsight. When I turned on the gunsight, I saw that the guns were pointing outward. It was impossible to hit anything like that. In that one day I could have downed three MiGs, but I came back disappointed without a single kill.

Nine days later, on March 25, I was flying Shahak, No. 77, one of four that were on intercept standby. The two pairs were Epstein-Tzuk and Marom-Baharav. After a brief patrol we were sent to engage a quartet of MiGs that was patrolling to the west of us. I spotted them first and informed the controller and Marom, the leader of the formation, that I had seen them. I closed on one of the MiGs and Michael Tzuk, my number two, asked and I gave him permission to cut behind them. He began a pursuit, with me covering him. Meanwhile, Marom downed another one of the MiGs with cannon and missile fire.

The controller informed us that another quartet of MiGs was joining the fight from the west. I saw two of them descending on us and coming toward Tzuk. They fired missiles at him. I shouted at him to break, and the missile passed by him. The Egyptians kept on firing their cannons. Tzuk broke hard and got away. I immediately took up the fight. They were a pair in attack formation. The Egyptian air combat doctrine that relied on flying in tight pairs did not do them any favours. For us, the threat of a pair was essentially the same as the threat of a lone aircraft. It made no real difference that there were two MiGs.

I closed after the rear aircraft as I pulled up and fired a short burst from 400 metres. The plane instantly exploded and went up in flames. I carried on after his number one, which had split off sharply. I chased after it. I closed in and, from 200 metres, coming out of a dive, I fired a volley that struck its left wing. The wing broke off of the plane and the aircraft went into an out-of-control spiral until it hit the ground. The whole time, Tzuk was accompanying me.

This was my fifth kill. I was now an ace.

In the meantime, Baharav went after the second pair of MiGs and, with his typical skill, downed both of them with a single volley.

We flew back and landed at Rephidim. Oded Marom, who'd succeeded Amos Lapidot as commander of the First Fighter Squadron, had downed one plane. Israel Baharav and I had each downed two planes. As usual, I was restrained about it and didn't celebrate the dual kill.

That day, a special surprise awaited me, too. IDF chief of Staff Haim Bar-Lev, along with Raful (who was a top paratroop officer at the time), and several paratroop battalion commanders, returned to Rephidim after a tour of the canal line. Raful, who was my battalion commander in the paratroops, was happy to see me, and even happier to hear that I'd just downed two MiGs.

"You see this guy," he proudly said to Bar-Lev. "That's Giora Epstein. He's one of ours, from the paratroops."

Those were my last kills in the War of Attrition. The Egyptian air force, having lost dozens of planes in dogfights over the Suez Canal, grounded almost all of its fighter jets. Nasser urgently asked his ally, the Soviet Union, to supply Egypt with SA-3 SAMs, the last word in Russian anti-aircraft weaponry in those days. For several weeks, in the dark of night, so as to avoid the threat of bombing strikes from us, the Egyptians deployed SA-3 missile batteries along the canal. These missiles were lethal at both low and medium heights. The air force found itself facing a new and unfamiliar threat.

The Sledgehammer squadrons that had just come into operational service were used to doing battle against the Egyptian missile batteries. It was a fight of a different kind, much, much harder, and exacted a heavy cost, especially from the Phantom squadron, No. 201, where many of the pilots had come from the Mirage squadrons. The air force lost 15 planes in the battles against the missile batteries. Some of the crews were captured and others were killed. It was a whole different story. Describing it, former IAF commander Ezer Weizman said: "The missile bent the wing of the aircraft."

The interceptors were hardly being used then. The Egyptians put aircraft up in the air very infrequently. We sat there on standby in Rephidim or Hatzor, or we flew patrols and monitored the reports from the canal area. As I said, nearly all the pilots of the Phantom squadrons who bore most of the burden of attacking the missile batteries had come from the Mirage squadrons, so we knew all the pilots who were hit.

One day I was on standby at Rephidim when a formation of Phantoms returned to the airfield after an attack on missile batteries by the canal. I was sitting in the cockpit of my Mirage, outside the shelter, waiting for instructions from the controller, when I noticed a Phantom approaching in an odd manner. He circled around and then straightened out with his nose pointing right at the shelter. I shouted at all the pilots to get out of there as fast as possible. The Phantom passed over it very low and went to circle around once more.

This time it came in fine. The pilot landed the plane on the runway and shut down the one operating engine. Only then did the pilot, Ra'anan Ne'eman, report that he'd been hit by a SAM as he was attacking the missile batteries west of the canal. Luckily, his plane remained intact, but two of Ne'eman's fingers were severed and he lost a lot of blood in the cockpit. He managed to exit the attack area, and at first tried to land the plane at Rephidim on his own with his injured left hand on the throttle. After failing on the first effort, he asked the navigator sitting behind him to operate the throttle[10], and so was able to safely land the plane.

A week before the Suez Canal ceasefire was signed, I was abroad, in the US, so I missed one of the most interesting battles in the War of Attrition: The dogfight of July 30, 1970, in which five Russian aircraft were downed. The Soviets' involvement in the canal sector had grown over time. Soviet troops manned some of the missile batteries, and several Soviet combat squadrons had also been deployed, mostly deep inside Egypt. On July 25, Soviet

---

[10] Israeli F-4s were US Air Force F-4E models, which featured flight controls for both cockpits as well as a nose-mounted cannon.

pilots fired a missile at a Skyhawk, forcing it to land at Rephidim.

The decision was made to launch a forceful response. The air force planned a classic ambush designed to lure the Soviet pilots to attack a formation of Israeli planes that resembled Skyhawk planes. In reality, it was four Mirages, joined by four Phantoms that flew in low to avoid detection by Egyptian radar. Another formation of four Mirages patrolled along the canal during the dogfight, while another formation was on standby at Rephidim. No less than 24 Soviet aircraft took part in the fight versus 16 Israel Air Force jets: 12 Mirages and four Phantoms. Five of the Soviet planes were downed. Three of the pilots were killed and two successfully ejected. As if that crushing aerial defeat weren't enough, the Soviets also took heavy losses on the ground. The Soviet pilots had ridiculed the Egyptian pilots who kept falling one after the other in every dogfight with Israel Air Force jets. Now, after all those Russian planes were downed in one battle, we heard about how there was rejoicing at all the Egyptian air force bases.

15 HAWKEYE

The War of Attrition ended in August 1970, and the air force emerged from it feeling hard-hit by the losses that resulted from facing the anti-aircraft missile batteries deployed along the canal line and inside Egypt. 'The One' Squadron – the Sledgehammer squadron from Hatzor – lost more flight crews and planes than any other squadron in the air force. I lost close friends. Other friends had fallen prisoner in Egypt. The loss of Shmuel 'Hetzkel' Hetz, who fell in battle, was a very tough blow. He was a friend, as were the other pilots. We were not a large force then, and most of the pilots, the more veteran ones at least, knew each other. After Hetz died, Motti Hod appointed Ran Peker as commander of 'The One', despite his lack of experience as a Phantom pilot. Given the tough situation that squadron was in, the air force commander was right to install an authoritative and experienced commander who was one of the force's top fighter pilots.

The War of Attrition reinforced my feeling that I had made the right choice in opting to stay as a fighter pilot in the Mirage rather than retrain as a Phantom pilot. I could have joined the first Phantom squadron, No. 69, but I didn't want to. The plane didn't suit me as well, I told myself. I still felt the same way later on when I also trained as a Sledgehammer pilot. I was one of the few who chose to keep flying the Mirage after being offered the chance to move to the Phantom. Many of the best veteran pilots in the force switched to the F-4.

There was another reason. Two people fly in a Phantom, a pilot and a navigator. My personal feeling as a pilot is against having someone else with me in the plane. When I wage war in the air, I want to do it alone.

In other air forces around the world, including the US Air Force, the Phantom was put to various uses, primarily offensive ones, because it could carry 7.5 tons of bombs. We considered it an attack jet as well as an interceptor or dogfighter. As an attack jet, it was superb. But in dogfights and intercepts, it had a lot to learn from the older Mirage.

I finished the War of Attrition with four more kills and five frustrated efforts involving planes that I could have shot down. There were two more planes that I had a hand in downing, but they were recorded as kills of the squadron, without being attributed to a specific pilot. When I reached a certain point in my career as a fighter pilot, as soon as I spied an enemy aircraft and told myself I was going to down it, that is what happened. I wasn't about to let any more technical problems like uncalibrated gunsights prevent me from making sure kills. My long-distance vision had proved itself in dogfights. In many instances, I spotted the enemy planes before the controllers saw them on the screen. They learned to trust me: "If Epstein says he sees an enemy plane, then there's an enemy plane there…"

My extraordinary eyesight gave me an initial advantage over any other pilot in a dogfight. The average range of vision for a fighter pilot is 8-12 miles. I could spot fighter jets that were as much as 24 miles away. The controllers didn't believe me at first when I told them I spotted planes from such a great distance, but they gradually came to see that it was true. Since the War of Attrition, I came to be called 'Hawkeye'. My ability to see an extra-long distance of course gave me a significant edge in dogfights. When you spot the enemy earlier, you enter the duel with a clear advantage.

David Ivry, the future IAF commander, described how once, from 13 kilometres away, I spotted the 'chute of a pilot who'd ejected. But to down enemy aircraft, you need more than sharp vision. You have to engage them and persist in the fight. As long as I had fuel and ammunition, I kept fighting. There are other pilots who feel that after one kill they could return to base and do that famous buzz flight over the airfield. They won't try to get any more kills. I'm not like them. Of course, another important quality is required: you have to be a good pilot.

After the War of Attrition, the pilot who held the record for the most kills was Asher Snir. Seven kills in the War of Attrition, in addition to five earlier kills in the Six Day War and in dogfights in the days following the war. Asher was a special figure. He didn't stand out that much in his early career as a fighter pilot but as time went on, he advanced a lot thanks to his ambition and his special personality. Asher, who was younger than me, developed into an excellent pilot in the Bat Squadron – the same squadron of Giora Romm – and reached his peak as fighter pilot during the War of Attrition, becoming one of the air force's top aces, and the first to record a double-digit number of kills. Brigadier General Asher Snir, a top air force officer and a close friend of mine, died of cancer when he was just 44.

In the US Air Force and in European air forces, as well as in Israel, the term 'ace' designated a pilot who had downed at least five enemy aircraft. Among the Mirage pilots, who flew the air force's main interceptor aircraft in that era, there were 32 aces. I joined this esteemed list on March 25, 1970. I had four kills during the War of Attrition plus one earlier kill in 1967 during the Six Day War.

During the War of Attrition, Iftach Spector succeeded Oded Marom as commander of the First Fighter Squadron, and I was in line for the position of first deputy squadron commander, having already filled that role and served as acting squadron commander when Spector was away for six weeks on behalf of the United Jewish Appeal.

Shortly before I was to take that position, Rafi Harlev, the base commander, summoned me and brusquely informed me: "Giora, you're not going to be Spector's first deputy squadron commander. You're going to be first deputy squadron commander in the Super Mystère squadron No. 105, the Scorpions, commanded by Arik Azuz." When I tried to object, Harlev would hear none of it.

"That's my decision and there won't be any changes."

Base commanders in the air force are powerful figures, and even well-regarded pilots stood no chance of getting around their decisions. It was hard for me to see why I wasn't getting the position that I'd wanted so badly, particularly considering all the successes I'd had in the War of Attrition.

It was a big disappointment, but I innocently thought that the reasons for the decision were purely professional. I only learned later on that this was not the case. It was all personal. It bothered me for a long time. Before assuming my new position, I had a few weeks off, and I asked Ran Peker to let me train on the Phantom. The weeks that I flew the Phantom and participated in exercises and dogfight drills only reinforced my feeling that, with my nature and the way I connect with the aircraft, I was really born to fly the Mirage. For four months, I flew in two squadrons, the Phantom squadron and the Mirage squadron. Three flights daily, alternating between the two.

Arik Azuz, commander of the Scorpion Squadron, a moshavnik from Nahalal and a close personal friend, was very pleased when Rafi Harlev told him he'd decided to assign me to be his first deputy squadron commander. He was in the midst of the officer's training course at Bahad 1 when the Sinai Campaign started, and the paratroops battalion in which he'd served as a fighter and a squad commander parachuted into the Mitla Pass.

Arik and several of his fellow paratroopers asked the Bahad 1 commander to be released from the course to go to Mitla. When their request was turned down, they ran away and made their way to join the paratroop force that went to Mitla. After the war, there was pressure to court martial the paratroop deserters, especially Arik Azuz who was considered the ringleader. Raful, the paratroopers battalion commander, came to his aid. He officially rebuked Azuz, but also saw to it that he could return to the officers' course. Later Azuz commanded a company in the battalion. After his discharge, he decided to volunteer for the pilot course and he completed that, too. Along with Arik Azuz there was another paratrooper, Arnon Livnat from Kfar Vitkin. Like Arik, he volunteered for the pilot course after his discharge. He was killed while piloting an armed Fouga trainer[11] during the Six Day War.

Arik Azuz was certified as a fighter pilot and advanced through a number of command positions. He was considered one of the best commanders in the OTU. While waiting to assume command of the Scorpion Squadron, he was a fighter pilot in the First Fighter Squadron. He was considered a very strict commander, one who was attentive to the smallest details.

At the time, the Super Mystère aircraft were in the process of being upgraded with a Skyhawk engine in place of the original French Atar engine, which was a gas guzzler. Other improvements were made in the firing mechanisms, in the air-to-air missiles and its ordnance capacity. The name of the plane was also changed to *Sa'ar* (Storm). With the upgrade, this aircraft boosted the air force's attack capacity. In dogfights it was inferior to the Mirage and the Phantom, but even so, I still earned a number of 'kills' in dogfight training drills versus pilots of the two other types of planes that were considered superior for this purpose.

I loved my time in the Super Mystère squadron alongside Arik Azuz. We were close friends, and the division of authority between us allowed me to do what I love best – dogfights and training pilots to be the best they can possibly be. It didn't take me long to see that the most important area for improving pilot skills was in aerial combat. A pilot who excels in dogfights will be an outstanding attack pilot. On the other hand, a pilot who excels in air strikes may not be that good in a dogfight.

In coordination with Arik Azuz, I introduced some changes to the pilot training programme to give them more time for dogfight training. Usually, dogfights began at the end of a four-month training period. I merged two training periods together and created more time for dogfights. Within a short time, I was able to identify the best pilots, and also help the weaker pilots improve and raise the level of their operational skills.

Another improvement that I introduced was going to do a dogfight that used double the amount of film. That way, you could complete one dogfight and immediately go into another. We placed a special emphasis on flight

---

[11] The Fouga was the French Magister trainer – two engines, two non-ejection seats, and a butterfly tail. In the 1967 War a squadron of these aircraft was camouflaged and sent out against Egyptian tanks; several of the lightly armed Fougas were shot down.

safety and escaping dangerous situations such as vertigo and disorientation. The drills proved themselves. Throughout my career as a pilot, I never ejected from a plane, and as a commander, I never lost a pilot.

A good number of young pilots who passed through the squadron under Arik Azuz and I went on to become part of the air force elite. We took them through all the different stages of training on their way to becoming certified fighter pilots. During this period, I spent more hours in the air than I had at any other time. I worked one-on-one in the air with pilots in whom I saw great potential. I held dogfights with them, commenting on their performance and correcting their mistakes.

The greatest pleasure I got from these excellent young pilots was when I led a formation from the squadron into dogfights versus Sledgehammers. We won most of these battles, despite the Phantom's superiority over the Super Mystère. Which just goes to show that in aerial combat, the aircraft is just the base. What you are able to achieve with it comes down to the pilot's performance. It's the quality of the pilot and not the plane that counts the most.

At the end of each training period, I knew which of the pilots would go far. I could see the skill in them, the way I knew it in myself. There were certain criteria that told me who was a good aviator: The best is a smart and natural flyer. Next on the scale is the natural pilot who's not as smart, followed by one who is smart, but not a natural, and finally the pilot who is not a natural and not that smart. And there were some like that in the air force. Among those I trained were some who went on to become aces, squadron commanders, wing commanders, and even IAF commanders. The cadets who trained on our team included Dan Halutz, the future air force commander; Gil Regev, who became a wing commander and attained the rank of major general as head of the manpower division; Avner Naveh who went very far in the air force, and Yossi Eliel, in whom I saw huge potential. He was a great guy and a superb fighter pilot who went on to command an F-16 squadron, and then was killed in an accident.

In those days, there was just one track in the pilot course – combat. Selection and screening were done as the course proceeded. Six hundred cadets started the course, and only about 10 finished it. Today the dropout rate during the course is smaller and there are numerous different tracks. A sociologist by the name of Nissan developed a special method for classifying new cadets in the pilot course, for identifying their potential and monitoring their progress to be able to spot the most outstanding ones at an early stage.

After an enjoyable year in the Scorpion Squadron, I went back to the First Fighter Squadron as the first deputy commander, working with Squadron

Commander Avi Lanir. Avi, a graduate of the Technion (the Israel Institute of Technology) in electronics engineering, had come to the squadron from the 'Syrian air force' – that's how we referred to Ramat David – and soon became the most popular fellow in the squadron, beloved by everyone – the pilots, the soldiers and the technical crew. A commander with a heart of gold, who truly found it emotionally difficult to expel pilots from the squadron.

As first deputy commander, I was a direct commander of the flight division, and being very familiar with the individual skills and capabilities of each pilot, I felt that the weaker pilots could not continue flying in a squadron of such high calibre as No. 101. For Avi Lanir, it was excruciating to even consider doing this to them. Each time I came to him with such a request, he found it heartbreaking and didn't bother to hide this from me, either.

"Let's give them another chance," he would say, and call the pilot I had in mind in for a talk. He would always encourage and teach them, with great love and sincerity. In the squadron, he gained a reputation as a scrupulous pilot who would never do anything the least bit wild, but few people knew that he had done time in military prison after doing a buzz flight over the house of his girlfriend Michal (later his wife) when he graduated from the pilot course.

There was another incident that entered the air force folklore – the tale of the black Mirage.

In April 1967, two months before the Six Day War, as a young Mirage pilot, Avi had taken part in the famous dogfight in which six Syrian MiGs were downed in the north. During the battle, he fired his cannons from a range of 200 metres at a MiG-21 that blew up. His plane was very close to the Syrian plane. He entered the explosion for a fraction of a second and emerged with his Mirage entirely covered in thick black soot, including the cockpit canopy, so that Avi could barely see anything at all. Despite the drastically reduced visibility, he managed to make it back to Ramat David, practically flying blind, and to land the plane safely with the aid of instructions from the pilot who was flying with him.

I arrived on the squadron in March of 1972. It was a quiet period in terms of operations, and the squadron was busy preparing for a festive event to celebrate the 25th anniversary of its first operational strike: on May 29, 1948, during the War of Independence, on an Egyptian tank column that was next to the Ad Halom Bridge near Ashdod. Ever since, that date has been considered the squadron's birthday, and it was celebrated each year. This year, for the 25th anniversary, a giant event was planned. Avi did a tremendous job organising it from scratch.

He coordinated a huge operation – locating every Machal pilot from the War of Independence still alive and having El Al fly them to Israel for free, with the air force seeing to every detail of their visit. The pilots who arrived in Israel were surprised to find that the hotel where they would stay was the same hotel they stayed in during the War of Independence. Avi even took the veteran pilots to the same bars they used to frequent 25 years earlier. In one of these bars, the owner wasn't that thrilled to see them at first. He still remembered the wreckage they left behind after nights of total drunkenness back in the old days. One of the Machal pilots who attended the event was Lou Lenart, the pilot who led the first quartet from the squadron that attacked the Ad Halom Bridge.

In those days, the air force was known for its big parties, but the squadron's 25th anniversary bash was still one for the ages. It was held on the tennis court at Hatzor, and most of the pilots from the force were there. One peak moment was when a large model of a Mirage rolled onstage to thunderous applause. The Machal pilots could barely hold back the tears on that unforgettable evening. I developed friendships with some of them. Lou Lenart, one of the squadron's early heroes, became my friend.

The time I spent working with Avi Lanir was wonderful. We flew and trained a lot, and forged a truly excellent squadron. One day, the entire squadron went on a trip to Jerusalem and I stayed behind on standby at Hatzor, when an order came through to send a quartet to patrol over the Golan Heights. It was clear that a live-fire event was going to occur. I summoned the squadron back to base immediately. Avi Lanir led the formation and in the dogfight he downed a Syrian plane, a MiG-21. I was frustrated that I didn't take part in the patrol.

We continued training in Sinai and on one training flight in 1972, we were flying at very low altitude when my partner, Avner Slapak, suddenly ejected with no prior warning. I didn't see a parachute and his Mirage immediately plunged to the ground. We started circling over the crash zone, searching for Avner. Avner hadn't said anything over the 'rina'[12], the personal radio used for distress calls by pilots who've ejected. I was thinking that we'd lost him, and I had to return to base since I was running low on fuel. Skyhawks and helicopters took over the search, and on one of their rounds they noticed in the wadi some rocks arranged to spell out SOS in big letters. Not far from there they spotted Avner with a Toto[13] rifle doing what looked like shooting practice and firing at rocks. They kept circling over him until the rescue

---

[12] A name chosen, as were other code names or nicknames, by an IDF computer at random.

[13] Also a name chosen at random by an IDF computer.

helicopter arrived and pulled him out.

One problem the air force tried to address following the War of Attrition was what happened when pilots whose planes were hit by surface-to-air missiles ejected and parachuted into the Canal Zone. The winds in that area were always westerly, so we tried to find ways to enable the pilots who ejected over Egyptian territory to use the wind to carry them into Israeli territory. From my experience as a skydiver with hundreds of jumps, most of them free-fall dives, I thought there had to be some way the ejecting pilots could use the westerly wind and have better control over their 'chutes so they could land in our territory. I knew that the ordinary automatic 'chutes with which the planes were equipped wouldn't allow the pilot who ejected at high altitude to have any control over what happened to them in the air, and that the only way to try to tackle the problem was to replace the usual 'chutes with those similar to the ones used in skydiving. These 'chutes have open chambers that give the skydiver better control and enable him to float for a greater distance. We experimented with various options, including cutting two rear cords of the 'chute while plunging, which would cause it to always fly forward.

While we were at work on these experiments, we learned of a new idea that had been looked at by the National Aeronautics and Space Administration (NASA) – a parachute for reclaiming rockets or rocket parts that were launched into space. A 'chute with a large canopy was attached to the rocket, its aerodynamic structure enabling the 'chute to glide farther and faster. The inventor had been turned down by NASA for various reasons, so he brought it to Israel to try to interest us in his invention. We decided to test the 'chutes with high-altitude jumps. David Duek, one of the best jumpers from the parachuting school, and I tested this 'chute from different altitudes, and what we found was that when exiting a plane at high altitude with a westerly wind blowing, you could drift for 20-30 kilometres, a distance that could make the difference between landing in Egyptian territory and landing on our side of the border. But there was still a problem that ultimately led us to give up on the idea. The velocity of the descent was so high that we feared that pilots who were not trained in skydiving would crash when approaching the ground at such a speed. Even I, a very experienced skydiver, had a few jumps where mishaps occurred that could have easily cost me my life.

Despite the failure of the experiments with this special 'chute, we did introduce certain improvements in the pilots' and navigators' parachute training when ejecting, and started to use larger 'chutes with a slower descent time.

One of the missions led by the First Fighter Squadron was aerial photography of targets in neighbouring enemy states. Aerial photography for intelligence purposes had begun as far back as the days of piston-engine aircraft in the First World War, and advanced by leaps and bounds with the entry of the first jet airplanes into the air force. British Meteor jets were equipped with special cameras and were able to take high-quality photographs at much higher altitudes than ever before. French-made Vautour bombers added a new dimension to aerial photography. The Vautours were the first planes to photograph the entire Middle East, including Iraq, Saudi Arabia and Egypt. At one point, the air force purchased three Vautour aircraft that were specially equipped for photography missions. After the first offensive wave of Operation *Moked* at the start of the Six Day War, pilot Uri Ya'ari was sent up in a Mirage to photograph all the airfields that had been attacked that morning by the air force. Throughout the war, the air force carried out daily photography sorties.

No. 119, the Bat Squadron, which over time had become a Mirage squadron, was traditionally dedicated to aerial photography. When the squadron made the transition from Mirages to Phantoms, aerial photography responsibilities were transferred to No. 101 Squadron. In late 1970, I'd trained for several weeks in aerial photography with the Bats. I learned about photography techniques and the special photography equipment that was installed on the planes. In the period following the War of Attrition, photography missions were an operational challenge.

As a member of the Bat Squadron, I flew a number of photographic sorties to check that we were doing everything right. In September 1970, on my first photography mission with equipment for medium-altitude photography, my camera captured the detonations of the four civilian aircraft from America, Britain, and Switzerland, that had been hijacked by terrorists and forced to land at Zarqa in the Jordanian desert. The images were of amazing quality; you could see the flames bursting from the planes at the moment of the explosions. This was the event that marked the start of what came to be called Black September – the expulsion of the terrorists from Jordan.

In the squadron, it was usually the more veteran pilots who were selected for the photography missions. By nature, these flights were more complex, with more complicated navigation that required special preparation. The pilot had to memorise the flight path, and the flights were at a higher altitude than any other flights that we flew.

When the Mirage squadron took over responsibility for the photography missions, it also received two more Mirages with special cameras installed in the nose. The cannons had been removed from these planes, but they still carried missiles. There were a number of different types of cameras. Those meant for low-altitude photography were called 'tarmil' and those for high-altitude photography were called 'tashbetz'. We photographed anywhere from low altitude all the way up to very high altitude. Most of the photography sorties covered long distances ranging from 100-150 kilometres. We flew at 60,000 feet over the canal, at speeds of Mach 1.8, and with the side cameras we were able to capture the entire Nile Delta up to Cairo West airport, and other distant targets in Egypt.

During and after the War of Attrition, when the danger from surface-to-air missiles increased and advanced SA-2 missile batteries were deployed near the canal (SA-2 and advanced SA-2, up to 60,000 feet and above 60,000 feet, respectively), the photography missions were flown at altitudes above 60,000 feet, out of range of the SAMs. The air force also used heavy Boeing C-97 Stratocruiser cargo planes and helicopters equipped with special electronic warfare technology to disrupt the missiles' radar systems and prevent them from hitting the photography flights. One time, in September 1971, the radar of an Egyptian missile battery locked onto a Stratocruiser that was flying over Israeli territory, about 22 kilometres east of the canal, and the missile intercepted it. Seven of the plane's eight crew members were killed. Only the flight mechanic managed to parachute from the stricken aircraft.

The air force tried to test ways to evade the more advanced missiles. I took part in some of these experiments in which we raised the Mirage's nose and flew in an arc all the way up to 75,000 feet.

There were two incidents in which aircraft on photography missions were hit. The pilot in the first instance was ace Eitan Carmi (9 kills). His plane was hit when he was 50,000 feet over Syria. He ejected safely, parachuted into the sea and was rescued.

The second instance was over Sinai, two weeks after the end of the Yom Kippur War. The aircraft had been flying at 60,000 feet, an altitude we knew was beyond the range of the SA-2 missiles. What we didn't know, was that the Egyptians had received more advanced SA-2 missiles that could hit targets at 60,000 or even 70,000 feet. The Egyptians prepared an ambush and fired at least 11 missiles from several batteries simultaneously at the Phantom that was on the photography mission. The pilot, Gideon Shporer (who later changed his surname to Shefer and went on to become a major general and head of the IDF Manpower Directorate) and the navigator, Ofer Tsidon, both wearing special high-altitude pressure flight suits, like astronaut suits, ejected. Shporer seriously injured both arms during the ejection. He landed in the swampland of the Qantara region, an area held by the Egyptians after the war, and was taken prisoner. Ofer Tsidon was killed, either when the missile hit the plane, or during the ejection.

The photography flights over Syria were more difficult than those in the south, as the geographic terrain made it impossible to fly in a straight line. We took off from Ramat David, climbed to an altitude out of missile range, and flew in a wide arc, filming Damascus with the aircraft at a 30-degree wing tilt so as to capture as large an area as possible. At the end of the route, we flew out to sea, passing over Latakia in west Syria. For these flights, we also wore special pressurised suits, and the gloves and space helmets of astronauts.

On two separate photography sorties in Syria, I was forced to make an emergency landing. The technique for those flights was the same: Climb to 36,000 feet, accelerate to Mach 1.3, climb to 48,000 feet at Mach 1.8, and climb to 50,000-60,000 feet.

The Mirage does not have a lot of internal fuel, and each drop tank held 880 litres that was meant to suffice for completing the mission and landing back at Ramat David. When flying reconnaissance missions in a wide arc, we would take off with a drop tank on the underside of the plane, and as soon as we reached supersonic speed, we jettisoned the tank. The order of the fuel transfer in the planes is automatic. The drop tanks first transfer the fuel via the wings to the fuselage, and then to the engine. When those tanks are emptied or jettisoned, the process continues: fuel comes from the wings and then from the fuselage. In both instances, I had problems with the fuel transfer from the drop tank to the wings.

The first time, as I was passing over Latakia at the end of the photography mission, I discovered that I was 400 litres short of the fuel I needed to return to Ramat David. I thought about doing an emergency landing at the airport in Larnaca, Cyprus. I reported my situation to the controller and started gliding toward home. I flew south over the sea, and descended slowly to 36,000 feet. I slowed my speed to save fuel. I crossed into Lebanese airspace at this altitude and, with the last drops of fuel, made a direct approach to land at Ramat David. The plane stopped halfway down the runway. It was completely out of fuel.

The second incident was quite similar, though this time I had just enough fuel left to clear the runway. When the incidents were analysed, we learned that, the first time, the drop tank hadn't transferred any fuel at all to the engine, and the second time it had only transferred a small amount.

Another experience I had occurred during a photography mission over Syria. I set off on a reconnaissance flight along the Syrian coast at an altitude of 35,000 feet, from Rosh Hanikra to Latakia in the north. During the flight, thick clouds gathered at high altitude, so to continue the mission I had to descend to a lower altitude. I finished the flight at just 18,000 feet, an altitude where the anti-aircraft missiles could hit the plane, a dangerous altitude for flying. Afterward, when they analysed the film, they spotted a missile battery next to the city of Tartus, whose existence we'd been unaware of.

The Egyptians knew about the photography flights and searched for ways to intercept us. After a while, when they had improved the interceptor capabilities of the upgraded SAM-2 missiles so they could reach 60,000 feet or higher, and after one of our Phantoms was hit during a photography mission, we developed methods to enable us to fly at a higher altitude. As part of these efforts, we were to attempt to climb to 75,000 feet. Iftach Spector and I did a series of test flights in the Mirage to see how it would perform at that altitude. The Mirage engine was not powerful enough to directly fly to that altitude. In drills, we climbed to 50,000 feet at Mach 1.8 speed, raised the nose and climbed to the maximum altitude – at which the speed begins to decrease. In these experiments we were able to attain an altitude of 75,000 feet.

In August 1973, I came to the end of my tour as first deputy squadron commander in the First Fighter Squadron. I now had two choices: to be a squadron commander in the flight academy, or a department head at air force headquarters in the Kirya. I chose the position at air force headquarters along with being an emergency pilot in the First Fighter Squadron. The knowledge and experience I'd gained from all the photography missions led to my appointment as head of the photography department at air force headquarters, in addition to my position as head of the department of long-range air strikes. Eitan Ben Eliyahu was appointed head of the missiles and enemy airfields department.

In late August and all through September 1973, the air force continued its daring high-altitude photography sorties over Egypt and Syria. In the photos, I discerned unusual activity in the area between Damascus and the Golan Heights, and west of the Suez Canal. There were unusual operational deployments happening on the other side of the line in the Golan Heights and on the Egyptian front. There was no question that these intelligence findings were real, but there was debate about their meaning. Benny Peled, who had succeeded Motti Hod as air force commander, was adamant – we were headed for war. However, Brigadier General Rafi Harlev, the head of air force intelligence, backed up IDF intelligence chief Major General Eli Zeira, who said, "These are preparations for an exercise. There won't be a war."

A month into my new position, I was involved – but from afar, much to my chagrin – in one of the greatest days of battle in the air force's history: the downing of 12 Syrian MiGs on September 13, 1973. Not in the air, but at a desk in air force headquarters. That day I issued an order for a photography flight over northern Syria. The air force feared that the Syrians would try to intercept the four Phantoms conducting the photographic sortie, so 12 planes were sent up – the 4 Phantoms, and 8 Mirages that waited by the Phantoms' return flight path. As expected, the Syrians launched aircraft, and in the ensuing dogfights over the sea, 12 MiGs were brought down. One of our Mirages was also downed, but the pilot was rescued.

That whole time, I was sitting in air force headquarters cursing myself for being there rather than in the air, in the fight.

16 WAR – AND I'M IN THE KIRYA...

In my new position at air force headquarters in the Kirya, I was continually in direct touch with the office of the air force commander, as well as with the office of the IDF chief of staff, regarding presenting plans and obtaining approval for aerial photography missions. Benny Peled personally monitored the aerial photos that came in from the Suez Canal and the Golan Heights.

The air force commander's opinion didn't change. In fact, it grew firmer each time he went over the images from the photographic sorties: we were going to war. He said the same thing at the meetings of the air force general staff. Of all the high-ranking air force officials, he was the only one who held this view. The attitude among the other air force officials was similar to that of the other IDF top brass, which was based on the assessment of army intelligence chief Eli Zeira and other top intelligence officers, that the two necessary conditions for war were not in evidence.

First, Egypt would not go to war as long as its air force lacked the ability to strike and harm Israel, and it was not equipped to contend with our air superiority. Second, Egypt would not go to war without Syria, and Syria would not go to war without Egypt. Military intelligence had no new information on any operational coordination between the two countries in preparation for war. The massive deployments on the borders – which we knew of from the photography sorties as well as field reports – were dismissed as being part of the final summer training exercises of both armies, separate exercises that were not related, similar to the way the IDF conducts seasonal but unrelated training exercises in both the Golan Heights and Sinai. The unusual concentration of troops on the Golan Heights was said to be due to the higher state of alert declared in Syria following the loss of 12 Syrian planes in the big aerial battle several weeks earlier.

On Friday, October 5, Yom Kippur Eve, I went down to Rephidim for routine standby duty. There were six planes at the base: four Mirages from the First Fighter Squadron at Hatzor and two Phantoms from the Bat Squadron at Tel Nof. I brought some new books with me to pass the time on Yom Kippur. No flights were planned for that day, so I looked forward to being able to relax and read and watch movies in the small air force club on the base.

At Rephidim, the forward airbase in Sinai, it felt like a regular weekend, combined with Yom Kippur. Barring any special incidents, it should be a day of rest. On Friday morning we were on normal interceptor standby, but that afternoon an alert was declared for the entire IDF and all leaves were cancelled. The word 'war' is not heard at Rephidim. Six planes on regular standby versus hundreds of Egyptian planes waiting in their underground hangars, ready for take-off.

When I arrived in Rephidim, 'Cheetah' Cohen, the base commander, briefed me.

"I'm telling you, Giora, there's going to be a war."

And I, the head of the photography unit, replied with all the confidence in the world, "Don't make me laugh. There won't be any war." As head of photography, I'd seen all the deployments on our borders, I'd seen all the pictures, I knew where every Egyptian and Syrian tank was, but still I sought to reassure him. There wouldn't be a war.

That Friday afternoon, Giora Furman, head of the air force operations department, called and asked me to return to air force headquarters in the Kirya. He told me the air force was going on alert and all pilots and flight crews were to report to their bases. He didn't mention the word 'war' either.

"Sure," I said, "but somebody will have to replace me here."

My replacement arrived at nine the next morning. Michael Tzuk landed at Rephidim, and I flew his Mirage back to Hatzor. Coming in for the landing, I flew low over Kibbutz Negba and signalled a greeting by rocking the wings. Sara and the girls were supposed to spend Yom Kippur on the kibbutz, but I wasn't sure that anyone there realised who this crazy person up there flying on Yom Kippur morning and waving hello was.

From Hatzor I took off in a Cessna for the Sde Dov airport in Tel Aviv, and the car that met me there drove me to Kirya headquarters. We drove down Ibn Gabirol Street in Tel Aviv which was totally deserted. Everyone was still at synagogue. Still unaware of what was about to happen in just a few hours. At that moment, I was only thinking about what to do if someone decided to throw rocks at the military vehicle that dared to be on the roads on this day. At air force headquarters, it was chaotic. Telephones ringing non-stop, people running here and there, maps and aerial images spread out on the tables. For the first time, I finally heard the word 'war'. According to the information I received, it would begin at six in the evening.

I received an order to immediately launch three photographic sorties at 14:10. All to Egypt. One from Port Said to the city of Suez, the next from

Suez to Abu Rudeis, and the third from Abu Rudeis to Sharm el Sheikh. Together with the unit officers, I planned the three missions, submitted the plan to department head Avihu Ben-Nun for approval, and then to the air force commander. Once the approvals were given, the orders were relayed to the squadrons that would perform the sorties.

Right then, air force headquarters underground command centre was buzzing like a beehive. Telephones still ringing, messengers still hurrying about, lots of shouting. All at once, the ordinary alert changed into an alert in anticipation of war. Each department was busy with its preparations. On a raised platform stood a small room with windows all around. This was the air force's emergency command and control post. Air force commander Benny Peled was still in his office upstairs. Each wing in the air force has a control officer who was in contact with the operations office of that base. The latest intelligence reports echoed the information I'd been given just a little while before: war on both fronts at six in the evening. The intelligence was constantly being updated. At 13:40, I saw planes moving into position on the board.

Ten minutes went by. The photographic flights hadn't taken off yet, and Pat, Captain Avraham Bundak, asked me to open the window that separated me from the intelligence personnel. He was inside the crowded command and control centre.

"Giora, the entire Egyptian and Syrian air forces are on their way to Israel…"

War. In an instant, we'd switched into another mode.

I immediately relayed the information to the office of the air force commander. Benny Peled ran down to the command and control centre.

"How do we turn on the warning sirens?" he asked.

I happened to know how. In one of my turns serving in the command and control centre, I'd learned how to operate the national warning siren system using five or six special buttons located in the air force underground command centre. I pressed them, and through the windows we started to hear the wailing of the sirens. This was the siren that marked the start of the Yom Kippur War. A genuine alarm whose meaning was clear, not just for us but for the hundreds of thousands now in synagogues and elsewhere around the country: This was war.

The telephones in the command centre were ringing off the hook. A thick cloud of cigarette smoke hung in the air. As the war went on, the smoke made it hard to breathe. It made the eyes sting and everyone was coughing so much they had a hard time doing their jobs. Eventually, compressors were brought in from El Al to draw out the smoky air, and an order went out banning smoking in the underground command centre and the command-and-control centre, with one exception: Benny Peled, who continued to burn through pack after pack of cigarettes.

In the first minutes of the war, the air force control units relayed reports on air strikes at the Suez Canal and in the Golan Heights. The air force base at Rephidim, which I'd left just hours before, was attacked by quartets of Sukhois coming in from the west one after the other, flying low.

At the height of the pressure in the underground command centre, Avihu Ben-Nun, head of the attack unit in the air force, said to me, "Giora, you know about aiding the ground forces. Go down to the general staff's command centre. In a room on the left you'll find the command centre for the artillery that's responsible for the aerial assistance to the ground forces. I want you to be the coordinator between them and the air force."

My 'expertise' in aiding ground forces was just a few weeks in the making, and began when Avihu Ben-Nun sent me on behalf of the air force to the Tze'elim base in the Negev to take part in a big exercise there by Yossi Peled's armoured brigade in conjunction with the air force. Up to that exercise, just a few weeks before the start of the Yom Kippur War, the air force never had anyone authorised to coordinate strikes and collaboration with the ground forces. In the past, the air force had had a rotating ground-air liaison, which was divided among the different squadrons. Young pilots were always sent for this duty, and given a jeep with a radioman and driver.

One day – this was back before the Six Day War – I was sent on this duty near the Jordanian border in the Beit Guvrin area. In those days, there had been a good number of live-fire incidents due to the attempt to establish facts on the ground in the territories that were in dispute between the two countries. To demonstrate sovereignty, Israel would send an armour-reinforced tractor to plough in the field there. The Jordanians or Fatah people would soon open fire. The IDF, ready for such a possibility, would return fire and the incident would quickly escalate. Sometimes, aircraft were even called in to suppress the sources of enemy fire, and the job of the coordinator on duty was to liaise between the ground forces and the air force.

In one of these incidents, the tractor came under fire and the driver ran off and abandoned it in the field. A force composed of four Sherman tanks under the command of Yossi Ben Hanan went out to the scene, and the air force was put on intervention standby. I rode in the jeep to the hill that overlooked the area, and three high-ranking officers – 'Chich' (Shlomo Lahat) the brigade commander, Yanush (Avigdor Ben-Gal), and Raful – arrived at the site in the field. A mobile command centre was set up, including a military half-track with a tall antenna for communication. Chich asked the radioman to get hold of someone for him on the radio – but the radioman couldn't. Chich and Yanush were holding walking sticks, like British army officers, and they whopped the hapless radioman on the head with them. I noticed that the frightened radioman's helmet was on inside-out, which was why he was having trouble following the order.

The next morning, Raful, who knew me back from my time in the paratroops, asked if I knew how to operate a D-9 tractor. I, of course, said yes, and right away I went into the field, climbed on the tractor, started it and drove it out of there. That finally brought the incident to a close.

But now, this wasn't some minor incident in the north, but a major war in which the IDF, the air force, and the entire country were caught unprepared. In the air force command bunker we were starting to receive reports about strongholds in the Canal Zone coming under attack and about desperate pleas for aerial assistance. This was my job, to take in the requests, pass them on and coordinate between the field and the air force.

I went to the artillery corps' command bunker. Four or five reservist artillery officers were in a big room there trying, not very successfully, to handle the hysterical cries for help that were coming from the combat zones. Commanders in the field, nearly everywhere that was under attack, whether by the Suez Canal or in the Golan Heights, were pleading for help from the air. The battle picture wasn't that clear yet, but from fragmented reports we were getting, it seemed the Egyptians were already crossing the canal, starting to build bridges and to surround some of the Israeli strongholds, while the Syrians in the north were sending in endless columns of tanks, against which we had just two regular armoured brigades in the Golan Heights. These were the first hours of the war. The air force, according to previous planning, was supposed to first take out the Egyptian and Syrian surface-to-air missile batteries, which made it impossible for our planes to have safe access to the combat zones to provide quick aid to the ground forces. The air force therefore had to deal with the missile batteries before it could help the ground forces.

But the commanders in the field didn't know about the air force plans and their requests for help kept streaming in. Telephone call after call, with desperate calls on the radio too. The reservist artillery officers struggled to provide quick answers. The procedure for calling in air support was clumsy and convoluted. Each platoon commander – whether in a stronghold at the canal, or in an outpost on the Golan Heights that was surrounded or being attacked from the air or with artillery, or tank commanders who suffered heavy losses in the first hours of fighting – called company commanders and requested air support.

The company commander relayed the request to the battalion commander, who passed it onto the brigade commander. The brigade commander collected all the requests for air support received from all the battalions in his sector, and passed them onto the division commander. The division commander then passed it on to the command centre, which relayed the request to the artillery command bunker in the Kirya.

On paper it sounds okay. There's a logic to the system. But while this procedure may have been fine for normal times, or even for the War of Attrition that ended three years before, it was not suitable for a war like this one. Not for a situation in which thousands of shells were landing on our positions every hour. Not when thousands of Egyptian soldiers were crossing the canal and trying to seize positions where there were just a few dozen soldiers who also weren't from the IDF's most elite units.

Hours sometimes passed from the moment the commander of a stronghold contacted the platoon commander until the request for help finally reached the artillery command bunker. The reserve officers passed the request on to me, and I was the one who had to allocate the aerial support.

As a result of the position Avihu Ben-Nun created and assigned to me, I became the Greens'[14] great hope. I received an allocation of Skyhawks to be used to aid the ground forces who were under attack and in trouble. The squadrons that provided aid to the forces on the line drew all the missiles and anti-aircraft fire. It was no coincidence that the Skyhawk squadrons lost more planes, especially in the first days of the fighting, than all the other air force squadrons. All the requests for help came to me. I wrote the operation orders and sent them by teleprinter to the air force bases, from which I'd been allocated aircraft, and two hours later the planes were in the air. Due to the complicated procedure, which I was not responsible for, and the winding path that these requests took before reaching me, there were many times when the help arrived too late, when, unfortunately, there was no more need for it.

Before I went down to the artillery command bunker, Avihu Ben-Nun promised me that the assignment I'd been given as coordination officer with the ground forces, was only temporary and that after a short time, I would hand off the position to another pilot, Yossi Henkin. I was so overwhelmed with trying to keep up with the aid missions to the ground forces, that I didn't have a free moment to see what was happening in the war as a whole, beyond my sphere of activity. In the command bunker there was a row of telephones that were directly connected to the armoured forces and artillery command centres. Any radio contact with the strongholds by the canal was kept open.

---

[14] 'Greens' are how other services refer to the Israel Army.

Every shell that exploded at one of these positions was clearly heard over the radio. I knew how desperate the situation there was, and how badly they needed air support, but often I was unable to help them. It was heartbreaking to hear some of the urgent pleas for help from the encircled strongholds. We knew there were soldiers there fighting for their lives and begging us for help, but most of the time we couldn't dispatch planes to attack on the canal line or on the Golan Heights, because of the anti-aircraft missile batteries. Direct-attack missions were considered suicide missions. Nonetheless, the Skyhawk pilots, including many reserve pilots, went above and beyond. After two straight days of fighting, some of them were utterly exhausted. One Skyhawk quartet became famous when it dropped cluster bombs that wiped out an Egyptian armoured battalion that had crossed the canal.

While I was fielding the calls for help from the ground forces in both sectors of the fighting, the air force was preparing for Operation Tagar 4, a strike on the missile systems by the canal. The operation, which the air force had been working on and practising since the end of the War of Attrition in August 1970, was set to take place in the early morning hours of October 7, on the second day of the war. It was a four-phase operation in which the air force planes would contend with the enemy's anti-aircraft systems, radar, and, in the Canal Zone, the missiles themselves. If successful, the air force would be able to assist the ground forces in Sinai.

The first stage of the operation, the strike on the anti-aircraft systems, meant to allow the air force's planes to operate unhindered, went well. But before the Skyhawks that carried out the strike returned to Israeli territory, Benny Peled received an order from the defence minister for the air force to direct all of its firepower toward the Golan Heights, where the defence line had been breached and it seemed like only the air force could now stop the hundreds of Syrian tanks from crossing the Jordan River. The three critical stages of Operation Tagar 4 were called off, and the force turned its attention to planning the strike on the northern front, with Operation Model 5 – attacking the missile batteries in the Golan Heights without the benefit of up-to-date intelligence or aerial photos.

On the second evening of the war, I heard about the heavy losses incurred by No. 201 Phantoms from Hatzor under the command of Ron Huldai, the squadron's first deputy commander, who in the first three days of the war stood in for squadron commander Yiftach Zemer who was abroad when the fighting started. The squadron lost six planes in one mission to attack the missile batteries in the Golan Heights. One of the pilots who was killed in this operation was Ehud Henkin from 69 Squadron, the brother of Yossi who was supposed to replace me as the coordination officer with the ground forces.

The sudden change of mission, from Tagar 4 to Model 5, illustrated the breakdown that was occurring on the political level and among the top ranks of security officials. The panic there was total. Moshe Dayan talked about the loss of the Third Temple. Motti Hod, the former IAF commander, was appointed commander of aerial operations in the northern command, and one of his first moves was to allocate two Skyhawk squadrons to the northern command to halt the columns of Syrian tanks that were advancing westward toward the slopes of the Golan Heights.

17 BACK TO COMBAT

After two tough days as the air force representative with the artillery, my replacement finally arrived and I returned to the air force command bunker. I went back to planning photography sorties and air strikes. I returned to long days and nights without sleep, with brief naps in rooms at the Ramat Aviv Hotel, which were made available to us for four-hour sleep and sandwich breaks. Often, we didn't even have time to eat anything.

Contrary to what was happening outside, work in the air force bunker was calm and focused. We prepared operational orders, we relayed the orders to the squadrons, and we did whatever was necessary for the missions to be performed. It was the Greens and the general staff that were driving us mad. I remember one night when we had to change the operational orders four times for the entire air force offensive system. The general staff couldn't decide what it wanted. They drove Benny Peled, the IAF commander, crazy and he drove us crazy. On October 7, the second day of the war, Moshe Dayan came to the air force command bunker. He was nothing like the Moshe Dayan of before the war. Nothing like the man who had projected so much confidence. His eyepatch had slipped down, revealing his empty eye socket. I urged the top air force personnel there to find a way to get him out of there, as his air of dejection and defeat began to affect us.

Planning operations is not in my DNA. I didn't fight for seven years to get back into the pilot course in order to serve as a staff officer, no matter how important the job, at a time when the country was in a life-or-death war. I am a fighter pilot, an aerial warrior. At a time like this, my place was at the front, in the air, not behind a desk at air force headquarters.

My colleagues and I were doing important work at the Kirya, in those fateful days for the air force, which was fighting and being tested as never before, but none of that compared to my desire to fly and take part in the fierce aerial combat. For the first time, I felt regret for having chosen this position over being an instructor in the flight academy, just because I didn't want to leave Hatzor. While I continued working at the headquarters, I started pressing Giora Furman and Avihu Ben-Nun to let me return to the Mirage squadron whenever there was a window of opportunity, to go out on a combat mission. The pressure helped, and it was agreed that if such an opportunity arose, I could leave for Hatzor in the afternoon after completing the operational planning and air strike orders for the next day of fighting.

On October 8, 11 and 14, I was able to leave to fly sorties with the squadron. On the first days of fighting, it was the Phantom squadrons that did the night patrols, because of their more advanced radar systems. Compared to the Phantoms that 'can see at night', the Mirage lacked radar and were essentially blind, and of no use for night patrols. However, as the war went on, and the great burden fell on the Phantom squadrons, it was decided to also use the Mirage squadrons for evening and night patrols. I flew two sorties in the last light of day. One was at night. In all three, I returned without results. No engagement with enemy aircraft. Disappointment.

On October 16, the 11th day of the war, I felt that I couldn't go on any longer working in the command bunker. The war had entered a decisive stage and I was still a fighter pilot left out of the fighting. Three days earlier, Lieutenant Colonel Avi Lanir, commander of 101 Squadron and one of my closest friends in the air force, had ejected over Syria and reportedly been taken prisoner. He had taken off for an intercept mission over Syria without participating in a pre-take-off briefing and obtaining the latest information on the location of the Syrian missile batteries. On his way to an engagement, his Mirage was hit by a SA-3 missile. Avi Lanir had apparently entered a missile area without heeding the two important points that the pilots were told in the pre-mission briefing: not to enter a missile area without seeing the target and without being certain that you can engage it; and only to enter a missile area at low altitude. Zero altitude.

Avi Lanir ejected from his stricken plane over the combat zone between the two sides. But a westerly wind pushed his 'chute toward Syrian-held territory. The tank crews that tried to rescue him saw that he managed to land, but was then captured by Syrian commandos and taken away in a military vehicle. In any case, according to the reports, he was not injured during the ejection or the landing. Information given to the air force indicated that Lanir was among the IDF POWs being held by the Syrian army. We kept hoping that his name would appear on the list of POWs in Syria, a list that was conveyed to Israel by US Secretary of State Henry Kissinger, who went back and forth between Jerusalem and Damascus in an attempt to achieve a ceasefire in what had become a war of attrition in the north, and to achieve a prisoner exchange.

To our great dismay, Avi Lanir's name did not appear on the list. Finally, in June 1974, when the captured pilots returned from Damascus, we received a report from pilot Ami Rokah, who had heard Lanir in prison. Rokah, who was injured when his plane was downed, had lain one bed over from Lanir in a room that was apparently used for medical treatment, with just a curtain separating them. Lanir told him that he'd been severely tortured. His arms and legs had been broken in an attempt to extract secrets from him. Avi Lanir didn't talk despite the terrible torture to which he was subjected, and he did not make it out of the Syrian prison. Lieutenant Colonel Avi Lanir, under whom I served as first deputy squadron commander before the war, did not give up the important secrets that he knew. Eight months after his plane was hit, the Syrians returned the squadron commander's body to Israel. Lanir was posthumously awarded the red-ribbon Medal of Valour for the great bravery he showed in Syrian captivity.

In the first week of the war, in addition to the heavy losses in the air, the air force command had another problem to contend with: two of the most important combat squadrons – the First Fighter Mirage squadron and The One Phantom squadron, both from the Hatzor airbase, were left without commanders. Avi Lanir had been downed and taken prisoner, and Yiftach Zemer, commander of The One, had injured his back when he ejected over the Judean desert, south-east of Jerusalem, after completing an air strike near Damascus, and wasn't able to resume command of the squadron. Amos Lapidot, the Hatzor wing commander, asked the air force commander to release Eitan Ben Eliyahu, head of the attack department, and myself, from our jobs in the command bunker. He wanted to appoint me to command the Mirage squadron and Ben Eliyahu to command the Phantom squadron.

Eitan and I had already arrived at the gate of the base in the Kirya, on the way to take command of the two squadrons at Hatzor, when the guard at the gate stopped us and said, "You must return to air force headquarters immediately".

Soon we were in the midst of a heated argument on an open intercom between Amos Lapidot, who urgently demanded that we get to Hatzor as quickly as possible to take command of the two squadrons, and air force commander Benny Peled and Colonel Giora Furman, head of the operations department, who were opposed to us leaving the Kirya. "You can't leave the air force's attack division without these two department heads," Peled and Furman angrily told Lapidot, as they informed him that they were not approving our appointments.

After a lot of shouting from either end of the intercom, a compromise was reached: Eitan Ben Eliyahu would go to Hatzor and replace Ron Huldai, who had been temporarily filling in for Yiftach Zemer. Huldai had admirably commanded the squadron in the tough early days and hours of the war, but Amos Lapidot felt the squadron needed an older and more experienced commander. Eitan Ben Eliyahu, who was three classes ahead of Huldai in the flight academy, was considered a more experienced pilot. As for the Mirage squadron, Peled, Furman, and Avihu Ben-Nun agreed that the squadron's first deputy commander, Israel Baharav, could fill in at a pinch for the captive Lanir. Baharav was wounded in the hands on the first day of the war when a tyre on his Mirage exploded just as he was taking off on a mission. The aircraft began to burn, the cockpit was locked shut and Baharav was badly burned on both hands when he managed to break a hole in the melted canopy of the plane. As a result of his injury, he had been grounded for part of the war. It was a very unusual thing for a Mirage to catch fire like that on the runway, and this was an aircraft – Mirage No. 59 – that had downed 13 enemy planes. It was grounded for the rest of the war and is now on display at the air force museum in Hatzerim.

The plan was put into effect. Baharav stayed on as the acting deputy commander and, despite his burns, returned to flying a few days before the end of the war. He was the leader of the quartet from Rephidim that took part in the last battle over Sinai on October 24. After the ceasefire, he was replaced by Herzl Budinger. To make it up to me for the appointment that was snatched away, I was told that on the days that I went to fly, I would assist Baharav in commanding the squadron.

In retrospect, the reason for the decision was clear to me: the situation in the Phantom squadron was much more of a problem than it was in the case of the Mirage squadron. The Phantoms bore the main burden in the war, and the squadron was in serious trouble after losing two pilots and planes, by the canal and over the Golan Heights in Syria. An experienced commander was urgently needed to revive the wounded squadron, take in new pilots and new aircraft, and lead it on more missions as the war continued. The Mirage squadron, the First Fighter Squadron, continued mainly to fly intercept missions.

I kept on with my duties at headquarters and took advantage as much as I could of the permission I'd been given to leave for evening and night-time sorties after my day shift at the Kirya. These were patrol flights along the eastern side on the canal, out of range of the missile batteries. Since the Egyptians rarely put planes in the air for attacks, the patrols ended without any engagements, which for me was quite a disappointment.

On one of the night patrol flights, the ground controller informed me that a large aircraft was flying parallel to me on the western side of the canal. It was a Tupolev bomber, though I couldn't identify it in the dark. A few seconds later, the controller told me that the Egyptian plane had fired a missile. I figured it was a Kelt missile, a Soviet cruise missile with a one-ton warhead or thereabouts. The Egyptians had previously used this kind of missile. Since the start of the war, several of them had been fired at military targets, but most fell or crashed without reaching their objective. On the first day of the war, a Saturday afternoon, two Kelt missiles were fired at Tel Aviv. The first fell into the sea and the second was intercepted by a Mirage flown by ace Eitan Carmi (9 kills).

A few more seconds went by and then, out of the darkness around me, I spotted the yellow light of the bomber's engine.

"Eye contact," I informed the controller. "Requesting permission to fire at the target."

"Negative. We have planes in the area. Do not fire."

From afar I monitored the path the bomber was taking. "He's flying toward you, toward 'Yaba Sinai'," (the air traffic control position in Sinai) I told the controller.

At one point, his engine turned off.

"Turn off the radar, he's coming straight at you," I shouted to the controller. The missile ultimately struck the bottom of a cliff, quite far from the air traffic control post.

The Egyptian bomber fired a second missile. Again I requested permission to fire at him and again it was denied. I immediately switched to the Rephidim channel:

"A Kelt missile is coming your way. Direct all your anti-aircraft fire at it."

Seconds later, I saw one of the most beautiful sights I'd ever seen. The sky lit up with bright tracers in every colour. Independence Day fireworks were nothing compared to this. The anti-aircraft guns intercepted the missile and destroyed it mid-air. I came back to land and called the controller, Yaba Sinai.

"I'm right behind the Kelt and you don't let me down it…?" I said angrily. He mumbled something in reply.

The war continued in the north and south. The air force was in the fight of its life. The interceptor pilots from the Mirage and Phantom squadrons were recording kills while I was stuck most of the time back at the air force command bunker. 'Flying Parkers' (Parker pens, in other words) – that's what I called positions at headquarters. I knew that I was doing important, necessary work, issuing orders for aerial photography and air strikes, but it's not what I wanted to be doing. Let me be in the air with my Mirage engaging with enemy aircraft. In dogfights. I did get to go out on a few night patrols – but without results. There were no enemy planes in the air during the hours I was patrolling. I heard about dogfights that happened in the daylight. My friends from Rephidim were at work in the air and shooting down enemy planes. I wasn't, and I felt so frustrated that the war would be over soon and I wouldn't have recorded a single kill. At some point, I felt like I was going to burst, and I went back to Giora Furman and Avihu Ben-Nun and told them: "If you don't let me fly – I'll desert."

On October 18, I set out on a patrol that in IAF slang is called 'putting out the sun', last patrol before the sun sets in the west. The patrol was to last for one hour and 50 minutes. We were a pair of Mirages in the air. I was the leader, and Yoram Geva was my number two. At a certain point, I asked Geva to take over the lead. In all of my previous sorties in the Canal Zone I never saw so much as a shadow of an Egyptian plane. While all the other guys from Rephidim were downing one Egyptian plane after another. The thought occurred to me that if Geva is leading, maybe my rotten luck will finally change and we'll go to an engagement. A nice idea perhaps, but Geva insisted that I lead since I was the senior pilot. The day before, on October 17, after the end of a shift at air force headquarters, I'd flown with Ra'anan Ne'eman to patrol the part of the Jordan River that passes through the southern Golan Heights, outside of missile range. That was my only sortie on the Syrian front.

The controller informed me of a target to the east and instructed us to go to the engagement at an altitude of 15,000 feet. I told him I would not enter the engagement at that altitude without seeing the target, and that I would only enter at a very low altitude. We descended to a low altitude, but I didn't see the target. The controller kept giving me directions. I was leading and Ra'anan was flying a little behind me, to the right. Suddenly he passed me and I spotted fire blow his right wing.

"Drop the drop tanks!" I called to him on the radio. He did so and the fire went out.

We turned back, flying nearly at grass level. On the way, we passed over Syrian outposts and over missile batteries. We were flying so low and at such a high speed that the Syrian soldiers couldn't react quickly enough to aim their missiles at us before we passed over them on our way back to the border. Over the border, I joined Ra'anan in close formation, and saw that one of his plane's missiles was hit by anti-aircraft fire and activated, the two-ton force of the missile's engine pushing his plane ahead. I also saw that the front of his plane had absorbed quite a bit of shrapnel. I told him to return to base, and I joined a pair of Mirages from the First Fighter Squadron. However, I ended up returning to Hatzor with no results.

The next day, I was in the air again, heading west. Our destination was the area by the Deir Suweir airfield. This is the place where Danny Matt's paratroops had managed to cross the canal two days earlier. They built a small bridgehead on the western side, where the first tanks from Haim Erez's brigade soon arrived. This is the spot where two entire divisions, Arik Sharon's division and Avraham Eden's division, which had crossed the canal over the unifloat bridge and continued fighting and expanding the bridgehead, were gathered. The ground forces had advanced westward, destroying most of the missile batteries in their path. Consequently, the air force had greater room to manoeuvre over the canal and it was possible to initiate air strikes and dogfights in a wider area.

It took the Egyptians about a day to discover the crossing. By the afternoon of October 17, they were attacking the bridgehead at Deir Suweir with all they had, from the air and with artillery. This was our big chance, and my big chance, to finally engage the Egyptian air force. This was why I'd been so determined to get back to Rephidim.

Right after take-off, I could feel how things had changed. Unlike before, the controller wasn't coming over the radio every other minute to warn of missiles that were locked on us. I enjoyed the change, the skies free of missiles. Our operating zone and hunting ground for interception was bigger than ever. All I needed now was some luck, for some enemy aircraft to appear.

The sun was setting. The day's light was fading fast and still there was no sign of the Egyptian air force. What a disappointment.

"Go in to land," the controller told us.

We broke direction and headed toward Rephidim, when suddenly the controller came on again.

"Negative. There are attacks in the yard at Deir Suweir."

As of October 17, the small yard at Deir Suweir, which came to be known as 'the yard of death', became the main battlefield on the southern front. It is a few hundred square feet in area and from the air, I spotted the convoy of IDF tanks and armoured vehicles on their way to cross the canal. The Egyptians had concentrated all their artillery on this area. Thousands of shells were fired, causing heavy losses.

I flew over the yard at low altitude and didn't see anything. As I turned right, I saw a burst of napalm on the ground that ignited our half-track. In the air, I saw a small halo of light. I knew this wasn't a fighter jet. I drew closer and saw a large helicopter. I reported it to the controller, who checked and got back to me.

"Authorised to shoot down. Not ours."

I reduced my speed, made a quick turn, and fired at him from a distance of 1,100 metres. I aimed slightly ahead, and the helicopter caught fire and crashed on the banks of the Great Bitter Lake. I landed at Rephidim and remained there on standby. I felt a bit of relief, at last I had a kill in the war, even if was just a helicopter. After the war, I went back to the spot and found the remains of the helicopter and the crew's graves there. It was a big Soviet helicopter, an Mi-8, that had been sent to hit our makeshift bridge over the canal. The helicopter flew low and dropped barrels of napalm, trying to hit our soldiers and vehicles that were massed near the crossing point. A second helicopter in the formation had managed to drop several barrels of napalm before it was hit by our ground fire and crashed in a eucalyptus grove west of the canal. I later learned that Defence Minister Moshe Dayan was just a few hundred metres away from the crash site.

I remained on standby at Rephidim the next day as well, October 19. It was the first time I'd stayed at Rephidim rather than return to headquarters in Tel Aviv. I was put in one of the standby pairs. Around ten in the morning, two of the pairs were dispatched toward the canal for interception. They engaged Sukhoi Su-7 and MiG-17 aircraft and shot down several of them. We were sent up on patrol after their fight ended, until formations could arrive from the north to replace us.

At 13:15, we were back on standby. I led in a Nesher[15] No. 61. Dror was my number two. We were dispatched to an engagement near Deir Suweir, above the bridgehead. The night before, the pontoon bridge was spread over the canal, and from the air we saw convoys passing over it, heading west. We flew very fast and reached the Great Bitter Lake before the Egyptian attackers. Our speed was so great, that when we saw the planes pulling from the west, we couldn't engage them right away. I had to make a 270-degree left turn while pulling up over the lake to go after them. They were flying in four pairs in a row, all Su-7s armed with rockets. We saw them enter an attack over the bridge, flying south to north. To the east of the bridge were long convoys waiting to cross to the western side of the canal. Tanks, armoured carriers, trucks, buses, and other vehicles. From the air, I saw one bus burst into flame when it was struck by a rocket from the Egyptian fighter-bombers.

I locked onto the third pair in the row and immediately fired a missile at the rear plane. The aircraft was hit, blew up and plunged into the canal. His number four broke hard to the left and fled without releasing any rockets. I left it and continued chasing the number two of the second pair that had just

---

[15] A Mirage derivative.

come out of a strike. I still had the detachable belly tank but was flying too fast to jettison it. I continued chasing him westward, gradually closing to within 300 metres behind him.

I fired a volley over him and the Egyptian pilot broke left at very low altitude and high speed, to try to shake me off. We were both flying very fast. I tried a few small volleys but missed him. I decided not to give up. I would keep on pursuing him as far as the 'Egyptian firewall', the anti-aircraft defence line about 10 miles west of the canal. Every Egyptian with weapons near the firewall, whether it was anti-aircraft guns, heavy machine guns, or light weaponry, would raise his weapon and shoot. In briefings we were repeatedly told that it was dangerous to cross this area and there was even an explicit order: Do not cross the firewall in pursuit of enemy aircraft.

I kept up the pursuit, unrelenting. We were both at zero altitude. Full burner, 700 knots. I closed on him. From the start, I told myself I would only chase him up to the firewall. He was flying at grass level, and to hit him with shells, I had to go a little lower than him, and it was not easy. From afar I saw the Egyptian anti-aircraft batteries. I was getting close to them. If I couldn't hit him now, I'd have to let him go.

I raised the nose and launched a volley that exploded in front of him. He broke, and then I fired another volley. Bullseye! The plane crashed to the ground. A red fireball rose into the air a few hundred metres behind me. I turned back east toward the canal and joined up with Dror who had also pursued a pair of Sukhois but failed to close on them. We headed back to Rephidim. I'd added two more kills to the helicopter that I shot down the day before.

At 16:30 I was back on interceptor standby at Rephidim, in the same plane – Nesher 61. I was leading the formation with Dror as my number two again. The second pair, Harish and Adres, was dispatched first to patrol around the canal, and now they joined me to form a quartet. The controller, Yigal Ziv, commander of the western control unit for the Rephidim sector, sent us up in anticipation of a strike on the bridgehead. After we crossed the canal line to the west, we were told to join the patrol of the Ahat Squadron (No. 201), the Phantom squadron that was circling at low altitude over the lake. After my experience in the previous engagement that day, which I entered at an overly high speed, I came in at a lower speed to catch up to the first pair of Sukhois.

We flew over the Great Bitter Lake and found the Phantoms. Ron Huldai was leading the patrol on the western side. We were starting to join them when we suddenly spotted an unidentified aircraft pair pulling from the south in a left, westward turn to about 8,000 feet. I reported it immediately and we took off after them. They looked to me like a pair of MiG-21s. I entered behind them right away and fired a missile at the plane on the right. The missile hit the target and the plane exploded.

I had started going after the second plane when, to the west, I saw a whole row of attackers, eight to ten Sukhois over the banks of the lake, turning left to strike. We immediately left the lone aircraft that had broken to the west and turned toward them, reporting to the Phantoms about what was approaching from the west. I was preparing to go after one of the Sukhois, when my number two asked permission to go in ahead of me. I gave permission, but then I saw he was referring not to the plane that I was closing on, but to another pair that was approaching a pair of Phantoms from the Ahat Squadron that had just begun a leftward turn.

Things got complicated. The Phantom pilots hadn't noticed the Egyptian planes and had begun to turn right. The Sukhois, armed with rockets, were trying to go after them. I shouted at the Phantoms to break, but my shouts over the radio did no good. At last, Dror hit one of the two Sukhois, and the other one fled. Later on, someone spread the story that I'd called to the Phantoms to break so I could be the one to shoot down the Sukhois. This nasty bit of rubbish became widely known, though of course, it was absolutely untrue.

I kept on pursuing my Sukhoi and when I got within 400 metres and wanted to open fire, number three suddenly pushed in between us and told me that he was taking him. I had no choice but to let him. To my surprise, he fired a missile at him from very close range, and because of the short distance, the missile did not lock onto the target. It passed under the Sukhoi. Number three and four, who'd begun patrolling before us, broke contact and went back to land, as they were running low on fuel. From 250 metres I fired a volley that immediately hit the enemy plane. It blew up, turned over and fell into the Great Bitter Lake. The pilot managed to eject, and for a few minutes he slowly parachuted down as the aerial combat continued around him. The whole time he was drifting down, he wildly waved his arms and legs, to signal to us not to hit him. Eventually, he disappeared from view. After the war I was told that he had drowned in the lake.

I went off in search of other targets and spotted a quartet of Sukhois fleeing west, with a pair of Phantoms chasing after the northern Sukhoi pair. At this stage, we were just two Mirages, since the number three and four in the formation had turned back to base for lack of fuel. I had gone after the southern pair and started closing on them, when the rear Sukhoi suddenly crashed. The second plane, which was further away, vanished to the west. I joined the

Phantoms in time to see Zohar down a Su-7 with a missile and Huldai fire a missile that missed, but the Sukhoi he'd been pursuing failed to get out of its break and hit the ground. We set up in formation again on the eastern side of the canal and returned to base.

Watching films of the shooting in the debriefing afterward, I saw that the two planes I'd shot down that afternoon were Su-20s, a swing-wing variant of the fixed-wing Su-7. In that one day, pilots from Rephidim shot down a total of 15 planes. Four of them were mine. That evening, Yafa Yarkoni, Arik Lavie and some other singers came to the base and we had a big party. Yafa Yarkoni brought a big cake that was really delicious. It was one of the most unforgettable nights at Rephidim after a successful day in combat, for the squadrons, and for me.

1

2

3

4

1. Giora, age 2, stands with his parents, c. 1940, at Kibbutz Negba in the southern part of Israel. Both parents were from Poland. His father had a much-loved Jewish name of Hillel, of a beloved rabbi born c. 110 BCE. His mother's name was Chaya.

2. Giora as an instructor in parachute school in Israel.

3. Now an experienced parachutist, Giora stands by the door before making his jump.

4. Giora free-falling away from a twin-boomed Noratlas transport [out of shot]. In the box at his waist are two important instruments. The white dial on his left is a 'stopper', which shows the time to when he must open his 'chute which the jumper himself still has to do. The altimeter is the black dial on his right.

5. Now with his parachute wings, beret and aiguillette, Giora is a full-fledged jumper.

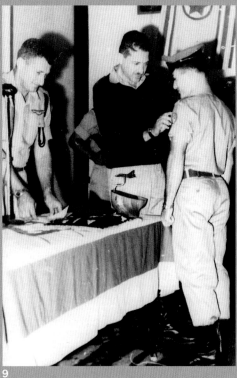

6. With his student Mobutu Sese Seko about to make his first jump. Mobutu was the president of the Republic of Congo, which he renamed Zaire in 1971.

7. Ezer Weizman, one of the founders of the Israel Air Force and eventually the CO of the IAF and then president of Israel, prepares for a flight in his special black Spitfire, still maintained in a memorial flight.

8. Camouflaged Super Mystères of 105 Squadron, 'the Scorpions', make their way to the active runway. Sometimes called the 'French F-100', a reference to the American Super Sabre, of the same period and performance, the Super Mystère was for the first half of the 1960s both an interceptor as well as a ground-attack aircraft, serving well in the Six Day War and also as an advanced supersonic trainer. (IAF photo)

9. Now a newly designated IAF pilot, Giora receives his wings from IAF CO Ezer Weizman on November 19, 1964.

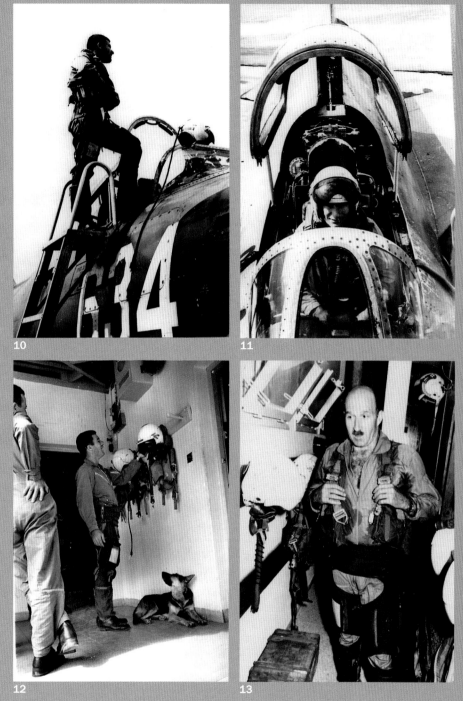

10. Newly winged IAF pilot Giora Epstein climbs into his Super Mystère. Notice his large flight helmet on the bow of the windscreen.

11. Now settled into his cockpit, Lt Epstein prepares to start his Super Mystère.

12. At the squadron, No. 105, Giora is already suited up and raises his helmet off its hangar rod, observed by the squadron mascot.

13. By 1967 and the Six Day War of June, the IAF had generated its share of personalities. Here, the CO of the IAF, Gen Moti Hod returns from a flight. A tough, thoroughly involved leader, he was sometimes known as the 'radiator', as evidenced by the sweat stains on his flight suit.

14

15

16

14. A colourful and capable Mirage ace, Iftach Spector focuses his attention behind his Mirage of 101 Squadron. He flew missions in the Mirage, then the F-4, eventually commanding No. 107 Squadron in 1973 and gaining a total of 12 kills. Reaching BGen rank, Spector is a recognised author and artist with several books and paintings to his credit. (Courtesy of BGen Iftach Spector)

15. One of the IAF's most legendary pilots, whose career was cut short far earlier than would be expected, Lt Col Avi Lanir was the CO of 101 Squadron when he was shot down on October 13, 1973, and imprisoned, dying in captivity after the 1973 war. His remains were returned from Syria in 1974. (IAF photo)

16. Major, later Colonel Oded Marom (10½ kills in Mirages), gestures in the universal manner of all pilots during a squadron gathering in the 101 ready room. Marom is an accomplished author with several books published in Israel. (Courtesy of Oded Marom)

17

18

17. Asher Snir flew Mirages and Phantoms, gaining 13½ kills and attaining brigadier general rank before dying in 1986 of cancer. He has been compared to the WWI French ace Georges Guynemer. (IAF photo)

18. First Lieutenant Giora Romm flew with No. 119 Squadron, 'the Bats', shooting down five MiGs during the Six Day War in June 1967 to become the first native Israeli ace. He had an illustrious career that including an A-4 squadron in 1973 after returning to Israel from captivity as a POW, and further senior commands during which he attained the rank of major general. (Courtesy of Giora Romm)

19. Taking a break before their next mission during the War of Attrition, 1970, 101 Squadron pilots enjoy coffee and donuts. From left to right: Shlomo Levi, Eitan Ben Eliyahu, Giora Epstein, and 101 CO, Oded Marom. While three of these pilots became aces, Ben Eliyahu (with four kills) would make MGen as the IAF CO 1996-2000.

19

20

20. Giora enjoys a joke with other members of 101 Squadron's ready room during the War of Attrition. From left to right [sitting]: Giora Epstein (17 kills), Lair Sela (3 kills), Shlomo Levi (10 kills), Yigal Shohat (POW in Egypt). Standing: Eitan Ben Eliyahu (4 kills), Oded Marom (10½ kills) and Israel Baharav (12 kills).

21. Giora [second from right] talks with squadron pilots. On the far right is IAF CO MGen David Ivry.

21

22. The bleak scene at Rephidim, the former Egyptian base in desolate north-central Sinai where IAF pilots stood alert after the Six Day War. Israeli troops are inspecting the control tower. They have run up the national flag on the tower's roof. (IAF photo)

23. This Egyptian MiG-21C is shown at the opening of the June 1967 Six Day War. It has been riddled with bullets after strafing attacks by the IAF during the initial wave. Its cockpit canopy is open indicating the pilot might have been inside at the moment the IAF attacked. Early model MiG-21s' canopies were hinged tilting forward providing wind-blast protection during the initial phase of an ejection.

24. In a dramatic frame, an Egyptian MiG-21 at the moment of its destruction by Nesher pilot and ace (5½ kills) Gidon Livni on October 18, 1973. (IAF photo)

25. A similar combat photo shows another kill with guns by an Israeli Mirage pilot in October 1973. (IAF photo)

26

27

26. A camouflaged Egyptian MiG-21 sports a typical camouflage paint scheme.

27. Mirage No. 52 takes off past two Super Mystères. Several Israeli aces flew this Mirage to victories, although Giora Epstein did not. The large fuel tanks were an important requirement for the fuel-hungry Mirage. (IAF photo)

28

28. This camouflaged Mirage is from No. 117 Squadron, the 'First Jet Squadron'. It has two kill roundels below its cockpit canopy.

29. A rare, inflight colour view of the top MiG-killer Mirage, No. 159 with 13 kill roundels below the cockpit. Giora scored a kill in No. 159 over an Egyptian Su-7 Fitter on September 11, 1969. Originally an unpainted silver Mirage with the red and white markings of 101 Squadron, it was part of a batch of Mirage IIIs sold to Argentina following the 1982 Falklands War. It was returned for display in the IAF Museum. The blue and red markings on the rudder probably indicate a 'shadow' reserve squadron.

30. Renewing an old acquaintance in 1974, casually dressed Giora stands beside Nesher 561 in which he scored an amazing eight kills (including two Su-7s, two Su-20s and four MiG-21s) in three missions during the 1973 war. Note the fighter carries a total of 12 kills.

29

30

31

32

33

31. Giora relaxes while on alert at 101 Squadron.

32. The relatively little-known story of training US Navy pilots to fly the then-recent agreement to lease IAI Kfirs as aggressors for VF-43 at Naval Air Station Oceana in Virginia Beach, Virginia, begins as shown here with VF-43 CO then-Cdr Jerry Hodge [centre]. Now the reserve CO of 254 Squadron equipped with Kfirs, Giora welcomes Hodge after the American returns from a flight in a Kfir at Hatzor. After flying three hops in a two-seater Kfir, Hodge flew three solo flights in a single-seater Kfir.

33. In 1976, at Ramat David, Epstein, who was then the CO of No. 117 Squadron, got to meet one of his childhood idols, RAF ace Douglas Bader, recently knighted by Queen Elizabeth. The two aces got along famously.

34. As shown, Sir Douglas Bader, the RAF's famous amputee ace (with 20 kills and several probables before he was shot down and captured by the Germans on August 9, 1941) visited Giora Epstein in 1976 and even got re-acquainted with an old friend, a Spitfire, in this case, Ezer Weizman's black Spitfire Mk IX.

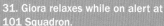
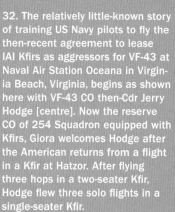
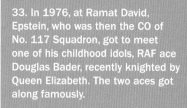

34

35

35. Lt Col Epstein, squadron CO of 254 Squadron at Hatzor in one of the unit's Kfirs.

36. The four American naval aviators from VF-43 at Uvda were [from left to right]: Lt Cary Silver, Lt Cdr John Stufflebeem, Lt Cdr Douglas Schlaefer, and Lt Lew Van Meter.

37. The five IAF instructors were [from left to right]: Maj Yosef Tzuk, Maj Betzalel Ofer, Maj Ilan Hait, Maj Yoram Geva and Lt Col Giora Epstein.

36

37

38. During the official acceptance ceremony back at NAS Oceana in 1985, and now in US Navy markings, one of the former IAF Kfirs is on display. (Peter B. Mersky)

39. A Kfir of VF-43 in flight. (US Navy)

40. Giora was invited to the 1998 'Gathering of Eagles' at Maxwell Air Force Base, Alabama. As an established personality himself, he met other such people like retired fellow ace Gen Chuck Yeager, the man credited to be the first to crack the sound barrier. General Yeager and then-Col Epstein, both turned out in tuxedoes for a formal event, pose for a photo.

41. Giora [left] also met several US astronauts including: Neil Armstrong [second from left] – the first man on the moon, Bill Anders [third from left] who flew Apollo 8 in December 1968, and Jack Lousma [second from right] – Skylab II pilot and commander of Columbia III, the third test flight of the space shuttle. Proudly standing in such distinguished company is Giora's longtime friend and aviation enthusiast Rick Turner [right].

42. Finally, during his eventful visit to the US in 1998, Giora enjoys meeting the Blue Angels beside one of the team's F/A-18 Hornets after watching their home-base air show demonstration.

40

41

42

43. Getting ready to leave his F-16 appropriately emblazoned with his 17 kill markers, Giora returns from his last flight in the IAF on May 20, 1997, his 59th birthday.

44. Right after his last flight, Giora is greeted by Ezer Weizman [centre] while MGen Eitan Ben Eliyahu, IAF CO [left] looks on.

45. On the day of his retirement, May 20, 1997, Giora presents Ezer Weizman with the wings Weizman pinned on then-Lt Epstein many years earlier on November 19, 1964.

43

44

45

העניקת דרגת תא"ל (מיל)
לגיורא אבן אפשטיין

6

18   7:57 PM

7

46. To round off his incredible experience, on September 9, 2018, Sara and Lt Gen Gadi Eizenkot, IDF chief of staff do the honours of removing his colonel epaulets during Giora's post-retirement promotion to brigadier general, with Giora's son Guy [right] looking on.

47. Giora with his wife and children who have been with him through most of this story [from left to right]: Dana, wife Sara, Giora, Guy, and Adi. The occasion is Giora's last flight as an El Al pilot on his 65th birthday, May 20, 2003.

BGen Giora Epstein, himself.

18 ONE VERSUS TEN

October 20, 1973. My second day on interceptor standby at Rephidim. Since the early morning, I'd been sent up a few times, but without seeing or engaging any enemy planes. Other formations had been sent up and came back in after notching kills in dogfights. I was feeling frustrated. At the operational briefing in the morning I'd talked about the importance of the mission and the need to strike enemy aircraft as soon as we engage with them, but how can I succeed in this mission if I don't even make contact? The three other pilots with me in the formation were Eitan Adres, a young pilot from the Scorpion Squadron, who was my number two, and the second pair, composed of veteran pilots Geva and Kal.

The hours passed and we remained on standby, growing more frustrated by the hour. From my experience at the canal the past two days, I figured if an Egyptian attack came, it would happen in the afternoon, just as it did on the previous days.

And indeed, around 16:30, Yigal Ziv, the controller, sent us into the air, but there was still no certainty of an engagement.

In such cases, there was always the fear that we'd end up just doing a patrol until planes come from the north to do the job. When we were in the air, the controller at last dispatched us to an engagement, having received information about Egyptian planes taking off in preparation to strike our ground forces near the canal. I was flying Nesher 61, which had become my 'lucky' aircraft, and leading the formation. We took off in quartet formation heading for the Great Bitter Lake, but so far we hadn't seen anything.

The controller instructed us to climb to 20,000 feet and continue heading west. After a few seconds of climbing to a higher altitude I spotted a pair of MiGs coming from south to north, about 10 miles from us. We jettisoned our drop tanks and turned right toward them. I flew after them and launched a missile at the rear plane. The missile hit the target and the plane exploded. I kept chasing the number one MiG for several minutes as he manoeuvred wildly, and then I saw one of the most amazing sights I'd ever encountered in this war. It was as if a field of mushrooms was sprouting before my eyes.

The horizon to our north-west had suddenly filled with MiGs. There were 10 pairs and they were all coming toward us. Apparently, the first two MiGs we'd chased were the bait meant to lure us into an ambush, 20 versus 4. Our good fortune was that we were at a higher altitude, and, as long as they were climbing toward us, they didn't have sufficient energy to exploit their numerical advantage. By the time they reached contact range they were a lot slower than us.

My number two, Eitan Adres, a young pilot with no kills yet, was able to shake off two MiGs that tried to gain the advantage over him. He got right on the tail of one and hit it with a missile. The missile he fired passed under his plane's nose, causing the compressor to stall. I was in the thick of the battle. One eye checking what's going on with the MiGs in front of me and behind me, and the other eye on Adres. I saw right away he was in trouble. He was flying too low, at just 300 feet, continuing to lose altitude, and I feared he would become an easy target for the Egyptian MiGs.

Over the radio, I calmed him down and guided him through what he needed to do: move the throttle to neutral and let some clean air flow into the engine. Adres managed to escape the dangerous situation. His engine came back to life and the aircraft stabilised. I told him to return to base. After such a situation, with an engine stall and restart, orders were to return to base. Still keeping an eye on my number two, I went after the second MiG. Geva passed by me, sitting just 200 metres behind another MiG.

"Why aren't you shooting him down?" I asked.

Geva realised that he was too close to the MiG. He increased his distance a little, fired a missile and the MiG fell. Kal, number four in the formation, was also chasing a MiG. He fired a missile and hit it, but he couldn't see if the MiG crashed. Since he was flying a two-seater Mirage with a smaller fuel capacity, he said he was getting low on fuel and turned east, back to Rephidim. Geva also had too little fuel by now and was forced to turn back.

I was left alone. One Nesher versus 10 MiGs.

What to do in such a situation? Give up? Head back to Rephidim?

Not me! I would keep fighting.

I chased after their number one. He must have been the senior pilot in this pack of wolves. His MiG was leading the whole formation. The chase went on for three or four minutes, and I was unable to get into a position where I could shoot him down. He kept doing unusual manoeuvres to elude me. This guy was either crazy, or a superb pilot. He descended and so did I. He kept moving around quickly to prevent me from being able to fire at his tail.

We kept descending at high speed, and the whole time I was unable to get my nose into position where I could fire at him. This was a classic dogfight. The whole time I was also checking to make sure there was no plane behind me. There were a lot of MiGs in the sky but I ignored them. If someone was going to shoot me down he had to be behind me, and only one plane can be behind me, no matter what. The number of MiGs that was currently in the air was irrelevant to the dogfight. As long as they were not behind me, they were no danger to me.

I was focused entirely on the MiG in front of me. The others didn't interest me. For now. I had a target and I was going to down it.

At one point in the dogfight we descended to 3,000 feet and the Egyptian MiG went into a 'Split-S' – an aerobatic manoeuvre that requires great skill, and is practised by every air force pilot: loop, rollover, straightening out the plane, flying upside down and pulling down into the second half of the loop. Each kind of plane has an altitude limitation for executing the manoeuvre, and I believe that for the MiG-21 it's 6,000 feet. The Egyptian pilot entered the Split-S at 3,000 feet, and it was hard for me to believe he'd be able to come out of the manoeuvre at that altitude. It was more likely that the manoeuvre would culminate with the plane crashing on the ground.

Because the altitude was too low, I didn't enter behind him. I executed a nose-down horizontal turn to pick up speed and follow him. During the dive he disappeared from my view in a cloud of dust and I was sure he was about to hit the ground. To my surprise, he managed to complete the Split-S, and I suddenly saw him emerge from the dust cloud. Afterward, I realised that since the altitude control of the MiG-21 is located on the tail, it gives it a certain advantage. This is what enabled him to get out of a situation that I really thought was lost.

As soon as I noticed him coming out of the dust at very low speed, I entered right behind him. I fired and he blew up mid-air.

Throughout my pursuit of the Egyptian MiG, which lasted three or four minutes, I was utterly focused on the target in front of me, but also thinking about those who might appear behind me. I shot him down, but there were still a large number of MiGs in the air. I still had work to do. I entered a turn and picked up speed. Now, I was at full burner. I soon spotted five more MiG pairs. This was what's left. We downed some of them, others fled or ran low on fuel. I'm still flying alone against them. The entire battle took place between zero altitude and 20,000 feet, within a diameter of five to ten miles.

I gathered speed and the MiG pilots apparently noticed that I was alone.

Our big advantage over them was that they followed the Russian doctrine of flying – close pairs that don't separate in combat. Our doctrine is different.

It's a hybrid of British education, American influence, and Sabra on-the-spot improvements. Our basic formation in aerial combat is composed of four aircraft. A single plane would never go up on patrol or attack, except at night. If aerial combat does develop, our aim is to be in a quartet that can immediately split into two pairs. And not necessarily the pairs that were set in the pre-flight briefing. With us, all of the planes take part in the battle. With the Egyptians, the number two's job is always to guard his leader. He does not take an active part in the battle. Except as a target for us, that is. Right now I was facing five pairs, but I thought of them as just five planes. As I said before, as long as they're not at my six o'clock position, they're not a threat. I can keep going even against five pairs as long as I have fuel, ammunition, and missiles.

The whole battle was waged west of the canal. We crossed the canal south of Ismailia and continued west to the Suez-Cairo highway. The air force had a nickname for this area – 'Texas'. This is where you draw your weapons. Whoever draws first, wins. It's a flat region where it's easy to fly. This is where most of the big dogfights in the War of Attrition and Yom Kippur War took place. There were another 10 MiGs around and I was in defensive mode, but constantly ready to strike if the chance arose.

I gathered speed as I turned, continually looking back to watch for planes behind me. They kept coming up behind me to get me in their sights, one pair after another. One went out and another came in. As soon as I saw they were within missile range, I tightened the turn so as not to allow them a firing angle and broke sharply when they were in gun range so they couldn't hit me. This is a familiar manoeuvre for our fighter pilots, one that we practise a lot. Let the enemy pass you, a classic manoeuvre using a horizontal turn. Whenever someone was in close range and I broke, the enemy plane continued forward at high speed. Then, I could lower my speed either by using the air brakes or by reducing engine power. If the enemy didn't relent, I would get into a scissors position – the two planes flying slowly alongside each other, trying to outmanoeuvre each other and get behind the enemy aircraft.

My battle – one versus ten – continued. I gathered speed and during a left turn, I saw a pair of MiGs closing on me from behind and firing like crazy from a range of about 500 metres at nearly a 90-degree angle. I broke sharply and they zoomed right by me, like a pair of missiles. I turned behind them right away to shoot them down, and saw flashes ahead of me. A pair of MiGs had fired missiles at me from about 400 metres. Instinctively, I ducked in my seat. There was no way I could react with a flight manoeuvre. The missiles passed over me, followed by the two Egyptian fighters. I turned after them, and closed in on the rear MiG, but then I saw another plane in the formation approaching me from the right. I went after him, and blew him up with my cannon. I immediately turned back and again saw another pair of MiGs closing on me from either side. I broke hard left then right, and they zoomed ahead. I got in behind them and fired my second missile at the rear plane. For some unknown reason, the missile just fell like a drop tank, essentially with no direction whatsoever.

I saw another pair starting to come in behind me. I broke and they climbed higher. I looked back and saw there was no one behind me. I gained speed and turned toward them. As I was climbing to them, I saw them turn over and lower their noses. I turned after the rear MiG while it was on its back. At the height of the climb, I hit it with a quick burst of cannon in the cockpit. The MiG's nose slowly lowered, and then it plunged straight into the ground.

This was the last pair of Egyptian MiGs. The number one of the last pair was far away from me, I saw him deep in Egyptian territory. I debated whether to keep on pursuing him. That could be my fifth kill in the same battle, my longest day of combat in the war. I still had 800 litres of fuel and about 30 shells in each cannon. I broke again and didn't see another plane in the air. Suddenly the skies were totally clear. No MiGs, no plumes of smoke from aircraft that were hit and caught fire, no parachutes. Nothing at all. I decided that four planes in one day was enough. I turned east and flew at low altitude. I was all alone in the sky. On the way back, I asked the controller if he had any more targets for me. He replied he had none.

The entire battle, from the moment we spotted the two MiGs that were sent as bait to lure us into a trap, had lasted nine minutes. I landed at Rephidim and brought the Nesher to the hangar. When I tried to stand up, I felt like my legs were glued to the floor. I was drained. The G-indicator on the cockpit showed the maximum. I'd experienced more than 10 positive Gs and 5 negative Gs. In Mirage training, positive G is 6.5 and the maximum negative G permissible is 2. Both of these forces, positive G and negative G, act on the pilot's entire body, from head to toe and vice-versa. The effect of positive G starts at the pilot's head and is usually created by emerging from a sharp dive and pulling quickly upward, while negative G moves from the feet to the head, and happens when entering a dive. Both have a significant physical impact on the pilot. With positive G, blood flows toward the feet, and if the load becomes too great, the pilot can become dazed and ill and lose consciousness. Negative G affects vision, to the point where a pilot may find that everything around him looks red. I had almost broken the dials of the G-indicators with the manoeuvres I'd gone through in this battle.

The mechanics who came to the plane could see how exhausted I was. The signs were clear. My face was sweaty and my legs were shaking and unstable. When they climbed the ladder to the cockpit, I handed them my helmet and unstrapped myself from the seat.

"I shot down four planes," I told them, but still I felt like I couldn't get up. They pulled the straps and helped me get out of the seat. I slowly descended the ladder, went to get a cold drink and then sat down to write down everything that had happened from the moment we took off. This would be used for the afternoon debriefings about the battles.

I heard from the other pilots who were with me about the results of their battles. It was an especially successful day for the standby teams at Rephidim and for the formations that came from the north. My battle, in which I was left as the lone plane facing 10 MiGs, was considered one of the greatest battles in the air force's history and not just in Israel. In the midst of all the excitement, there was a telephone call from headquarters. It was Giora Furman.

"Okay, that's enough, come back to headquarters now."

"I'll return as soon as my replacement arrives."

After the replacement arrived, I flew to Hatzor, and from there to air force headquarters at the Kirya in Tel Aviv. When he saw me, air force commander Benny Peled embraced me and gave me a big kiss on the cheek.

"You did very well. You boosted the air force's performance," he told me. Overall, the mood at headquarters was very different now from what it had been in the first days of the war. The days of heavy losses. The days when we learned of formations that did not all return together. About friends who were killed or taken prisoner. It was a different feeling then, on the ground and in the air.

For the next two days, I stayed at headquarters in the Kirya. The air force continued to enjoy clear skies without the threat of missiles, and the kills continued on the southern front. I was having mixed feelings. On the one hand, I'd already shot down nine aircraft in this war, but I still felt that I hadn't experienced combat as part of a squadron. I hadn't fought as part of the First Fighter Squadron to which I was so attached. I had managed to get out of headquarters in Tel Aviv on occasion, I'd flown and earned kills, but it wasn't the same as being part of a combat squadron in war. That was something I'd yet to fully experience.

The battles in the south resumed and I was feeling more frustrated than ever stuck at headquarters. This was the last place I wanted to be right now. I was sending out orders to the combat squadrons, and my heart was with the guys who were going on those missions. The Mirage and Phantom squadrons earned more kills in the skies over the canal, especially in the southern sector, where the IDF was in a race against time to tighten the blockade on the Third Army. The Egyptians, in a desperate attempt to halt the ground forces that were expanding the bridgehead to the west of the canal, were putting planes in the air, and our air force was excelling against them. Giora Furman and Avihu Ben-Nun heard from me on the evening of October 22, when I repeated my threat that if they didn't release me immediately to my squadron, I would be deserting.

The next morning, after insisting yet again, I was finally released. I went right to the squadron and up on patrol, where I waited for the controller's voice to come on the radio and send me to an engagement. I scanned the skies, hopeful that the enemy would appear, but none did. It was a day of 'ironing' – patrolling – without results. Other pilots had more luck. The guys at Rephidim kept the tradition going and shot down more enemy planes.

19 THE FINAL BATTLE

On October 24 at 17:00, I was on standby with the squadron. Just ahead of the scheduled take-off for our patrol, another pair was assigned to go up with us. My number two was Dan Sever, and when we were in the air, Avraham Salmon and Michael Tzuk were teamed up as well. They were both from the First Fighter Squadron. I was in a two-seater Mirage IIIB. This aircraft could perform just the same as the single-seater Mirage, but it carried 350 litres less fuel than the single-seat Mirage I was used to flying. A 'plain' Mirage without the drop tanks had 2,550 litres of fuel. When you added the two large drop tanks on the wings, you got another 1,300 litres in each one. You could also have a belly tank that held 880 litres, plus two supersonic wing tanks with 550 litres each.

Following the controller's instructions, we flew toward the canal to relieve a quartet from the No. 144 Phoenix Squadron that had been patrolling the area. We were the ones who were supposed to 'put out the sun'. When we got near the canal, we were transferred to the Shomrei Ha'arava radio channel and the controller told them to go home. As they were turning east toward home to land at the Etzion airfield by Eilat, and we were taking their place on patrol, I heard the controller shouting to them on the radio: "Hurry to an engagement, heading 220, south-west." The quartet from the squadron released their drop tanks as they headed toward the engagement, to a dogfight.

"And what about us?" I asked the controller.

"Clear the channel and keep patrolling," he replied.

"How about *you* just patrol…" I retorted.

I switched to another radio channel and turned right away toward the area where I thought the dogfight would develop. I told the controller we were heading to the dogfight and not leaving the channel. I again requested coordinates but got no response. We sped up, jettisoned the wing tanks and raced south-west, toward Jebel Obeid, west of the city of Suez. On the way there we saw a pair heading east and climbing. For a second I thought they were MiGs, but when we got a little closer I saw they were a pair from the Phoenix Squadron quartet, the leader and his number two, in afterburner. They had

1,000 litres left in their tanks, and with the burners on they were using 250 litres a minute. By the time they got to the dogfight, they'd be out of fuel and have to turn back. The two other pilots, Menachem Eliyahu and Shlomo Erez, hadn't lit their burners and still had enough fuel to remain in the fight. Each of them downed a plane and then went back to land. We headed further west and from afar we saw two explosions in the air, followed by three big explosions on the ground. Deployed parachutes were visible in the air as well. That's where the fight was.

When we got closer we saw a large number of MiGs in the thick of a dogfight against several Mirages from Rephidim. Despite the call over the radio to jettison drop tanks, I didn't jettison the belly tank. Since I was in a two-seater Mirage, with less fuel in the main body of the plane, I also needed to preserve the fuel I had there. We entered the fight. The sight before us was incredible. This was the largest dogfight over the canal during the Yom Kippur War. A spectacular battle unrivalled by any other in the war. Ten Mirages – a quartet from Rephidim, a pair from the Phoenix Squadron, and my quartet from the First Fighter Squadron at Hatzor – versus 24 MiG-21s.

The Egyptians also apparently felt the war was nearing its end, and had put a lot of aircraft in the air in the hope of boosting morale. They were quite frustrated by their failure to down our planes and were resorting to a familiar tactic. Air force intelligence spotted a MiG-21 squadron west of the canal preparing an ambush for the Phantoms that were on an attack mission over the highway to Cairo. The Phantoms were ordered to break contact and turn east, and the Egyptian hunters became the hunted.

I was in combat once again. We may have been outnumbered, but even when I was fighting alone, one against ten, this didn't bother me. Now the ratio was a bit better than that. I spotted a pair and sped right over to it. I fired a missile that exploded but failed to ignite the MiG that kept on flying, trailing a cloud of smoke and fuel behind it. I regretted the time I now had to waste on a stricken MiG. I cut it off to get within cannon range.

When I was 500 metres from it, the Egyptian pilot realised there was no point and decided to eject. I told him thank you over the radio, and instantly turned my attention to another MiG. I closed on him with a turn and, after a few manoeuvres, I got into a good position for firing while diving. I fired a missile that hit him. The missile passed by the nose of my Mirage, causing me to stall. I immediately brought the control stick to neutral and radioed it in.

I heard Menachem Eliyahu from the Phoenix Squadron tell me he saw me on the right. I gave him the go-ahead to enter the fight and immediately climbed toward a MiG that was passing from left to right. I saw a Mirage fire at it and then leave the MiG intact and continue on. I wondered why he hadn't kept after it, and I soon discovered the answer: There was no pilot in the plane. When I got close enough to the formation, I saw that the MiG was completely intact, flying smoothly without smoke or fire, but its cockpit was empty. It might have been my MiG-21, the one whose pilot had ejected at high altitude not long before. I reported it and kept on. I found another MiG and, after some sharp manoeuvres up and down, I closed on him and hit him with cannon fire. This was the third MiG I'd downed that evening. Not far away, Israel Baharav, the leader of the quartet that took off from Rephidim, was waging a dogfight against seven MiGs. He shot down two of them.

All of a sudden it was quiet. No more planes. No nothing. There were no more targets. We'd downed 14 or 15 of the 24 Egyptian MiGs. All the rest had fled. For the Egyptians, the ambush had succeeded in drawing us in, but the results were not much to their liking. I still had plenty of fuel left. My decision not to jettison the belly tank had proved smart. I asked the controller for more targets, but he said he had no new targets for me at the moment. I started heading home to Hatzor, bringing Sever with me into the formation, when I heard Salmon report that he was low on fuel and going to land at Rephidim. Tzuk was behind us, coming from the Kutmiya area, and also on his way home.

Amos Lapidot, the wing commander, called me on the radio: "What are the results?"

"We have seven requests [to confirm the downing of enemy planes]."

Lapidot told me that the quartet from Rephidim also had seven requests.

We landed at Hatzor and heard that the ceasefire went into effect that evening at 18:00, shortly after my final battle ended.

To my dismay, only 11 kills out of the 16 we requested were confirmed. As for the other five MiGs – they said there was no unequivocal proof that they were downed. I think intelligence was mistaken in saying that only 20 planes took part in the battle. The correct number should have been 24.

I flew 28 missions in the war. The three kills credited to me on the last day of fighting brought my total number of kills in the war to 11 planes and 1 helicopter – making me the pilot with the most kills in the war. In all, I now had 17 kills to my name. The all-time ace in the Israel Air Force.

20 LESSONS IN THE AIR

The war had ended. Personally, I might have felt pleased with the number of enemy planes I shot down, but at the same time, I couldn't ignore the failures and mistakes committed by the air force, and there had been more than a few. At a debriefing for all the interceptor pilots, I made my criticism known. I didn't give anyone a break – not the air force command, the general staff, or the pilots who could have achieved much better results in the war.

Most of the interceptor pilots hadn't fully grasped that this was a real war, a war to save our home, a war to save the State of Israel. A genuine war of survival. Some seemed to think of it as a direct continuation of the War of Attrition, not really understanding that it was the biggest and most brutal war the country had withstood since the War of Independence in 1948.

The war should have been managed differently. The air force could have been given greater prominence in the war than it was. When the commanders of the tank brigades that fought on the canal line and in Sinai and in the Golan Heights, or the commanders of the surrounded strongholds, asked where the air force was in the war, they had good reason to do so. We needed to think about this and to come up with an answer. Too many errors in planning preceded the war and occurred during the conduct of the war itself. The air force command, as well as the general staff, failed to appreciate the big change that had taken place in the Arab armies since their crushing defeat in the Six Day War. Some people were even comparing their air strike on Saturday afternoon to our Operation *Moked* that opened the Six Day War.

Benny Peled, the air force commander during the war, was one of the smartest people I'd ever met, but in the first two days of the war, serious mistakes were made because he hadn't been in the air force during its most difficult period in the War of Attrition. From 1969-1971, he was essentially out of the force. He was studying engineering at the Technion and was on loan to Israel Aircraft Industries. He lacked direct experience with what the air force had to contend with during the War of Attrition, and in dealing with the Egyptian SAMs, which changed the rules of the game to a great extent. He wasn't sufficiently involved in the discussions of what lessons the air force should draw from the War of Attrition and how it should prepare for the next war.

Aside from the mistakes, especially in the first days of the conflict when he was put under tremendous pressure from the general staff, Peled also made some courageous decisions that made the pilots recognise we were in a very serious war. One of these was the readiness to absorb losses on aid missions to the ground forces, particularly to the armoured forces in the Golan Heights, before the missile batteries there were wiped out. It was Benny Peled who set the policy that if necessary, you keep going no matter what. Even if it means taking heavy losses, and there were a number of such occasions.

The force had prepared for a pre-emptive strike in the morning hours, but had to cancel it on orders from the politicians. Nearly the entire fleet of planes, including the Phantoms, had been put in the air, armed for this type of combat, but did not assist the ground forces in the critical hours when the enemy went on the attack.

According to all the air force's calculations, the four Mirage and Nesher squadrons – more than 70 planes in all – should have been sufficient to defend the country's skies and to await attacks by the enemy air forces. However, after the surprise attack by the Egyptian and Syrian planes, a strike that did not extend beyond the combat sectors or threaten population centres or air force bases, the order was given to dispatch the entire air force. IAF planes patrolled the country's skies over every base and every city, rather than making a focused strike on the enemy forces in the war's early hours. The air force lost two critical hours in which it could have attacked the forces that were preparing to cross the canal in the south, and the Syrian armoured columns that had begun advancing toward the anti-tank trench in the Golan Heights. If that would have been done, perhaps the outcome of the first two days of combat would have been different. In those two critical hours, the Egyptians and Syrians were able to operate in clear skies, with none of our planes in the air, similar to the situation of our ground forces in the Six Day War.

The Egyptians were a more dangerous enemy than the Syrians, but air force headquarters, under pressure from the government, especially Defence Minister Moshe Dayan and the general staff, did not put into effect the plans that the force had prepared for in the event of war. Every fighter pilot in the air force knew the plan for Operation Tagar 4, for an air strike on the Canal Zone, inside-out and had practised it countless times. As soon as Dayan started talking about the destruction of the Third Temple[16], the air force received Dayan's order – via chief of staff David 'Dado' Elazar – to shift the weight of its activity to the northern front. Operation Tagar 4 was halted and the air force embarked on Operation Model 5 – striking the Syrian SAM batteries to help the armoured forces that were in dire trouble in the Golan Heights.

Contrary to its entire combat doctrine, the air force embarked on Operation Model 5 without having the latest intelligence information, without planes being sent up first to do aerial photography of the strike zones. No. 201 Squadron set out to strike on the Golan Heights without up-to-date aerial photos and in very poor visibility. A preliminary photography sortie would have revealed the movements of the mobile SA-6 batteries, which had shifted location. Most of the planes that were shot down during that offensive in Syria were hit by anti-aircraft fire on their way to attack bases that no longer housed any missile batteries.

As a prerequisite for launching Operation Model 5, the IAF commander should have insisted on obtaining prior intelligence and updated aerial photos taken just before the strike, showing the locations of all the missile batteries. The pilots who took part in the operation were only given flight paths and out-of-date aerial photos when they were already in position for take-off.

The air force had the plans for Operation Tagar 4 in the south ready. All that was needed was for the plans to be executed properly, without improvisation. In stage one, the Skyhawk squadrons were supposed to neutralise the anti-aircraft batteries in the planned area of attack – and this was carried out successfully. In stage two, the Phantom squadrons were supposed to attack the missile batteries' radar centres, and then in the next stage, the missiles themselves. This was to be followed by clean-up work – going back to attack targets that weren't hit or destroyed the first time around. Once these stages were complete, the air force could focus on aiding the ground forces in the south.

In effect, the Skyhawk squadrons that were dispatched first accomplished their mission, but the second wave, the Phantom squadrons that should have attacked the missile batteries, never took off. Why weren't they allowed to do at least one round of air strikes in the Canal Zone? Benny Peled, the air force commander, should not have given in to Dayan and the chief of staff. He was the air force commander, the professional who best understood the situation from the air. It was his duty to insist on completing at least one round

---

[16] Solomon built the First Temple in 950 B.C.E. The Babylonians destroyed it in 586 B.C.E. The Second Temple was built around 517 B.C.E. and was destroyed by the Romans in 70 A.D. The State of Israel, founded in 1948, was often considered the Third Temple. On October 7, 1973, the war was going badly for Israel. A distraught Moshe Dayan, Defence Minister, muttered that the Third Temple (Israel) was in danger. His request to demonstrate Israel's nuclear capability was immediately denied by Golda Meir, the PM.

of Operation Tagar 4 before redirecting the air force to the Syrian skies, for a move that turned out to be mostly an improvisation in conditions of total panic.

The air force commander's big mistake was caving to the pressure from Dado, the chief of staff, and the general staff. The general staff did not function well. Its orders to the air force were chaotic, so we were repeatedly forced to alter the operational orders that were relayed to the squadrons. All of the above refers to the first three days of the war. Later, once the initial shock wore off, Dado pulled it together and took control of the campaign in such a way that I consider him the true hero and victor of the Yom Kippur War.

In the early stages of the war, Giora Furman, head of the operations department, did argue with Benny Peled. On one of the first days of the war, after Peled returned from a meeting with the general staff and ordered us to change the operational orders that we'd prepared, Furman tried to convince him that it was a mistake.

"Why all this run-around?" he asked angrily.

Furman's criticism, and that of others – I presume that Avihu Ben-Nun, head of the offensive department, also saw this and tried to persuade Benny Peled to change his mind – created tension between Benny Peled and Giora Furman. During the final third of the war, Benny dismissed Furman from command of the operations department.

At the summation debriefing for the interceptor squadrons in the war, I argued that most of the pilots hadn't really grasped what this difficult war was all about. We in the air force, and the rest of the country, too. There were pilots who shot down one plane and returned to base satisfied. It hadn't really sunk in that this was a war, not just a day of combat. As soon as you shoot down the first plane in a dogfight, you should be searching for more engagements. You have to search out the enemy in the air in order to bring him down. That is what I did. That is what I would expect from every other pilot in the force. In the big battle, in which there were another three pilots with me, each of us downed one plane in the beginning. After that, they all returned to base. I was left alone, fighting against 10 MiGs, and I downed three of them. If they'd have stayed with me, we could have shot them all down. Eighty per cent of pilots cease fighting when they hear the controller say, "Cease combat". I had an instance like that, too. The controller instructed me to cease combat, just when I saw four MiGs in the air. I asked for permission to continue. Without waiting for an answer, I shot down two of the four MiGs.

Not all pilots showed the same determination. I told the interceptor pilots that if the air force had fought the way it should have, we would have downed twice as many enemy aircraft. I didn't hide my view that some of them had kept on as if it were still the War of Attrition. It was a sport. A playing field where we'd developed combat methods like splitting the pair in a fight. There was an express order from the air force commander, Motti Hod, at the time, that no matter what, you don't let yourself fall in a dogfight. Anyone who felt he could be getting into a risky situation, or who couldn't achieve a quick result, should break contact. This was correct for the War of Attrition. It was not correct for a war for the country's survival.

At the air force-wide debriefing, I didn't pull any punches. I said just what I felt. It was the Skyhawk and Phantom pilots who bore the brunt of the burden and the danger, who performed the toughest missions, and suffered the heaviest losses. Along with the ground forces – the armoured forces, the paratroops and the infantry – and other units who bore the burden of halting the enemy in the difficult conditions in which the campaign began. In the air-to-air area, I said, we were not in a bad position, and in many cases, the pilots did not have the right attitude. They should have gone out there with a knife clenched in their teeth. That wasn't always the case.

The criticism was harsh, but genuine. Yes, the war ended with a big victory by the air force and the IDF. But these things still had to be said. Even if they were hard for people to hear.

21 BACK TO THE ROUTINE

In the post-war debriefings, we discussed and analysed my dogfights and other pilots' dogfights. I'm the air force record holder for kills, with 17, and evidently also the world record holder in downing fighter jets in combat. Next on the list is Avraham Salmon, with 14½ kills. Amir Nachumi with 14 then Asher Snir with 13½, and Israel Baharav and Iftach Spector with 12 kills each. A few months after the war, I learned that Benny Peled, the air force commander, had recommended me for a commendation and the committee had decided to award me the blue-ribbon Medal of Distinguished Service. As a rule, the IAF did not give many recommendations for medals and commendations. Sara was very excited to hear of the decision. I, much less so. Pilots who received medals were not publicly identified by name, and the medal would be presented by chief of staff Motta Gur, who succeeded David 'Dado' Elazar, after the latter resigned his position in wake of the Agranat Commission's findings.

After the war, I remained at air force headquarters as head of the defence division. We went on living at the Hatzor air base, and in June 1974, our son Guy (a 'war baby') was born, joining his two older sisters, Adi, born in 1968, and Dana, born in May 1970. That same month, the whole country held its breath when a Red Cross plane landed at Ben Gurion Airport and brought back IDF POWs from Syria. Among them were 25 pilots who'd been captured during the war. Israel had only received the list of prisoners from Damascus a short time before. As usual, the Syrians had saved their bargaining chips in the negotiations over the separation of forces in the north until the last minute and had refused to provide the names of the prisoners they held. We kept waiting to see if, somehow, Avi Lanir, commander of the First Fighter Squadron, would get off the plane. Maybe there was a mistake on the list and we'd be happily surprised.

It didn't happen. The plane landed. Some of the pilots walked down the stairs of the plane, others were brought down on stretchers. Lieutenant Colonel Avi Lanir was not among them. He was one of the 53 pilots who were killed in the Yom Kippur War. The most senior pilot ever to fall into enemy captivity.

I'm not known as an emotional guy. I keep my cool at tough moments, and I'd experienced plenty of those in the Six Day War, the War of Attrition, the Yom Kippur War, and during aerial mishaps. Tough moments where I've lost close friends, pilots who came up with me in the pilot training course, or flew with me in different squadrons. Avi Lanir's death was especially hard for me to take.

Division head at air force headquarters is usually a position for a lieutenant colonel. I was serving as head of the defence division as a major, having only recently been promoted to that rank. The air force defence division is the biggest of its type in the IDF, and deals with every type of defence: ground defence, electronic warfare, firefighting, missile interception, nuclear, biological and chemical weapons. This is a job that only pilots can deal with, but it's hard to compare it to flying and to aerial combat, and I sometimes found myself flying Parker pens over the desk.

After the Yom Kippur War, Highway 4 was opened. Up to then, the drive to Tel Aviv went via Yavne.

I left Hatzor very early every morning, and when I arrived, I had breakfast in the officers' mess. As a member of the air force team, I was entitled to receive a box of 28 chocolate bars each month, an old British tradition that the air force happily adopted, claiming that pilots needed extra energy. My family back at the kibbutz enjoyed the fine chocolate most of all. Once a week I came back to life. On Fridays, I was in the First Fighter Squadron. This was the day that the squadron practised aerial combat. I also occasionally got to do photography sorties in the Mirage.

I introduced some changes to the division, in coordination with Avihu Ben-Nun, head of the offensive division, and Amos Amir, head of the operations division. I issued an order that no one from my division went to meetings after 16:30. I transferred the intercept department to the offensive division, and it became a combat division. As part of the lessons of the Yom Kippur War, the air force grew, and most of the new investment was in the attack squadrons – the Phantoms and Skyhawks. The culture of pre-flight and post-flight briefings continued, even as the force underwent structural changes. One of the main lessons drawn from the war experience was that the air force would no longer issue operational orders in high-pressure situations. There could be no repeat of the Operation Model 5 mistake – the air strike on October 9, 1973 on Syrian general staff headquarters, in which many civilians and several diplomats were killed. That to this day is considered a major failure for the air force.

The analyses of the strikes on the missile batteries in the war reinforced the need for developing electronic warfare to scramble the radar of the missile batteries. As someone who'd accumulated a lot of experience in photography flights at altitudes beyond the missiles' intercept range, I was well aware of the importance of the electronic warfare that later enabled us to develop methods for evading surface-to-air missiles at lower altitudes. Initially, the scrambling devices were installed on helicopters and cargo planes, and later in the Phantoms as well. As head of the defence division, I attached great importance to this. We had two officers in our department who specialised in electronic warfare and had studied electronic engineering at the Technion. I was able to convince one of them to take time out from his studies to establish an electronic warfare division in the air force. The decision proved itself and the whole area of electronic warfare and scrambling the SAM radar systems was given a serious upgrade, with good results.

After the war, the air force attracted great interest. Military analysts, strategists and experts in the field of aerial combat openly marvelled at all that the force had accomplished, including the downing of 350 enemy planes. In professional aviation journals the world over, articles were written about my particular achievement – downing 17 enemy aircraft in dogfights. Years after the war, the History Channel produced a series of films on classic dogfights by aces from different air forces around the world. One of these films depicted my dogfight against an Egyptian MiG-21 pilot on October 20, 1973. The producer of the film described me as the world record holder in the downing of fighter jets in aerial combat.

After the war we received requests to host delegations from other air forces that wished to learn from us and our experience in the war. Each of these delegations, especially the ones from the United States, the country that had aided us so much in the war, were gladly welcomed and assigned a squadron commander or other senior officer as a guide. One of the most intriguing delegations that I got to host after the war was made up of American media people who were visiting a number of Middle East countries, including Egypt, Jordan, Syria and Lebanon. I became friendly with two of them: Dan McKinnon, owner of a small television station in San Diego, and Randy Cunningham, a big hulking guy known as 'Duke' who'd been a TOPGUN instructor and commander of VF-126, the Aggressor Squadron at NAS Miramar, near San Diego. Duke was the US Navy's only pilot ace in the Vietnam War – as a Phantom pilot based on the aircraft carrier USS *Constellation* (CV 64), he shot down five enemy planes.

Avihu Ben-Nun had asked me to serve as their host, and Duke and I naturally had a special kinship. He told me all about his experiences as a pilot in the US Navy. In one of our conversations, he asked me how many planes I'd shot down. "I have a few kills," I replied.

As part of their visit, I took them on a tour of the Golan Heights. Lying near the road where we stopped was some debris from a Syrian MiG-17. The two ignored the signs warning of minefields and ran to grab some pieces to take home as souvenirs.

At the end of the visit, I took them to the airport. Duke asked me again, "Tell me the truth, how many kills do you have?"

"Seventeen," I said. They were both stunned. It looked like all the air went out of them at once.

A year later, they both came back to Israel for another visit, this time as private citizens. By then I was commander of No. 117 Squadron at Ramat David and I took Duke up with me in a two-seater Mirage for a drill of a dogfight against a Phantom. Years later, on one of my visits to the United States, Duke, who was still an active pilot and instructor in the famous TOP-GUN Fighter Weapons School, which specialised in training US Navy pilots, introduced me to the other pilots as Israel's biggest ace and boasted to them that on his visit to Israel he had flown in a Mirage and 'ripped' the Israeli pilots in a dogfight…

My friendship with Duke grew stronger over the years. At one point, he decided to run for Congress as a Republican from San Diego. Since running an election campaign requires a lot of money – the estimate at the time was two million dollars – Duke organised fundraising events and asked me to come to one. As I was still an active pilot then, I consulted with the air force commander, Avihu Ben-Nun, about the invitation. Ben-Nun advised me that it was better that I pass as long as I was still flying with the air force.

Two years later, when Duke ran for Congress a second time, I was no longer an active pilot, and I agreed to make an appearance. I gave a speech before several hundred invited guests, many of them wealthy Jews who'd paid $5,000 each to attend the event, and I explained how important it was for there to be pro-Israel representatives, like Duke, in Congress. The evening was successful, and Duke went on to be re-elected. After the event, Duke also took me on a visit to TOPGUN and I got to meet with the pilots there. The meeting was planned to last just 30 minutes, but I ended up sitting with them for three hours. They peppered me with questions about my dogfights, and I gave detailed answers to each one.

My other friend from that delegation, Dan McKinnon, was a former heli-copter pilot who specialised in rescue missions. In one remarkably complex operation, he had rescued 40 civilians from a ship that was about to sink. He came from an affluent family, his father was a personal friend of President Ronald Reagan, and Reagan appointed him head of the Federal Aviation Administration. He went on to enter the history books of American civil aviation when he brought in military air traffic controllers to break the big strike by civilian air traffic controllers in 1981. He later founded a small airline called North American.

On one of my trips to the United States, together with Sara and my son Guy, Dan invited us to the Naval Aviation Museum in Pensacola, which had parts of aircraft carriers and real planes used by the US Navy. Later on, he arranged a special surprise for me: an air show by the Blue Angels aerobatic team. After they landed, the team commander told me that had he known before about my record as a pilot, he would have invited me join them in the show. To make up for it, he made me a very tempting offer: He'd add me to the aerobatic team and in return, I'd agree for one of my kills to be credited in his name. Of course, he was joking.

France was one of the few countries whose request to send a delegation of experts to Israel was turned down. Israel and the Israel Air Force had not forgiven the French for the 'betrayal' of the Six Day War and the embargo imposed by Charles de Gaulle. After some protracted negotiations between the two countries' defence ministries, an agreement was reached to have reciprocal visits. The French would come to us and an Israeli delegation would travel to France.

Israel had a special interest in two weapons systems that the French were about to supply to Arab countries, the F-1 Mirage that performed somewhat similarly to the American F-104, and the Magic 531 air-to-air missile manufactured by the Matra company. The Magic 531 was a heat-seeking missile that was of particular concern to the air force because of its special design that enabled the eye of the missile to identify the heat of an enemy aircraft's engine from any direction. Our missiles were only effective from the rear. The French missile was in an advanced stage of development and our defence ministry was worried about Arab air forces gaining a technological advantage with this missile.

The defence ministry informed the French that it would allow their delegation of experts to visit Israel and hear what the air force learned from the Yom Kippur War, on condition that Israeli pilots could fly the F-1 Mirage, and that we would learn the specifications of the Magic missile.

At the time, I was commander of No. 117, the First Jet Squadron at Ramat David, and the air force decided that since we'd flown French Mirages, we would host the French delegation. Ahead of their arrival, the French sent us a list of questions that interested them. When we read the questions, we burst out laughing. All the questions were related to the Six Day War. As if the Yom Kippur War had never happened.

The two French experts who arrived were veteran pilots. One was a wing commander of the operational units at a French airbase, and the other was the commander of a Mirage squadron – the attack model. They stayed at a hotel in Haifa and came to Ramat David each morning with an intelligence officer who acted as their escort. We gave them information that had been pre-approved by air force intelligence. At the end of their visit, it was decided that another officer and I would go on a reciprocal visit to France, around the time of the Paris Air Show at Le Bourget, an international airport also used by the French air force.

During the visit we flew in a four-seat Fouga to visit different French airbases. At one of the bases, we were shown the Mirage IV – a bomber that served as a prototype for the supersonic Concorde passenger jet. The Mirage IV was built to fly twice the speed of sound, and with the capacity to carry a nuclear bomb long distance. The French also showed us another plane, a Mirage 3A, that could carry small atomic bombs. Their gaze was entirely to the east, to the Soviet Union and the Warsaw Pact countries. For the first time in my life, I saw a Mirage with a navigation computer. Though still primitive, the thinking was advanced.

The French hosted us in fine style with gourmet meals prepared by a famous chef and served in dishes shaped like champagne bottles. The ice cream was also served in small champagne-bottle-shaped dishes. In Rouen, we were treated to a history lesson all about the French national hero, Joan of Arc.

I was hoping to fly an F-1, but the French said they didn't have one available. I had to make do with a simulator. I found that the aircraft felt to me more like a flying gas tank. A long-range plane with high engine power and wing load, but weak air-to-air performance.

Throughout the visit, the French avoided anything related to the air-to-air missile that we were so interested in. At the final meeting with division heads in the French air force, I thanked them for their wonderful hospitality but reminded them that they were also supposed to give us information about the missile. I saw they were embarrassed and hesitant. But later, thanks to the friendship that had developed between us, during that luncheon we were able to obtain very valuable information for our air defence system.

The intelligence officer who was with me at the meal was given an informational booklet about the missile. It described the 12 test launches that had been done so far, none of them successful. After analysing the material, we concluded that while the missile was quite advanced it needn't be cause for concern for our air force.

From there I went to the Paris Air Show at Le Bourget. Israel Aircraft Industries and other companies were present at the show, and we were guests of McDonnell, manufacturer of the F-15s that the IAF was about to receive. At the air show, I had an exciting experience. At a luncheon hosted by the French company Dassault, I met some of my childhood heroes. Great pilots of the past who were living legends. People who had a lot to do with inspiring my passion for flying. People like Pierre Clostermann, author of *The Big Show: The Greatest Pilot's Story of World War II*, the most fascinating biography of a fighter pilot I'd ever read.

Besides Clostermann, there was Alan Deere, author of *Nine Lives*. Deere had been downed nine times and lived to tell the tale. And Douglas Bader, the amputee English pilot whom I'd first met a few years earlier in Ethiopia, before I returned to the pilot course. Bader's plane had crashed during a training flight when he was 21 and he lost both legs. But he recovered and resumed flying and was an ace fighter pilot during World War II. On one mission over Germany, his plane was hit and he bailed out, leaving his two prostheses behind in the plane, which crashed to the ground. When he was a POW in Germany, an unusual agreement was reached with the British to parachute in two new prostheses for him. A British plane orbited over the POW camp as the Germans obeyed an order not to shoot it down, and the two new prostheses were dropped. When we met in Ethiopia, I was a young parachuting instructor and he was already an aviation legend. Aside from a handshake, he didn't pay me any attention. This time it was totally different. I was presented to him as the top ace of the Israel Air Force and he was quite impressed.

Another encounter that stood out was with the German ace Erich Hartmann, credited with downing 352 planes during World War II, mostly on the eastern front. In one battle there, he downed five Russian planes in less than 20 minutes. The base he commanded was conquered by the US Army and he was handed over to the Russians. When the war ended, he would not agree to return to Germany until the last of the German POWs was released from Russian captivity. He went on to become commander of a Phantom squadron in the new Luftwaffe and its attaché in Washington.

22 COMMANDER OF THE FIRST JET SQUADRON

A few months before my position at headquarters was due to end, the air force decided to appoint me commander of No. 117, the First Jet Squadron at Ramat David, the only Mirage squadron left in the air force after the Yom Kippur War. Even though the position was supposed to be filled by someone with the rank of lieutenant colonel, I came to the squadron in August 1974 as a major, and only received the promotion a year later.

The First Jet Squadron had a glorious history in the air force. It was the squadron that received the air force's first fighter jets, British-made Meteors, that Israel's first prime minister, David Ben-Gurion rechristened with new Hebrew names: *Sufa* and *Sa'ar*.

The arms embargo imposed by French President Charles de Gaulle following the Six Day War had affected the IAF the most. Before the war, the Dassault plant in France had produced 50 upgraded Mk. 5 Mirages, based on specifications Israel had given to the French that included additions and improvements specially adapted for the Israel Air Force. De Gaulle froze the deal and instead of the planes coming to us, they were given as a gift to Libyan President Muammar Gaddafi.

Somehow, Israel managed to obtain the blueprints for the plane it had been blocked from receiving, and on the basis of sketches received from a Swiss engineer who worked at the Dassault plant, in addition to other sources of information – including some key figures at Dassault – Israel Aircraft Industries (IAI) developed the Nesher, the Israeli version of the French plane, which was one ton heavier than the old Mirage fighter, and carried more fuel and munitions. The Nesher was used by the air force in the War of Attrition and the Yom Kippur War. Most of my kills during the Yom Kippur War came while flying a Nesher.

In addition to increased production of the Nesher, in early 1974, before I took command of the squadron, IAI began producing a new fighter jet – the Kfir. The Mirage and the Nesher were considered too weak, and the air force, together with IAI, examined the possibility of installing American Phantom J-79 engines in place of the original Mirage and Nesher engines, which were not that strong and had to be changed after 72 hours of flying.

The Kfir was a hybrid of the Shahak and an American engine. In laboratory tests conducted by IAI, the engine transplant was a success – and the two-seater test plane thus came to be known as the 'Blaiberg', after the heart transplant patient operated on by South African surgeon Christiaan Barnard. In 1975, the Kfir went into mass production and gradually replaced the Neshers. The First Jet Squadron was the last one that still used the original Mirages.

When I took command, I replaced Yehuda Koren, who was an ace with 10½ kills to his credit, and who commanded the squadron during the Yom Kippur War and led it on air-to-air missions, mainly on the Syrian front, where it downed many enemy aircraft in dogfights. Together, we watched the honour guard for the outgoing and incoming commanders, and from that moment on, I set about rebuilding the squadron the way I saw fit. In a fighter squadron, operational quality and safety are a direct result of the atmosphere, cohesiveness, morale, and camaraderie among the pilots. I sought to instil the same philosophy with the squadron's technical and maintenance crews and administrative personnel, so that together we became one body, one squadron, which aimed to be one of the top in the air force. The air of camaraderie in a squadron was very important to me.

For example, on one of my first days with the squadron, I noticed that the custom was that the squadron secretaries were not permitted entry to the air crew's dining hall. I immediately changed that. I assembled all the squadron secretaries and operations secretaries and told them that from now on, we would all share meals together. That continued throughout my time as commander.

During my three years as squadron commander – 1974-1977 – there were no wars or major military clashes, but one of my most important tasks as a combat squadron commander was to ensure that there was no let-up in preparedness after the difficult war the squadron had been through. One of the first things I resolved with the wing commander was that, as squadron commander, I would decide which pilots served with me in the squadron. If I felt that a pilot was not suited for the squadron, I would have the right to transfer him elsewhere. In no way would I compromise on the quality of my pilots. When I saw that a pilot wasn't performing up to par, I gave him some chances to prove himself, but if I still felt that he wasn't at the right level, I transferred him to another squadron. When I finished commanding the squadron, I could take pride in the fact that, under my command, not a single plane had crashed and I hadn't lost a single pilot. The same was also true for the squadron I commanded later on as a reservist.

Most of my pilots, whether in compulsory service or the reserves, came from kibbutzim and moshavim in the north, including a good number from communities located close to Ramat David. The new pilots I got had previously been in Skyhawk squadrons, and there were some that I saw right away had the potential to be outstanding pilots. One of these was Ilan Ramon. From the start, I could see that this young pilot had good flying abilities and a high level of technical capability. He was a very likeable guy with a baby-faced appearance, and even after he was selected to become an astronaut in the NASA space programme, I kept on calling him 'the kid'.

As squadron commander, I introduced a lot of changes, operational as well as administrative. For instance, contrary to the standard practice in the air force of people calling each other by their surnames, I insisted that people call each other by their first names. A minor detail perhaps, but to me it was important in creating the atmosphere and feeling of connection I wanted to see in the squadron. I also was totally opposed to the penalties that were routinely meted out to pilots in other squadrons for exceeding flying limits. I set a new rule that, in my squadron, no one would pay a cent. The pilot's salary, I said, belonged not to him but to his family, and if we took it away, we were really punishing his wife and children. There was a lot of argument in the air force over this policy of mine, but I remained adamant about it.

The Ramat David airbase was very similar to the Hatzor airbase where I'd served up to now. It was a small and intimate base, located in the Jezreel Valley, in one of the most beautiful areas of the country. My family's move to Ramat David went pretty smoothly. Sara left her job at Kaplan Hospital in Rehovot and got a new job in medical administration at Ha'Emek Hospital in Afula. Her office was very close to the place where I was born. The two girls adjusted quickly to school and preschool in Nahalal, and two months before the move to Ramat David, our son Guy was born.

From my very first day with the squadron, I made it very clear that I aimed to make it the leader in flight quality and air operations. In training drills, I also put a special emphasis on excellence in dogfights and on attacking ground targets, something that was given less importance in the Mirage and Nesher squadrons. To attain the results I wanted in the air, I also put a great deal of focus on everything related to ground operations – I wanted highly skilled and motivated technical crews who identified with the squadron and felt close to the air teams. I believed that creating social-familial cohesiveness in the squadron would help make it what I wanted it to be.

There were plenty of examples of this. We had a bus driver named Attias who'd worked with the squadron for a long time. He was a civilian working for the IDF whose job was to transport the pilots to the hangars. He was a very friendly older fellow who also prepared meals for the crew who were on call in the mornings. Ramat David sits atop a huge underground lake with water that flows out into streams year-round, and Attias used to catch fish in one of these streams and grill them for breakfast. The problem was that the water was polluted with oil from local factories. The fish had an unpleasant smell and could only be eaten after being soaked for a long time in a lot of lemon juice. Aside from the fish, though, Attias, who was a really wonderful guy, would grill steaks that he served on special wooden trays.

It wasn't just Attias. Veterans of the squadron tell the story of how one day they found the squadron commander washing dishes at the sink, chopping vegetables into tiny pieces for a salad with onion and olive oil, and asking the squadron secretaries how they liked their omelettes. And that's not to mention the fresh rolls and coffee at the end of breakfast.

The squadron's social events soon became famous throughout the air force. The mother and sister of one of the pilots were singers in the Gevatron choir and every so often, different groups from the Gevatron would perform for us.

The squadron's training programme was varied. As I've said before, I always believed that good performances in aerial combat will also affect capabilities in ground strikes. The results achieved by the squadron after several months of training proved that the method works. From training drills within the squadron in which I participated like all the other pilots, we moved on to competitions versus other squadrons in the wing, and then against combat squadrons from other bases.

In the corps-wide machine-gunning competition, I and another pilot named Eshkol, a kibbutznik who later became religiously observant and went on to become a big rabbi in Bnei Brak, hit four bullseyes on an old half-track that was used as the target. The competition included navigation through a series of landmarks, with examiners on the ground continually measuring and record-ing the results. The round ended with a bombing sortie – dropping four bombs on a target, and then with a round of cannon fire at the target. At the end of the day, when the results for all the competitions were tallied, the First Jet Squadron was declared the winner, and the squadron that came in second had only earned about half as many points as we had. After the competition, I received a letter from the head of the combat training division asking that we not take part anymore in the air force machine-gunning competition, since as an air-to-air squadron we recorded results to which no other squadron had even come close. As the squadron commander, I couldn't think of a greater compliment.

For me, the most exciting competition was the aerial combat against other squadrons. Within the wing, we competed against the Phantom squadron – No. 69, the Hammer Squadron. The score at the end was 70:30 in our favour – a total knockout.

Mirage pilots especially liked dogfights at low altitudes, while the Phantoms had an advantage in dogfights that took place at high altitude. In most parts of the country, dogfights were restricted to an altitude of 12,000 feet, except for the Dead Sea where you were permitted to descend to 5,000 feet, an altitude that I really liked. At the start of each such battle there was a joint briefing and afterward, at the end of the day, there was a debriefing for both squadrons, in which we analysed all the films. Each 16-mm film listed the name of the pilot and how many 'kills' he had that day.

During my time as squadron commander, I was involved in founding a civilian skydiving club. After the skydiving championship in Moscow in 1955, several instructors had talked about starting a club as part of the flight club, but nothing came of it. One day, two skydivers, Jews from South Africa, came and introduced themselves to me. Having heard about me and my free-fall diving skills, they wanted to know if I would help them open a skydiving club in Israel.

With special permission from the air force I joined the project and, once all the necessary permits were obtained, we opened the skydiving club. On Saturdays, I took Sara and the kids and went to skydive at Ein Shemer. Each member of the club was given a rating based on his level of skill and experience, and I received the highest rating. My membership card said number one. A few years later, the club moved its operations to Sde Dov in Tel Aviv. Until 1988, I continued going there and skydiving on Saturday mornings.

One surprise for me while I was commanding the First Jet Squadron was a visit from Douglas Bader. It was the third time I got to meet my childhood hero. One day, I got a call from air force headquarters telling me a former Machal pilot was going to be celebrating his son's bar mitzvah at the Western Wall and at Masada, and that one of the many guests coming from abroad would be Douglas Bader.

I decided to prepare a surprise for him, and when he came to the base I brought him to see something special – the black Spitfire that Ezer Weizman had flown in air shows. An aircraft nearly identical to the plane Bader had flown in World War II. Douglas couldn't contain his excitement. He climbed into the cockpit and it looked like he was about to take off again. He told me about his experiences in the war and about how he parachuted into enemy territory without his prostheses. Later, he told me that he now had three sets of prostheses, and joked that he selected which to use depending on which woman he was going out with.

Toward the end of my time with the squadron, I was sent to Chile as a guest of the Chilean air force. A nice way to finish three intensive years at Ramat David. After the military coup in which the communist President Allende was overthrown and General Pinochet came to power, Chile wanted to renew its army and air force. The Americans had decided to impose an embargo and were not supplying F-5s, even though Chile had already paid for them. It was just like the move by Charles de Gaulle when he imposed an arms embargo on Israel following the Six Day War. Israel sold the Chilean air force Shafrir-2 air-to-air missiles for their Hunter airplanes. I came to Chile with experts from RAFAEL to instruct the Chilean air force pilots and technicians in the use of the missiles. The city of Antofagasta, next to the airbase where we instructed the locals, was in a flat desert and reminded me somewhat of Rephidim. The missiles were installed on the Hunter aircraft, and I went up in the air with the pilots to teach them.

The Chileans went to great lengths to make sure that I enjoyed my visit. They put a special plane at my disposal and I was taken on an unforgettable tour of the country's south. A vast nature reserve with mountains, lakes, icebergs and an untamed landscape that draws hundreds of thousands of backpackers from all over the world.

On the return flight, we landed near a remote village to pick up a gravely ill teenager and transport him to a hospital in the capital, Santiago. I was very impressed by the devoted care the boy received, but sadly, he did not survive the trip to Santiago and died on the way.

In Santiago, before the return flight to Israel, I was invited to attend the wedding of a fighter pilot that was being held in the local officers' club. All the officers and pilots wore their fancy dress uniforms, with medals and colourful sashes on their chests, and golden daggers at their thighs. I tried to keep a straight face and not burst out laughing.

I have many memories from the various events to which I was invited during my years as an active pilot, in regular service and in the reserves. One was an event called 'Gathering of the Eagles'. It's a special event held once a year, during the final week of the US Air Force's commanders' course, in which 600 troops, most of them majors, take part. The course has a tradition that goes back many years: The entire course lasts a year and during the final week 20 guests are invited to attend, mostly from the US Air Force, and they get to tell the cadets about why they were invited to appear there. I was invited in 1998, and I was the second person from the Israel Air Force to appear before this distinguished forum. I told them about the dogfights I had on October 19 and October 20, 1973. One of the regular guests who was invited nearly every year is Chuck Yeager, another one of my childhood heroes, and that week I got to spend a lot of time with him.

Another special event I was invited to was in 2003, marking the 100th anniversary of the Wright Brothers' first flight. It included an exhibition of nearly every kind of aircraft that was produced since 1903. I was there with Sara for two days, and on the last day, there was a gala evening attended by the who's who of American military and civil aviation, including all the American astronauts who'd flown with the space programme. The emcee for the event was the famous actor Harrison Ford, himself a pilot who owns 13 private planes. Sara made sure to get a picture with him.

A few years later, I got to see what it was like to fly in a MiG-21—the plane I'd chased as a fighter pilot and one that I'd shot down a good number of times. I had an Israeli friend who now lived in the United States, and he introduced me to a former US Air Force pilot who had bought in Czechoslovakia several Soviet fighter planes, including a MiG-21, a MiG-23, and an Ilyushin bomber. This pilot, Joe, invited me to fly the MiG-21. It was quite a strange feeling to sit in the cockpit of what was the main fighter jet of the Egyptian and Syrian air forces in the 1960s and 1970s.

I commanded No. 117 Squadron at Ramat David for three years. Three years of operational quiet, but a lot of training and preparation for whatever might come in the future. I received a good air-to-air squadron when I came in, and I left my replacement an even better squadron, with top fighter pilots. One thing I was proud of was that I was able to convince quite a few pilots to sign on for a further period of regular service in the air force.

I completed my tenure as squadron commander without having lost a plane or a pilot. I now held the rank of lieutenant colonel and it was time to move on to the next position.

23 THE HEART WANTS THE FIGHTER SQUADRON; SARA WANTS EL AL

In August 1977, I was about to finish my time as commander of the First Jet Squadron. I was 39, older than most of the people who hold senior positions in the air force, and the higher you climb the command pyramid, the more crowded it gets. The horizon left to me for senior positions was shrinking, and I had to hold another senior aviation position to make colonel.

The air force was about to change commanders. David Ivry would soon be taking over from Benny Peled. This was terrible timing for me. A time when both the incoming and outgoing commander were not going to be making major appointments. The key person at such times was Rafi Harlev, head of the group in charge of air force training and instruction. We'd met when I was with the squadron in Ramat David, and he asked me what I wanted to do when I finished with my position there. I told him that I did not see myself in a position at headquarters, flying Parker pens from one side of the desk to the other, and that I would prefer another command position in a combat squadron. Harlev heard me, but still he told me firmly that he was designating me for a staff position as a lieutenant colonel. I was unwilling to accept this and requested a meeting with the air force commander. Harlev ended up leaving the air force a few months after our conversation, when he was passed over for the top command position.

A meeting took place not long afterward. Benny Peled held me in high esteem. He listened as I explained why, with my talents, I preferred to command a squadron. I am sure that he agreed with me, but he couldn't ignore the poor timing.

"You're right," he told me, "but I'm right at the end of my tenure as air force commander and I don't want to dictate senior appointments to David Ivry, who is supposed to replace me. I suggest that you go talk to Ivry."

David Ivry, whom I also knew well, going back to my early days as a fighter pilot, agreed that I was better suited to command a combat squadron, but he explained that since he had yet to officially take over the position, he could not make those decisions.

I felt like I'd fallen through the cracks. This one is about to leave and doesn't want to make a decision and that one hasn't assumed the position yet and doesn't want to make a decision, and here I am, stuck with the position that Rafi Harlev is assigning me, another staff job. Feeling that I was left with no choice, I went back to Benny Peled and told him that, given the situation, the best thing would be for me to leave active service and just be a reservist pilot.

"What will you do as a civilian?" he asked.

I honestly hadn't thought about it and I had no idea what I would do. Benny Peled suggested that I come back to him in another week.

A week later, I went to see him again. Peled, who was about to be appointed CEO of Elbit Systems once he finished commanding the air force, suggested I join him and take a senior management position with the company. When I protested that I had no training for that kind of job, he was insistent.

"Each air force base has to send two pilots to university studies, and if you want, the army would pay for you to study at the Technion, and afterward you could take a suitable position at Elbit."

He also suggested that I seek a senior position with the Mossad or the Shin Bet, or go abroad for a year to the National War College. I told him that at my age, there was no way I'd get a position in the Mossad or Shin Bet, that it could only be administrative, and if that were the case, I might as well stay in the air force. As for studying at the Technion, it was more than 20 years since I finished school on the kibbutz, and I didn't see myself going back to school now. I wasn't very keen on the last suggestion, either.

"I have another idea for you," Peled said. "Go to El Al. Air force pilots get priority when El Al is accepting new pilots. It's been a long time since they offered a training course for pilots making the switch to civil aviation and they are just about to start a new course like that." El Al was an interesting option I hadn't thought about before, and a recommendation from the air force commander, even the outgoing one, would of course carry great weight with a company where nearly all the pilots were former air force and many continued to fly in the air force as reservists. I promised Benny that I would think about it and get back to him.

I went home and consulted with Sara, who was excited by the idea of my joining El Al. Although my first choice was still to be an active pilot in the air force, I started to look into the idea. I spoke with Yosef Tzuk and Betzalel

'Tzulik' Ofer who were already captains with El Al, and they both advised me not to wait. At the time, the average age at which one ceased to be an operational pilot in the air force was 34, and after age 45 you needed special permission to keep flying. Even if I stayed in the air force, in another five years I'd have to stop doing the kind of flying that I loved so much – and then what?

Sara was even more excited about the idea after talking with some El Al pilots' wives. We're going to El Al! But it wasn't quite that simple, as it turned out. Benny Peled had a list of 21 candidates, all air force pilots, all about my age but with more seniority in the military. El Al only had positions available for 11 new pilots. When I heard this, I went back to Benny Peled.

"With these numbers, my chances aren't very good," I said.

Benny wasn't fazed. "Giora, don't forget that I'm the one who decides who goes to the El Al course. Nobody else. If you decide that you want to go to El Al, that's where you'll go."

At that time, the summer of 1977, we had just finished building our new house in the pilots' quarters in Ramat Hasharon, and we started moving our things there from Ramat David. We even had a telephone line in the new house, even though the average waiting period in the area then for a line was three years. The benefits of being in the air force.

One weekend, a couple of weeks after that conversation with Benny Peled, Sara and I came to the new house. Sara was arranging things in the house and I got on the ladder and started painting the walls. Ready for any type of work, as usual. I was standing on the ladder when the telephone rang. It was Avihu Ben-Nun, commander of Wing 4. Avihu and I had a good relationship going back to when he headed up the offensive division during the Yom Kippur War and I was a department head there.

"Giora, what are you up to?" he asked.

I told him that in a few days I was handing over the squadron command to Kobi Richter, and that I'd decided to be discharged from the air force and go to El Al.

Avihu listened and then he said, "Come see me in my office in Hatzor. There's something I want to talk to you about." I went there, and he asked me to wait in his office while Benny Peled finished saying goodbye to the people at the Hatzor base as he prepared to step down as commander. When Avihu returned from the farewell ceremony, he got right to the point.

"Giora, I want you take command of the First Fighter Squadron."

I felt like I'd just been hit over the head with a sledgehammer. It was one of the few times in my life that I felt thrown off-balance. There was no position in the air force that I wanted more than to command this squadron. When I'd checked with Benny Peled, David Ivry and Rafi Harlev about it a few months earlier, I was told that the position was already filled and a new commander had been appointed.

"What about the new commander?" I asked.

Avihu told me that a decision was made to transfer him to another position. "I want you to take the position."

Oh, Avihu, Avihu, where were you two weeks ago….

Like I said, there was no position in the air force that appealed to me as much as commanding the First Fighter Squadron. The squadron in which I was shaped as a fighter pilot. The squadron in which I recorded all 17 of my kills of enemy planes. But now, when I was finally being offered the job, I'm afraid that it was too late.

"Sara already sees herself in El Al and living in Neve Rom. It would be hard for me to make her move back to Hatzor for another two or three years with the squadron," I said, trying to explain. "Also, let's say I take command of the squadron for a few years and then leave the air force – who can promise that I'll be accepted at El Al once I'm over 40?"

Avihu reassured me about the age issue. David Ivry, the incoming air force commander, would sign a letter together with the CEO of El Al and the transportation minister pledging that when I finished my term in the squadron two years hence, I would be accepted into the El Al training course. It was mighty tempting. If only I'd received this offer a couple of weeks ago.

"I have to talk to Sara," I said. "She's already dreaming of the good life as the wife of an El Al pilot."

Avihu told me that David Ivry was waiting for me in his office in Tel Aviv. I drove straight there. Ivry repeated the offer. I explained the problem due to the timing of the offer. I left there after I told him I would see what Sara thought. When I got home to Neve Rom, I found Sara in tears on the living room floor. Unbeknownst to me, Avihu had driven to our home to try to convince her.

I urged Sara to stop crying. "Let's go back to Ramat David and there we'll talk about it."

We talked about it that weekend. First, Sara knew how much this job meant to me. How it would be my dream come true. But she was ready to be some-where else. In El Al. After so many years as a fighter pilot's wife, she now envisioned herself away from the family lodgings at the base. Later on, I learned there was another reason that she hadn't shared with me right away.

"You've tempted fate for so many years, Giora. You've stretched the risk to the limit. It's enough. For you and for me. I went through all those hard times together with you." And she added: "I don't think you can really rely on that written commitment. Two years from now when you leave the air force, the situation in El Al might be different. What will you do if they tell you then that El Al isn't accepting any new pilots? What will that letter be worth then?"

As it turned out, she was very right about that. El Al fell into a serious crisis. For several years it froze all new hiring and even laid off 11 pilots who'd already completed their training as first officers. No matter how many letters and signatures I would have had to show, there was no way they would have hired me had my entry into the company been postponed by two or three years.

I felt that I couldn't press her to defer the move to El Al and to return to Hatzor. My dream was so tantalisingly within reach, but I wholeheartedly agreed to give it up.

24 A NEW LIFE IN EL AL

In the summer of 1977, I started a new chapter in my life with El Al. For me, the world of civil aviation was a whole new challenge. After the initial stage of the training course in which we studied the aircraft's structure and the instructors didn't say a word about actual flying, we moved on to training on a simulator that gave a picture of the plane's instruments.

As usual, I was anxious to get to the flights themselves. This was the most interesting part for me. Each cadet in the course was assigned a veteran El Al pilot as his personal instructor. We flew as co-pilots in the seat beside the captain, with the first officer sitting behind us. In those days, most of the company's passenger planes were Boeing 707s, a plane considered reliable but also a gas guzzler. The plane's crew included the captain, first officer, flight engineer, navigator, and radio operator. We were all crammed into the little cockpit.

When we flew within Europe there was no need for the navigator and radio operator, but in flights over the Atlantic Ocean, communications were a lot more difficult. You could only pick up shortwave frequencies. The navigator would identify the flight path by the stars and use an instrument called a sextant, a navigational instrument invented in the 18th century and still in use in every aircraft despite all the modern technological advances. The navigators used charts of the stars to navigate the plane over the ocean. When we approached the coast of the United States, contact was made with the American air traffic controller who guided us through the final flight segment until we landed at John F. Kennedy Airport in New York.

The El Al flights were so different to what I was used to in the air force. I didn't expect nor did I get the same feeling of flying that I'd experienced in fighter jets. In passenger airliners, take-offs are manual, even in the newest aircraft. With most passenger planes now, landings can be done automatically, except for at certain airports that lack the necessary automation equipment. In those cases, landings are also done manually.

After a series of training flights in which I flew 170 hours with an instructor, I reached the stage where I was able to take the tests to be certified as a first officer. I was the first one in the course who was deemed ready to take the test, which is done during a flight. Unlike the training flights with the instructor, during this flight, the examiner acts as if he's not there, and also creates problems that I, as a pilot, must discover and deal with. For example, when I asked him to switch to a certain channel, he deliberately selected the wrong channel.

I felt that I performed as required on the test flight, but the tester thought otherwise and said that I hadn't done well on the things not directly related to flying the plane, and failed me. In accordance with procedure, I went to the fleet director and requested a different instructor. I was assigned a new instructor and after another brief series of test flights in which I performed take-offs and landings, I received approval to take the test a second time.

This time I passed without any trouble. I was certified as a first officer with El Al, as a pilot with the national airline. A new chapter of my life began as a first officer, a pilot in the Boeing 707 fleet. I flew the 707 for eight years. Later, I moved to the 767/757 fleet, which I flew in for 16 years; the 757 was a smaller plane than the 767, but had an identical cockpit.

In those years, El Al was a government company with poor relations between the employees and the government-appointed administration. When I started flying with El Al, the company flew seven days a week, including Saturdays, the Jewish Sabbath. The destinations were always changing. A morning flight to Tehran (today that sounds so hard to believe, but until February 1979, the Tehran route was one of the busiest) and the next day a flight to London or Amsterdam or some other European city. I did my best to be free on Fridays. Those were my days for the air force – training, drilling aerial combat or other manoeuvres. I was still a reservist pilot, and those hours in the air, back in a fighter jet, prepared me for the coming week of routine flights with El Al.

In January 1979, when I was still fairly new with the company, I took part in the big mission to rescue Israelis and Jews from Tehran. The Islamic Revolution in Iran took the whole world by surprise, both in terms of the suddenness with which the Shiite genie burst out of the bottle, and its intensity. The Iranian army, one of the largest and strongest armies in the Middle East, collapsed like a house of cards. The Iranian air force alone, with its new American F-4 fighter jets, could have stopped the popular uprising that erupted in the streets, but when the moment arose, the air force commanders, just like the tank commanders and the special forces commanders, didn't have the nerve to act. Many of them were executed after being sentenced to death by the revolutionary courts that were soon established.

In the capital Tehran, it was chaos. The revolutionaries, stunned by their success, waited for their leader Khomeini to arrive from his place of exile in Paris. Meanwhile, many thousands of foreigners were desperate to find a way out of the country. Among them were business people, diplomats and secret agents from Western countries, as well as hundreds of Israelis – emissaries, diplomats, businessmen, employees of various companies, and a large group of Mossad intelligence personnel, whose lives were now in danger. In addition, there were a good number of Iranian Jews who now feared for their lives and wanted to leave the country while it was still possible. Many of them waited in safe houses, waiting for word to make their way to the airport. The Israeli government considered their rescue a matter of national importance, and the mission was to be carried out by El Al, the national airline, which still ran a regular route to Tehran despite the chaotic situation in the country. The Mossad oversaw the rescue mission, using El Al planes and coordinating with the people who needed to be rescued.

I was a relatively young pilot in El Al, but I'd done a good number of flights to Tehran so I was chosen, along with other pilots in the company, all air force veterans, to fly the rescue planes to Tehran and back. At Tehran's international airport, it was also total chaos. The revolutionary guards were gradually taking over the airport, and after they seized the control tower, it ceased to function. Planes from various airlines that were in the air at the time became flying message-relay stations and helped guide other planes in to land in emergency conditions on runways with minimal lighting. As soon as one plane landed, a second plane that had been relaying information to other planes in the air, prepared for landing and handed off the job to the next plane in line.

As there were a large number of people we needed to rescue, El Al allocated several planes each day to the operation. When we landed we steered the plane to a designated location, far from the eyes of the revolutionary guards. The doors opened and throngs of people poured into the plane, far more than the normal passenger load for a 707. The embassy staff, Mossad personnel and others who were in Iran on state business, came to the airport straight from their hiding places and slipped into the plane as quickly as possible. Hundreds of local Jews joined them. Some tried to save some of the assets they'd accrued in Iran and showed up at the plane lugging expensive carpets. The aisles were crammed with people and carpets.

The waiting time on the ground was very short. We kept the right engines going the whole time as we waited for a report from the ground crew that we could close the doors, taxi and take off. We did not refuel there. We left Israel with enough fuel to fly to Tehran and back. All the Israelis and many Iranian Jews whose lives had been in danger were rescued from there. Most of them by El Al. Each time we took off and exited Iranian airspace, you could hear the cheering and the sighs of relief from the passengers. We, too, the flight crew, felt that a heavy burden was lifted from us.

The wages and benefits at El Al were better than those for pilots in the air force. My salary enabled us to enjoy a higher standard of living than before and to afford things that were beyond our means when I was an air force pilot. El Al pilots, especially captains, had a very high social standing in Israel, and beyond. There was a special kind of glory attached to being an airline pilot.

I often found myself working around the clock. During one of my first years with El Al, I flew 28 weekends in a row, mostly passenger flights. Weekends were the high-capacity time and, at the time, none thought that El Al, the national airline, could operate any differently from the European airlines that made most of their revenue on long weekends. It was the same in El Al. But from the time that Israel was founded, the ultra-Orthodox parties had demanded that El Al not fly on Shabbat and Jewish holidays. All the Mapai governments, one of the movements in Israel after 1982, had refused to go along with this. The ultra-Orthodox protested, but it didn't stop them from supporting the government.

In May 1977, the Likud Party won its first national election and Menachem Begin became prime minister. In his first term, he didn't institute any major changes, but in the coalition agreement he signed with the ultra-Orthodox parties following his re-election in 1981, he pledged to halt El Al flights on Shabbat and Jewish holidays. In August 1982, while the IDF was deep into the Lebanon War, the Knesset passed new legislation and over the next six months, El Al gradually ceased all of its flights on Shabbat and holidays. Everyone knew this would mean a loss of tens of millions of dollars a year. The loss of revenue would adversely affect employment conditions in the company (for whom a significant portion of wages was derived from working on weekends) and lead to lay-offs. However, Begin, who cited religious reasons for the decision even though it was clearly due solely to his coalition needs, wouldn't budge. And a Labour Court ruling saying the company could continue flying on Shabbat had no effect, either.

In light of a threat of a strike by employees, particularly members of the ground crew who realised they would no longer be able to earn weekend overtime, which was a significant portion of their pay, the government decided to pre-emptively ground El Al. Starting in September 1982, all of the company's flights were halted for four months.

Sara and I were on holiday in Europe when this came about. We had planned to return home via Rome and were unaware of the shut-down. In Rome, we ran into an Israeli couple we knew and they asked us how we were getting back to Israel.

"We're returning on El Al flight 356 from Rome, of course," I said confidently.

That's when we first heard that El Al was grounded and that all the flights had been halted the week before. Fortunately, at the Rome airport we met some Arkia (a smaller Israeli airline) pilots I knew, and they brought us into the cockpit and flew us back to Israel.

The grounding of El Al and the subsequent placing of the company under receivership enabled the government to make changes in its administration and in the workers' status. Rafi Harlev, a top air force pilot who'd previously served as the company's deputy CEO, was appointed CEO that September and began to rid El Al of 'surplus workers'. His decision, which caused great agitation among the company employees, including the pilots, called for serious cutbacks in the workforce through a combination of lay-offs and early retirements. Pilots were affected as well. Twenty-one pilots were on the list slated for lay-offs. Harlev cut mercilessly, with no regard for the fact that many of the workers were former air force pilots, including some he had personally commanded and many of whom, like me, still flew as reservist pilots in the air force.

I was a graduate of the most recent pilot training course offered by the company, and management announced that the 11 pilots who'd joined the company after that course would be laid off, along with 10 other pilots. My name was on the list. It was a tough time for Sara and me. The reputation I'd earned as a fighter pilot, all the successful missions I'd flown, all my achievements as the record holder in downing enemy aircraft, as commander of the First Jet Squadron – none of it mattered when my name appeared on the blacklist. I wasn't alone. I was part of a group of pilots who'd given the best years of their lives to the air force and to the country, all of us now senior officers in the reserves, and now we were going to be tossed out.

The uproar that erupted over the firing of the pilots spread beyond El Al. It was natural that we, the pilots, would lead the fight against the lay-off plan, which we felt was arbitrary and rather than helping to strengthen El Al would wreck the company. The pilots' committee decided to speak directly with Prime Minister Menachem Begin. I was chosen along with two other highly regarded air force fighter pilots to represent the pilots at the meeting with the prime minister. Begin was very respectful and listened to us patiently. We explained that you couldn't summarily fire pilots who were air force combat veterans, who'd won the Six Day War and saved the country in the Yom Kippur War. I don't know what Begin did after that meeting but we left his office feeling that there was a readiness to talk and to think about other solutions for El Al's business recovery.

As the negotiations dragged on, several of the more senior El Al pilots decided to take early retirement, so the list of designated lay-offs shrank a bit. Eventually, enough pilots agreed to retire that the pilot lay-offs were cancelled and we remained with the company.

25 GOODBYE TO THE MIRAGE

The El Al flights became routine. Day turned to night and we were in the air on the way to destinations in Europe, or on the transatlantic flight to New York that took more than 12 hours. At the time, New York was the only American city to which El Al flew.

El Al was a job. The air force was my soul. My heart was still in the air force. For the first two years after my discharge, I continued flying as a reservist pilot in the First Jet Squadron. At some point, the air force decided to close down that squadron and its reservist pilots were assigned to emergency flights in No. 109, *Ha'emek* (the Valley) Squadron, and the Mirages were transferred to No. 253, Negev Squadron at the new Itam airbase that was built near the city of Yamit in the Sinai. Amos Bar, who was my first deputy squadron commander in the First Jet Squadron, was the one who built the squadron at Itam.

As part of my reserve duty, I retrained to fly the Kfir. The ground part of the course was held at Ramat David, an airbase in the north, and the certification flights were done at Etzion. The first deputy squadron commander for the Kfir squadron at the Etzion airbase, another new air force base, had trained with me on the Mirage but was dropped from the First Fighter Squadron not long after he completed the pilot course. One day he invited me to a traditional Friday night dinner. I didn't know he'd started to become religiously observant, but it dawned on me when I saw his kids doing the ritual hand-washing before the meal. Today, he's a famous rabbi in Bnei Brak. And he wasn't the only one. Four pilots from the squadron later became religious.

The commander of the Etzion base, who'd been the commander of the First Jet Squadron in Ramat David before the Yom Kippur War, was pleased to see me.

"It's great that you've come to our squadron," he said as he welcomed me.

I told him that I was only here for training.

"Well, then you won't fly here," he said, not necessarily in jest.

I thanked him and went to complete my certification on the Kfir with 101 Squadron.

In April 1981, the air force closed down the Mirage squadron at Itam, in wake of the peace agreement with Egypt and the withdrawal from Sinai. This closure also marked the beginning of the swansong of the Mirage throughout the air force. This was the aircraft that, starting in the mid-1960s, had given the air force the edge in aerial combat, that had been the main interceptor in the dogfights in the Yom Kippur War, the plane that was my great love as a pilot and with which I'd achieved the extraordinary feat of downing 17 enemy aircraft.

In the early 1980s, the air force had just a few dozen Mirages left, and decided to put them all together to form one reservist squadron based at Hatzor, No. 254, Midland Squadron. I was appointed commander of this squadron, to which 24 Mirages were transferred. All the pilots, with the exception of the first deputy squadron commander who was in regular service, were reservist pilots and war veterans. Building and operating the squadron was a challenging task. Many of the reservist pilots were also El Al pilots, like me, and their days of reserve duty in the squadron had to be planned in accordance with their civilian flight schedule.

We put together a core group of 20 reservist pilots, and once we finished building the new squadron, about 200 reservists served in it. In addition, there was an adjutant in regular service, the operations secretaries, and 15 active-duty soldiers in the technical department. Most of the mechanics were reservists from El Al, as were the three flight engineers.

We operated like a regular air force squadron. We flew four days a week. Every day, four to six reservists reported for duty and each one flew at least three flights for the day.

As commander of this special squadron, I sought to shape it like any other, with the best pilots who were veterans of the Mirage and Nesher squadrons. Some had fought in the Yom Kippur War and others were younger. As in the First Jet Squadron, I worked to boost the operational performance, camaraderie and morale. The squadron functioned like this for three years, and its first real test came with the first Lebanon War in 1982. I urged the air force commander to include us in the intercept missions in the skies of Lebanon and Syria, but the directive was that only the F-15 and F-16 squadrons would take part in interceptions over the border. I couldn't understand why we were being left out. The Syrian air force had MiG-23s, which I felt were inferior to the MiG-21s we'd fought against in the past. But that was the decision, and all of my appeals to air force commander David Ivry to let us fly over Lebanon and Syria were turned down. We were assigned patrol missions along the border.

One day I was patrolling as the leader of a quartet formation over the Hermon Mountains when the controller instructed us to fly to an engagement over Lake Qaraoun inside Lebanon. The F-15s and F-16s that had flown an operational mission there had run low on fuel and returned to base. It would take time for a new quartet to get there and we were sent to fill in the gap. We reached Lake Qaraoun but we didn't see any enemy aircraft. Suddenly, my number two spotted a pair of planes. We got into position behind them but something seemed off to me. I shifted to the side and saw that these were our own F-16s.

We weren't the only ones who didn't take part in this war. In all of the first Lebanon War, only one Syrian plane was shot down by one of our Phantoms. The pilot, of 105 Squadron, the Scorpions, was Ben-Ami Peri who, with four previous kills, made ace with this kill on June 11, 1982. The Phantoms, like the Mirages, had been told to let the newer planes do the job. With the exception of that one plane, all the Syrian aircraft shot down in the first Lebanon War were downed by our F-15s and F-16s.

During the war I got a telephone call from the squadron's technical officer who told me he'd received an order from the equipment squadron to transfer four Mirages from the squadron to Israel Aircraft Industries, so they could be sent to the Argentinean air force. Argentina's air force had been hit hard that year – 1982 – during the Falklands War with Britain, and wanted to renew its fleet of fighter jets. Israel was in the midst of upgrading its fighter jets and agreed to sell Mirages to Argentina.

I told the technical officer that he was not transferring a single plane to IAI as long as we were in a state of war, and before I could look into this matter. The Wing 4 commander at Hatzor didn't know anything about it, either. After checking with the air force equipment division, I learned that this was, in fact, the directive. I insisted that they leave my squadron with at least four quartets of Mirages, but after the war, an order was issued to transfer the rest of the planes to IAI. The squadron was rendered inactive for four months in which I had all the pilots and mechanics undergo a retraining course on the Kfir aircraft, and we kept flying those planes for the next two years.

It was tough for me, having to say goodbye to the Mirage. I decided I would fly the last plane from Hatzor to Ben Gurion Airport. I took off from Hatzor and flew along the coastline, planning to turn inland to land at Ben Gurion. Suddenly, the oil pressure warning light began to flash. The emergency procedure when this happens is very clear: shut down the engine immediately. I did so and glided into Ben Gurion. When I landed and climbed down from the cockpit, I saw a huge puddle of oil beneath the plane. The oil pressure hose had burst.

That was how my last flight in a Mirage ended.

I felt a very deep attachment to this aircraft. I'd logged more flight hours on it than any other pilot in the air force. To me, the Mirage was the plane that does what you think it should do. I loved flying it, I loved training on it, and I loved fighting with it. I was a Mirage pilot from 1966 to 1982.

My three years in the Midland Squadron were one of the most enjoyable parts of my service in the air force, and I believe the same was true for the other reservist pilots in the squadron. It was an air-to-air squadron, the kind that pilots love best. We nicknamed the squadron 'Le Club' because it was like Club Med for pilots. I brought the reservist pilots that I wanted into the squadron. I did more days of reserve duty in the squadron than I did during any other time in my air force service. Some as a volunteer. On nearly every free day I had from El Al flights, I was at the squadron. The principle I handed down to the pilots was that everyone should give the squadron three days of reserve duty per month.

26 THE BATTLE OVER THE F-16

Around the same time the new squadron was founded, several other veteran pilots and I went to Commander David Ivry with an unusual request to allow us to retrain as F-16 pilots. The F-16 was the more advanced fighter jet that replaced the air force's older French-made aircraft.

"No problem, on condition that you sign on for three years of regular service," was Ivry's reply.

We said we were ready to sign on for regular service as reservists until we completed the certification period, but he wouldn't agree to that. It wouldn't be practical for me to leave El Al for three years, so I decided to drop the subject. The other pilots came to the same conclusion.

The success of the reservist squadron that I commanded, which was very economical and efficient, led the air force to decide to keep a squadron of the old-generation Kfir aircraft operational. This squadron was called Kfir Gderot.[17] We transferred 14 of these planes from Ramat David to Hatzor. The second-generation Kfir jet, the Kfir Canard, differed from the first-generation Kfir. It had larger, duck-shaped devices on the forward fuselage designed to improve the aircraft's manoeuvrability. The new version was better than the older model, but the Kfir Gderot pilots were so skilled that it didn't really make a difference. Our main speciality was aerial combat and we often 'walloped' the pilots from other squadrons in training exercises.

Despite all the compliments the squadron received, the age of the aircraft, combined with the fact that the air force was now moving forward with squadrons of the latest F-15s and F-16s, led to the decision that it was time to end the era of the old-generation Kfir aircraft. Thus, in December 1984, the Kfir squadron was shut down, with financial cutbacks being given as the official reason.

After the squadron ceased operations, the Americans asked to lease the Kfir aircraft from us to use them to simulate enemy planes – MiG-21s – in

---

[17] Gderot means 'fence' and refers to the small canards placed on the Kfir's air intakes to improve the fighter's performance in air-to-air manoeuvres. The Kfir was a heavy aircraft and the canards were soon enlarged to further improve the Kfir's performance to make it more like the Mirage.

training exercises. American pilots came to Israel. Their first stop was IAI, where they learned all about the Kfir aircraft, and then we trained them to fly the plane. These American pilots, who were all incredibly handsome, stayed in Eilat and came to the Ovda airbase every morning. People who lived in Eilat at the time used to say that two things happened: not a single virgin was left in the city, and all the bottles of Jack Daniels ran out. Once their training was completed, the planes were packed up and shipped to the United States, and eventually to VF-43 at NAS Oceana in Virginia Beach, Virginia. I was asked if I wanted to check them after they were unloaded at the port. I agreed, and did two test flights there.

That year, Israel's economic crisis worsened, and the government decided to make deep cuts in the defence budget. As a result, the air force shut down three combat squadrons. The Midland Squadron was one of them. I turned the closing of the squadron into a big party. I invited all the reservists' families to a festive luncheon at Hatzor and we put on a special evening event for the pilots and the technical crew, with the air force commander in attendance. It was a very memorable evening.

For a while, I went back to being a reservist pilot in the First Fighter Squadron, which in those days was flying the Kfir Canard. I knew that this assignment was temporary and that this squadron, too, would soon be affected by the air force cutbacks. When the squadron was shut down in preparation for receiving more F-16s, I switched to the Smashing Parrot Squadron, No. 149, at Ovda. This squadron was also living on borrowed time. The First Fighter Squadron switched to the F-16C, called the 'Lightning'. The Smashing Parrot Squadron moved to Hatzor when the Ovda base closed following the peace agreement with Egypt.

Squadrons were closing down, aircraft were being taken out of service, but it never occurred to me that it was time for me to retire from the air force. Most of the pilots my age had already retired and stopped doing reserve duty. I was looking for the next challenge – to become an operational F-16 pilot. This was now the air force's front-line jet, the plane that replaced the Mirage as an interceptor for aerial dogfights.

In 1982, after the Lebanon War, a new air force commander took over. Amos Lapidot succeeded David Ivry. At the farewell party for Ivry at Tel Nof, I had a little surprise ready for him: I handed him the insignia of No. 254 Squadron and said that since he was now a reservist pilot, I was inviting him to join the squadron. I could see that Ivry was quite moved.

"I'm not sure Amos Lapidot will like it," he briefly hesitated.

"I'm not asking him," I replied.

David Ivry, who continued in the army as deputy chief of staff, certainly picked up the gauntlet: He came to the squadron once a week and flew like any other reservist pilot.

After Ivry had moved on, I decided to revive the idea of retraining on the F-16. Amos Lapidot repeated the condition stipulated by the air force: I would have to sign on for three years of regular service. I told him I'd already given the air force three years of such service when I commanded the reservist squadrons.

Lapidot promised to look into the matter and instructed that a committee be formed to consider the possibility of veteran fighter pilots transitioning to the F-16. After seven months, this was the conclusion: If a veteran reservist pilot retrains on the F-16 and flies it for at least a year, that's clear profit for the air force. Each flight hour in the F-16 costs the air force $10,000 and since less time would be needed to train veteran pilots compared to young pilots, this was a strong economic advantage, in addition to the benefit of having experienced pilots flying the air force's newest fighter jets.

I went to the El Al deputy CEO and requested unpaid leave to attend the retraining course that was to be held at Ramat David. The request was approved, as long as I continued to fly the 767 on weekends.

One day, after I had just flown back from Europe, I got a call from air force headquarters informing me that Amos Lapidot had changed his mind about the approval he'd given me to train on the F-16.

"Let me speak to him please," I said.

"He can't speak to you now," I was told.

I insisted. "I am a lieutenant colonel in the air force and I will file an official request to meet with the air force commander."

"Go right ahead, but he won't meet with you."

I didn't understand why Lapidot had reneged. From talking with some friends, I learned that several other air force pilots had pressed him not to approve it, claiming that at my age, 46, it wasn't worth it to train me on the F-16.

It was because of jealousy and spite.

I'd known Amos Lapidot for many years, including the time he served as commander of the First Fighter Squadron and as the Wing 4 commander during the Yom Kippur War. Our families had a nice connection, too. We lived in the same neighbourhood. I called his wife Amalia and asked her when Amos was getting home that day, and invited myself over for coffee. When Amos arrived, he was surprised to find me sitting in his living room.

"Amos, do you know that you're the air force commander?" I asked.

He was surprised by the question.

I persisted. "It seems like no one has told you this. Explain to me how all kinds of people can change the decision of the air force commander. Are they princes? I remember another time when we were princes for years in the Mirages and we never kept a good pilot from advancing."

Amos hesitated, and I continued.

"I know you've been influenced by certain people in the air force. Give me a list of 10 people in the force whose opinion matters to you. I'll call each one of them and ask them to give their opinion on whether I can retrain on the F-16."

"Fine, the bureau chief will prepare a list for you."

I contacted Yossi Eliel, commander of the Negev Squadron, No. 253, the F-16 squadron at the Ramon airbase, a pilot for whom I had great respect. I asked him if he thought I could do the retraining, and if yes, to please call the air force commander and tell him so.

Eliel replied straight away, "If you come to my squadron, I'll have you retrain tomorrow."

Eliel called Lapidot with his opinion and warmly recommended that my request be approved. Others also called to express the same opinion.

A few days later, I received a surprising phone call from Yossi Eliel.

"Giora, I'm embarrassed to call you like this. I received an order from the base commander to change the opinion that I relayed to the air force commander."

I knew, of course, who had given him the order. It was the commander of the Ramon base. I also knew the reason, and that it related to something in our distant past. I thanked Eliel and told him I understood the situation in which he was caught. I wasn't angry at him. I understood that he could not go against an order from his base commander. I liked Eliel. He was one of the young pilots who'd passed under my command, and I'd always felt he had the potential to become a commander, that he was a pilot who would go far in the air force because of his special abilities and personality. Sadly, not long after our talk, in July 1986, Yossi Eliel was killed when the F-16 he was flying crashed on the runway at the Ramon base during a training run for an aerobatic show that was supposed to be part of the flight school graduation ceremony.

A week after my second conversation with Yossi Eliel, the air force commander's bureau chief called me again.

"I have the opinions you asked for. Seven were in favour, three were against. Amos received the results, but he is not changing his mind. You are not going to retrain."

It was hard for me to accept this decision, but I knew there was no way that Amos Lapidot would change it.

A few days after that, I met with Avihu Ben-Nun, who by then was head of the planning division, with the rank of major general, and a sure candidate to be the next air force commander.

"I heard they cancelled your switch to the F-16," he said.

I confirmed it. "Ask Amos…"

"If only we had a lot more pilots like you who wanted to fly the F-16."

"Careful, I'll hold you to your word," I said.

I came to terms with the fact that I wouldn't get to fly the F-16.

I transferred to the Smashing Parrot Squadron for two years, flying Kfirs. There is where I made my last flight in the Kfir. As I had done in earlier times when I served in other squadrons, I used every day off from El Al to fly as a reservist pilot. I especially loved the dogfights between the Kfir pilots and pilots from other squadrons. One morning, there was an aerial combat exercise between the Kfir squadron and the Golden Eagle F-16 Squadron, No. 140. I led a formation of six Kfirs against four F-16s. Of our six, one trio was for patrol and blocking and the other was for defence. At one point during the battle, I spotted F-16s coming to engage us from 15 miles away. As I tracked them by eye, I saw one of them plunge and crash to the ground. The pilot was David Ivry's son. The exercise was immediately halted. We returned to Ovda and the F-16s returned to Ramon.

In 1988, I was invited to Kibbutz Ma'abarot for the wedding of Giora Furman's daughter. Avihu Ben-Nun, who'd been appointed air force commander by then, was also among the guests. I went over to him and reminded him of our conversation about me retraining on the F-16.

"Now I want you to keep your promise," I said.

It was four years since Amos Lapidot had prevented me from moving to the F-16. I was almost 50, a very advanced age for an air force fighter pilot. But that didn't matter to me. I felt that I could do as well on this plane as much younger pilots. Avihu called over Eitan Ben Eliyahu, who was also at the wedding.

"Giora here wants to retrain on the F-16!"

"You'll get an answer," he promised me.

Just one week later the answer came. The air force commander's bureau chief informed me that I was approved to retrain on the F-16 at the Ramon base. Happy news. It reminded me of other times in my life I'd received happy news, like the first time I was accepted into the pilot course, and the second time I was accepted into the pilot course.

Three months before the start of the retraining course, I turned 50, and a birthday party was held for me at the Ovda base. I was surprised by the scope of the event. Pilots and other people I'd worked with throughout my years in the air force and the parachuting school had been invited. A version of 'This is Your Life' was presented, recalling my childhood and school days on the kibbutz, my time as a parachuting instructor and my long career as an air force fighter pilot. Even someone like me, who always tries to keep his cool, couldn't help but be moved.

In August 1988, I reported to the Ramon airbase for the retraining course to be a pilot in the Negev Squadron. But before that, I'd had to overcome another hurdle: the medical exams. I was sent to the Tel Hashomer cardiology institute where a stress test was administered. The doctor in charge of the institute brought me the results. "For your age, your heart is in excellent condition," he said, not noticing my quick sigh of relief.

"And how old would you say I am, doctor?"

He looked at me and smiled, "Between 38 and 40, right?"

When I told him my real age, he could hardly believe it.

The course lasted six months. I took unpaid leave from El Al and served as a reservist in the air force under regular service conditions. After I was certified, I was assigned to the Golden Eagle Squadron, also based at Ramon. I was the oldest pilot in the air force who had re-trained for the F-16, and the only El Al pilot in the squadron. On weekends, when possible, I flew for El Al. At the time, I was a pilot in the airline's Boeing 757 and 767 fleets. I was offered the opportunity to certify to fly the 747, the airline's jumbo jet, but I chose not to. When I had transferred from the 707 fleet, I'd spent three weeks in ground training, following certification on an advanced simulator at the Boeing plant in Seattle which was nothing like the simulator we used in Israel as 707 pilots. At the end, I was certified to fly as a first officer on the 767.

After a year with the 767 fleet, I went back to flying the 707 for a year, and was a member of the crew that brought El Al's last 707 to an airport outside Los Angeles to have silencing equipment installed. New civil aviation rules in Europe and the United States banned the aircraft from landing in airports located near city centres. The plane that was flown to Los Angeles had a silencing mechanism installed on its exhaust line and afterward it was transferred to Arkia Airlines.

Generally, certification as a flight captain occurs five years after certification as a first officer, but because of all the problems in El Al, which had been operating under receivership for some time, the airline was not hiring new pilots and senior pilots were not retiring. So I was certified as a captain after just 18 years of flying with the airline. Even after the certification and after I was awarded the four gold stripes, because of a shortage of first officers, I flew for two years more as a first officer with the status of captain.

I found the F-16 to be an incredible plane with amazing capabilities. It was the best of its kind around, like the Mirage, in its time, it had far exceeded enemy aircraft in its capabilities. The F-16's capabilities were far beyond those of the Mirage, but our enemies had also been busy upgrading their air forces over the years. They, too, had more advanced aircraft, with more advanced technological systems. As always, the key factor was the pilot. The result of the dogfight depended on him.

Flying an F-16 was different than any other plane I'd ever flown. It felt like it was the computer more than the pilot that was flying the plane. Naturally, I made many comparisons to the Mirage on which I'd flown so many hours. The stick was on the pilot's side and barely moved. Pilots complained that it wasn't comfortable for them. You pulled to the left as hard as you could and the plane would turn in accordance with the parameters – velocity, altitude, temperature – but it is impossible to exceed 9 G. The computer would not allow it. The Mirage easily passed the 7 G limit. On the F-16, exceeding the G limit would damage the plane.

But the more I got to know the new plane, called the 'Hawk' – the Americans called it the 'Fighting Falcon' – the more I came to admire its capabilities. In dogfights, even with a Mirage behind it, it could down the rival plane within 20 seconds – though, again, it all depended on the pilot. In the past, I'd had dogfights where I flew a Mirage and was able to down a Kfir or an F-16. Despite the new plane's extraordinary capabilities, I still felt that the experience of flying the Mirage was more powerful.

In January 1991, when the first Gulf War started, I was in the Golden Eagle Squadron at the Ramon base. I was at the base when the first Scud missile attack on Israel occurred. When those first missiles fell, pilots who were with me there readied to take off for Iraq. Everyone was on standby. Suited up and ready to go as soon as the order came, so I calmed them down. Most of them were young, they hadn't tasted war before and they were keen to head out. I explained to them that it was night-time. If they didn't go to sleep now, they wouldn't have energy in the morning, if and when they were needed.

On the second and third day of the Scud attacks, the air force was on attack standby in western Iraq. In the combat squadron operations rooms, briefings were held and targets were marked. We were prepared for intercept missions, of course. We waited on standby, but the order for take-off never came. Under pressure from the Americans, Prime Minister Yitzhak Shamir cancelled all the attack plans in western Iraq. Israel was kept out of the Gulf War. The Iraqi air force, which we'd expected to meet over the skies of western Iraq, fled to Iran.

During the war, I got to spend a few nights at home in Ramat Hasharon. When the warning sirens went off, everyone who was at home put on their gas masks and Sara stuffed damp towels under the front door. To me, it was an amusing scene. There were nights when I flew for El Al, which was the only airline that was still flying and was part of the war effort to transport emergency equipment. One experience from those nights was a take-off from the air when I was on approach for landing and opposite us were American Patriot missile batteries that were trying to hit the Iraqi Scuds. It was quite the sound and light show, but the results were not that impressive. Not a single Scud was intercepted.

Not long after the war, the air force had a surprise for me: Commander Avihu Ben-Nun had decided to promote me to the rank of colonel. Ehud Barak, the new IDF chief of staff, gave me the new insignia together with Ben-Nun. Sara and the children were present for the event, and were very excited, of course.

For the first time, my family started to talk to me about retiring from reserve duty in the squadron. Most fighter pilots stop flying at age 40-45. Yosef Tzuk – who was my close friend and who made air force history by being the first pilot to down a MiG during the 1956 Sinai Campaign – had stopped flying in 1988, at age 50, but he was definitely the exception.

I flew the F-16 for nine years. Grandpa fighter pilot. Older than the parents of most of the young pilots at the base. I would soon be turning 59, an age where my pilot instincts would begin to decline. I barely felt it, but I did start to sense the reactions of the other pilots, that maybe it was time for me to start thinking of retirement from active combat flying. "It's a shame, but maybe…" some hinted.

The squadron commander was much more blunt.

"Giora, maybe the time has come for you to stop flying," he said to me one day.

I was almost 59. He was 39.

I realised that my time as a fighter pilot was nearing an end.

27 THE LAST FLIGHT

On my 59th birthday, it did end. My last flight in the air force. A special day for me and for the air force.

As usual, I did not get emotional. That day I flew as part of an F-16 formation. I attended the pre-flight briefing at the Ramon base like any other pilot. The only difference compared to every other flight in my life was this would be my final flight as an air force fighter pilot.

The air force held a very beautiful and impressive event in my honour. All the top figures in the air force, including the IAF commander, Major General Eitan Ben Eliyahu, were there. Everyone that I invited came. President Ezer Weizman made it known that he would come to bid farewell to the pilot who so stubbornly insisted on getting into the pilot course and remaining a fighter pilot. Former air force commanders attended, too, along with friends and fellow pilots that I had flown with over the years. There were people I dearly wish could have been there for this occasion, but some were no longer with us, and others could not attend due to poor health. My whole family, including my sisters, flew down from the north.

There was something I wanted to do for President Ezer Weizman. Ezer was the one who had personally presented me with my pilot's wings at the ceremony in the Tel Nof cinema hall on that stormy night in November 1964, when I graduated as the outstanding cadet and he was the air force commander. Now, in 1997, I decided to surprise him. At the farewell event, I wanted to give Ezer back the beautiful gift I received from him. My pilot's wings. He deserved it. He'd played a significant part in the decision to put me back in the combat squadron. I asked my daughter Dana to prepare a small velvet box, and I placed my pilot's wings inside it. A personal gift from me to the president of the State of Israel.

That day, the weather in the Negev was summery and there was a light wind. The squadron completed its scheduled exercises and readied for landing. The F-16, the plane I'd flown for my last nine years in the air force, glided into a soft landing at the military airfield. I taxied the plane over to the stage that had been set up for the farewell ceremony. The pilots of the Golden Eagle

Squadron and the squadron commander, all 'kids' compared to me, had landed earlier and arranged themselves around the stage.

The air force had prepared a special gesture in my honour. A surprise I never expected. Seventeen roundels were painted on an F-16, symbolising my kills of enemy aircraft. None of those kills had been in the Hawk, but now, when the Mirages and Neshers I'd flown and in which I'd recorded all of my kills were already history and could only be found in the air force museum at Hatzerim, or as part of a display at other air force bases, this was a wonderful idea – painting my kills on the F-16, the plane I'd fought so hard to fly.

There was another wonderful tribute. My son Guy was invited to take part in the farewell flyover. Wearing a flight suit, he was in the back seat of an F-16B, flew in the flyover in my honour, and then waited for me with all the other pilots at the squadron plaza.

I turned off the Hawk's engine, folded the flight maps and saw the mechanics coming up the ladder to open the cockpit canopy. I took off my pilot's helmet and from the cockpit I looked out at all the guests who had come for the ceremony. Within seconds, I was going from one embrace to the next, and hearing President Ezer Weizman making the kind of remarks that had made him such a beloved figure in the air force back in the day. Sara and the kids and the other pilots could hardly contain their excitement.

Ezer Weizman hugged me and said a few words that really moved everyone in the audience. Including me. I surprised him when I pulled out the little box.

"Thirty-four years ago you gave me these wings. Now I give them back to you…"

Everyone applauded. I saw that Ezer was touched. Both he and the air force commander spoke about Giora Even-Epstein, the pilot who had shot down more enemy fighter jets than any other air force pilot in the world. Ezer placed my gift in a special spot in the gift room in the president's residence.

Thirty-four years before, I'd 'put one over' on the pilots who graduated the course with me. They were all drunk on vodka and whiskey, while I kept walking around with Coca Cola in my cup. On my last day as a fighter pilot, at a bar at the Ramon base, the other pilots were drinking and I, as usual, had my Coca Cola in hand, raising it again and again for each toast.

An era that had begun as a childhood dream had reached its end. The boy from Kibbutz Negba who fell in love with the skies from the books he read about the history's great flying aces, had indeed conquered the skies. It wasn't always easy, plenty of obstacles had stood in my way. But I'd overcome them all. I was born to be a fighter pilot, and I tried to be the best fighter pilot possible. That was my aim, my focus. That was what I trained for.

When I was in the air, in war or in training, I wanted to do what I was trained to do: to down enemy planes. To win. I did it my way. With me, there were no buzz flights or whoops of victory after each kill. But I let nothing stop me on my way to victory. My wife Sara often says the desire to win is so ingrained in me that even when I'm playing with our little grandchildren, I won't give in. I have to win and when they don't let me win, I get mad.

The air force was my home for 34 years. Even after I finished my regular service, I continued flying for many more years. More than any other fighter pilot in the air force. When I took off the uniform, I held the rank of colonel. Pilots who'd been my cadets for years attained even higher ranks. I didn't have any big dreams of reaching the top of the air force command pyramid. I didn't want general staff positions. I didn't want to fly Parker pens. I wanted to fly, then to fly some more. I wanted to be the best possible, and if there's any truth in what President Weizman, a former air force commander, and other air force commanders who followed him said, it seems I didn't disappoint them.

I broke quite a few records in the air force. At the time, I was the oldest cadet to be accepted into the pilot course; I finished the course in 13 months, quicker than any other pilot, I was also the pilot with the most parachute jumps. I was the first and evidently the only pilot to take part in the World Skydiving Championship. I was the oldest pilot to retrain on the F-16, and when I retired, I was the oldest active combat pilot in the force. And of course, I had the highest number of kills of enemy aircraft.

It was time to give someone else a chance to break some of my records. I said goodbye to the IAF when I was 59, but not to flying. I kept flying for El Al for another six years after I left the military. In El Al, too, I flew until the maximum possible age according to aviation regulations, which was 65. For a time, my son Guy and daughter Dana were flight attendants with El Al, and we would head to Ben Gurion Airport together. The long dry spell at El Al during which no new pilots were hired finally ended, and new pilot training courses were opened, which attracted many air force veterans. Often, the first officer sitting beside me was one of the 'kids' who'd been one of my cadets or a young pilot who'd flown with me in the combat squadrons. A heavy hint that the time for retirement was nearing.

Even though I'm no longer in the cockpit, of a fighter jet or a Boeing passenger jet, I still relive those incredible moments in the air that I got to experience. Every so often, the History Channel airs the terrific movie about my dogfight over the Suez Canal on October 20, 1973. The channel, which produced an excellent series on famous dogfights in history, also produced two films about the Israel Air Force. The second film covered Ran Peker's battle against a Jordanian Hunter plane in the Battle of Sumu, and my dogfight over the Suez Canal. Even I, who know every second of what happened in that battle, feel a thrill each time I see the film. Each time I hear the superb analysts who narrate the animated segments describe me as the world champion in downing enemy fighter jets in dogfights in three wars – the Six Day War, the War of Attrition and, above all, the Yom Kippur War.

In the first years after I stopped flying, a strange thing happened to me: I started dreaming at night about things that all involved very serious safety events – crashes, emergency landings and so on. One day, at the funeral of a mutual friend, I saw Menachem Shmul, the IAI test pilot who told me that he experienced something similar when he stopped flying in the air force. The dreams stopped after a few years and since then I sleep well at night.

After the time I was invited to the 1998 'Gathering of the Eagles' at Maxwell Air Force Base in Alabama, in the United States, a photographer named Ron Kaplan called me and said that a good friend of his named Rick Turner, who was a huge fan of the Israel Air Force and the First Fighter Squadron, wanted to commission a painting about me. This conversation exposed me to a whole new world I'd never heard of: oil paintings of famous aerial battles and the pilots who were involved in them. In the aviation world, this is a very popular hobby and there are thousands in the US and England who collect these paintings – the original oil painting as well as print copies of them – and are ready to pay serious money for them.

Rick put me in touch with a painter, Roy Grinnell, who worked with many American aces depicting their missions, and together we decided the subject would be my fourth kill in the October 20 battle of the Yom Kippur War. In the painting, the sky is red, just as it was during the battle, right before sunset. At the bottom of the painting is a description of the famous battle.

Five hundred copies were printed and one time when I was in New York, I sat and signed every one of them, and they were later sold for $120 each. Then I was drawn in further to this new field.

In the Israel Air Force, the whole subject of historic preservation had been neglected for many years. I decided to use paintings to commemorate the Israel Air Force's heritage and to ensure also that the Mirage, the plane that flew in the air force for 20 years, from 1962-1982, and won three wars for it in hundreds of dogfights, would also be memorialised with an impressive painting.

Rick and I started searching for the right painter for this project. I looked at quite a number of them, but none of them seemed good enough. Finally, I was introduced to the work of a British painter named Robert Taylor, who I learned was like the Leonardo Da Vinci of aircraft artists. He is a man who is an entire industry unto himself of paintings of this kind, and who usually has a three-year waiting list for his services. I contacted his agent and he agreed to take on the project.

As we were discussing it, an idea came to me to commemorate my friend, the commander of the First Fighter Mirage squadron, Avi Lanir, who did not return from a mission over the Golan Heights in October 1973. I obtained the family's consent and spent a lot of time going over the sketches from the British artist depicting the plane, painted with Avi's number at the height of a dogfight.

When the painting was completed – the original oil painting hangs in the home of Avi's son Noam Lanir, who purchased it from the artist – I received 500 prints of it and I got the 27 Mirage pilots who are aces to sign them. Later, I also asked to get a black-and-white version of the sketch. I got 300 of these prints and had all the Mirage pilots who are 'double aces' with more than 10 kills sign them. Each print was later sold for $320. The writing at the bottom of the picture describes Avi Lanir, commander of the First Fighter Squadron who was captured in Syria and tortured to death, carrying the secrets he held to the grave.

After the big success of the painting commemorating Avi Lanir, Robert Taylor's agent contacted me and asked if it were possible to do a painting of a Phantom, too. Not being a Phantom pilot myself, even though I did train on that plane, I handed the task over to one of the Phantom pilots. He didn't do a very good job with it, so I took it upon myself to complete the project. I had these prints signed by 21 Phantom pilots whom I selected. Eight were generals, including Dan Halutz. The British 'went crazy' when they saw the list of signatures on the picture. Nearly all the prints were sold in England and the United States, but I hope that this field of painting depicting the combat legacy of our air force, and of our most accomplished pilots, will gradually catch on in Israel as well.

28 THE HEART

I can count on the fingers of one hand the number of times I've been sick. Really sick. Not things like the broken leg I suffered in a parachute jump or a finger that accidentally got stuck somewhere it didn't belong. That doesn't count. Maybe because I have such a high pain threshold. I hardly ever feel pain and someone who doesn't feel pain doesn't go looking for doctors and hospitals. I had major heart surgery on May 30, 2012, 10 days after my 74th birthday, and from the moment I awoke in intensive care I felt no pain or fear. I don't need shots of aesthetic for dental treatment.

Two years earlier, and at age 72, seven years after I stopped flying with El Al, the medical diagnosis hit me like a bombshell: "You have heart disease. The name of the condition is cardiomyopathy. The illness affects the left ventricle of the heart."

More than 50 years had passed since Dr Baruch, the air force flight surgeon, had disqualified me from the pilot course. I knew that there was something abnormal about my heart. Back then, they called it an 'athletic heart'. Every year, I'd passed the annual physical exam in the air force. In all of them, my electrocardiogram (EKG), which measures electrical current generated by the contraction of the heart, was totally stable, unchanging. From age 59, after I stopped flying in the air force, I had cardiac exams every six months at the Mor Institute, for El Al. When the tests were done when I was 62 and still an El Al pilot, the doctor at the institute told me he knew my EKG was different.

"I saw your medical file from the air force and I want to see what is different about it."

This doctor sent me to do an echocardiogram, which uses sound waves. I'd had several of these tests when I was in the air force and there were never any special findings. The doctor I was referred to was a flight cardiologist who had once been a cardiologist in the air force. He diagnosed me with heart failure, my heart rate was too slow, but that didn't stop me from continuing to fly as an El Al pilot until age 65. The level of heart failure did not prevent me from functioning as usual. Without any side effects.

At age 72, it came. One Saturday I suddenly felt strong pressure in my chest. Sara immediately gave me an aspirin and called an ambulance. On the way to Beilinson Hospital, the paramedic in the ambulance determined I was having a heart attack and gave me the initial treatment to keep the situation from worsening. At the Beilinson emergency room, they diagnosed a myocardial infarction and I was taken to the operating room for a catheterisation.

I recovered and was discharged from the hospital. One evening a few months later, I was sitting watching television when I had a mild stroke. All of a sudden, in my right eye, I was seeing colourful lines and stars that were moving from the right side. It went on for a short time and gradually faded. I told Sara I must have a problem with my eye and that I needed to go to the eye doctor the next day. But Sara was firm.

"No eye doctor, Giora. We're going to the emergency room right now."

Tests showed that my field of vision on the right side was affected and there was concern that a blood clot could have caused the blockage of a blood vessel in the brain. I was given an injection of a blood-thinner but it didn't help. Another test revealed a small blockage of blood vessels in the brain. My vision on my right side has been impaired ever since. I was hospitalised for a few days and our friend, an Israeli doctor who lives in Boston, happened to be in Israel just then. We told him about the medical findings and he said right away that something didn't add up. He asked us to meet with a friend of his, an American doctor who'd made aliyah and was now in charge of a department at Ichilov Hospital.

This doctor also told us that something didn't add up. He decided to admit me to Ichilov for comprehensive echo scans. These tests showed no connection between the vision impairment and the blocked blood vessels in the brain. An expert professor did more tests and discovered that the left ventricle of my heart was pumping a significantly low amount of blood compared to normal. Consequently, blood clots had formed and one had reached the brain. At the end of our meeting, he scheduled an appointment for me to have a pacemaker put in.

The next day, I had an appointment at Beilinson Hospital for a regular check-up. I showed the doctor my test results from Ichilov and he quickly called the director of the cardiology department's heart failure unit. After reviewing the test results, he decided to admit me then and there. Two days later, the pacemaker was implanted, but my condition didn't improve. It kept deteriorating. I had shortness of breath and growing fatigue. The heart failure on the left side of my heart was worsening, and the pacemaker was doing nothing to relieve it. I read up a bit on my disease. Basically, the left side of the heart loses its ability to contract and so the heart cannot pump out to the body all the oxygenated blood that comes from the lungs. The symptoms are a gradual decline in stamina, increasing shortness of breath while active, leading to shortness of breath while at rest, and nocturnal episodes of shortness of breath accompanied by a feeling of suffocation.

That's exactly what I was feeling.

At one medical appointment, given my worsening condition, Dr Tuvia Ben-Gal, director of the heart failure unit, suggested the possibility of implanting an artificial heart pump. This was the first time I'd heard of this medical innovation, which had been successfully used on cardiac patients in many countries and on a small number of patients in Israel. Dr Ben-Gal said this treatment was practically my only chance to go on living. He also told me more things I hadn't known about my illness.

Apparently, what Dr Baruch spotted 50 years earlier was, in fact, an abnormal heart. Even then, the EKG had indicated heart disease, but since there were no echocardiograms in those days, no precise diagnosis of what I had was ever made.

"If there would have been an echo test in 1956," said Dr Ben-Gal, "there's no way anyone would have let you fly."

Lucky for me.

Dr Ben-Gal explained that normally I could have gone on living with the disease, but the problem was greatly exacerbated due to the heart attack I'd had a few months before. What I had thought was a mild heart attack had in fact nearly destroyed my heart. A normal heart empties 50 per cent of the blood that accumulates in the left ventricle – this is called the ejection fraction. Mine was much lower than that. The result was an expanded heart, and a weakness that made it impossible for me to function.

"Without the valve that I propose we implant, you'll have no more than a few weeks left to live," the doctor told me. As I was already over 70, a heart transplant was not an option. At the time, no organ transplants were done on people over 65. This age limit was later cancelled.

My heart failure continued to worsen, and as soon as the ejection fraction fell below 20 per cent, the doctors were adamant that I had no other choice. They had to operate immediately and implant the left ventricular assist device (LVAD) artificial heart pump, a medical device that was developed in America. I consented to the surgery, which was long and complex. After a short time in the hospital, I came home to a new life. Today, eight years after the surgery, I depend on two batteries that I place in a vest I wear that looks like a flak jacket. The batteries are connected to the pump implanted in my chest below the diaphragm, which sends the blood from my left ventricle directly to the aorta, something my heart could no longer do on its own.

It's been doing an excellent job of it since.

I don't think of myself as disabled. I have a disease, but it doesn't hinder me from functioning just as I used to. I have no pain, and my condition has actually improved. My ejection fraction has risen from 20 to 30 per cent. The only limitation I have is that I need to charge the batteries once a day. That's all. People who are unaware of my condition don't notice any difference in my behaviour. I can travel, drive, hike. The doctors at Beilinson were very impressed by how I coped with the new situation. A situation that requires an understanding of the physical changes that have occurred in me, a capacity to cope with it and the desire to triumph over it and go on as if nothing has happened. Thanks to medical advances, I could live with this device until 120, says Dr Ben-Gal. I also started serving as a 'promoter' of the device. Beilinson arranges for me to meet with patients who are in a condition similar to mine, so I can explain to them about the treatment and about the quality of life following the implant. Some have even given me certificates of appreciation for this important help.

My wife Sara and our three children, Adi, Dana and Guy, and our grandchildren are the most important part of my life. They watch over me when needed. We're what you could call an air force family. Sara was an operations secretary in the mid-sixties and our children followed a similar path. Adi and Dana were operations secretaries and then operations officers in the squadrons. Guy began his army service in the pilot course, and when he was cut from there, he continued on in the air force as an officer in an anti-aircraft missile battery. Our eldest granddaughter serves in the Air Force Museum in Hatzerim.

I asked my doctor how I could have done so much with my faulty heart – gruelling training with the paratroopers, all of the skydiving, and especially thousands of flight hours and the continuous strain that puts on the heart and the entire body. There is no clear answer, apparently. Maybe I'm just built differently. Maybe the disease was dormant for so many years until one day, in wake of my heart attack, it began to act up.

I can't imagine what my life would have been like had I not been able to fulfil my dream to fly, to soar up into the skies, to fight and to win.

In the air force, some people said: If you managed to do all that with a damaged heart, who knows what you could have done with a normal heart?

GLOSSARY

- **Aliyah** – Emigration to Israel undertaken by Jewish people from outside of Israel (i.e. from Europe or America).
- **Bahad** – Term for a training base.
- **Gadna** – Military programme preparing youth for military service.
- *Gar'in* – A Hebrew term used for groups of people who moved together to Palestine.
- **Gibush** – Term for a training period in the Israeli forces.
- **Golani Brigade** – Israeli regular service infantry brigade.
- **Hachshara** – Youth camp in Europe for preparation of emigration to Israel (commonly known as aliyah).
- **Haganah** – The main paramilitary organisation of the Jewish Yishuv in Mandatory Palestine between 1920 and 1948, it then became the core of the Israel Defense Forces (IDF).
- **Haggadah** – Passover text.
- **Hashomer Hatzair** – Secular Jewish youth movement founded in 1913.
- **HeHalutz** – A youth movement founded in 1918 by folk hero Joseph Trumpeldor (1880-1920).
- **Kibbutz (singular)/Kibbutzim (plural)** – Term used for a settlement.
- **Kibbutzniks** – Members of a kibbutz.
- **Knesset** – Legislative branch of the Israeli government.
- **Konenut gimel** – Highest state of alert in IDF.
- **Krav Maga** – Form of self-defence originated from Israel.
- **Mapam** – Left-wing political party.
- **Moshav (singular)/Moshavim (plural)** – Term for an agricultural settlement.
- **Mukhtar** – The head of local government of a town or village.
- **Olim (plural)** – Immigrants to Israel
- **Palmach militia** – Elite fighting force of the Haganah.
- **Sayeret Shaked** – IDF Southern Command special forces unit.
- **Shin Bet** – Israeli internal security service.
- **Yishuv** – The Jewish community or settlement in Palestine during the 19th century and until the formation of the state of Israel in 1948.

INDEX